THE
EIGHTEEN-SIXTIES

ESSAYS

by

Fellows of
the Royal Society of
Literature

Edited by
JOHN DRINKWATER

CAMBRIDGE
AT THE UNIVERSITY PRESS
1932

CONTENTS

INTRODUCTION

By *John Drinkwater*

It was Mr Granville-Barker who proposed to a little
lunch party at the Garrick Club that the papers delivered
to the Royal Society of Literature should be written
year by year with some co-ordination of aim. After
much discussion it was decided that this could be most
suitably achieved by concentrating upon a given period.
In order to make the scheme more specific, the period in
each case was to be a decade. The firstfruits were brought
together in *The Eighteen-Seventies*, edited by Granville-
Barker himself, and were followed by *The Eighteen-
Eighties*, edited by Mr de la Mare. The present volume,
which turns back to the 'sixties, is the third of the series.

Within the very simple editorial plan the writers,
needless to say, have been free to follow their own bent.
But the editor in each case has had a double purpose to
fulfil, and it has been his business to see that not the
treatment but the choice of subjects was made with
this purpose in mind. The intention of each of these
volumes is to give nothing like an exhaustive survey, but
a faithful impression of the period in question, and,
further, to give this impression without re-examining
the major writers whose work is familiarly known to
everyone who cares about literature at all.

In the eighteen-sixties, for example, the representative
English poets clearly were Tennyson and Browning,

but here we have Mr Abercrombie on Henry Taylor
and Mr Wolfe on Clough. To read these two papers is
not to get a complete view of poetry in the 'sixties, but
it is to discover certain intellectual and spiritual qualities
that were emphasised by that period, and to see them in
their merits and their limitations more precisely than we
could in the work of the more universal men. Similarly,
Mr de la Mare, in his paper on Wilkie Collins, evokes
powers that, while they were certainly not beyond the
scope of Dickens and Thackeray, find a more particular,
a more easily disengaged expression in the smaller
master.

This consideration in the 'sixties has less force when
we pass from the poetry and the fiction. These good poets
and this good novelist are here richly rewarding to their
latest critics, and not the less so in that they must without dispute take second place to giants of their own time.
When Mr Granville-Barker comes to write about the
theatre in the 'sixties he is free to make the most of any
giants that he can find. But that is only because there
were not any. The transit from Planché to Gilbert is
perhaps as important as anything that was happening in
the English theatre at that time, and yet there will be
few readers who do not come to Mr Granville-Barker
for their first knowledge of the process. Here are no
Olympian ardours to remind us of the Elizabethans or
Ibsen, but here is an account which in its liveliness reminds us that even in the lapses of its inspiration the
theatre remains an enchanted place.

Mr Graves, on the other hand, has caught a giant
right enough. His giant is a little fellow with a hump-

back, but whatever we may think about him he remains indisputably a giant. *Punch* in the 'sixties was a social force, and he has remained one ever since. Mr Graves, most devoted of historians, is the first to allow that there have been occasions when *Punch* has been foolish, even sometimes a little ill-tempered. But no one can be nearly a hundred years old, and still going strong, with an account quite clear of indiscretions. For good and ill, common sense passes in the world as the first characteristic of the Englishman, and common sense has nowhere so constantly been raised to the level of wit as in the pages of *Punch*. To some natures even witty common sense is incurably tiresome, and most of us have moods in which we can find it so, but on the whole *Punch* remains, as it has never for long failed to be, the acutest and the most amusing satirist of daily life in England. It is not too much to say that it has not only reflected but has had a definite influence upon the English habit of mind. This volume is fortunate in having as the chronicler of that influence in the 'sixties a writer who has himself done so much to invigorate it in our own time.

Dr Boas has his giants too. But his immediate concern is with the less-considered aspect of their statures. It would have been beyond the scope of this book merely to remind us that the great historians of the 'sixties were great historians, but it is precisely to our purpose to remind us that in writing history they were adding to the riches of English literature. If my own Mr Dallas is no giant, he is certainly no pigmy. He is a big loose-limbed sort of a fellow, so big indeed as to make it surprising that he should have been able to efface himself from all common and almost from all critical knowledge for fifty years and more. He is just the sort of recovery that one is glad to have made for such a book as this.

I have left to Sir John Fortescue and Sir Oliver Lodge the responsibility of bringing this discursive account of the 'sixties to a really distinguished close. That I should be Sir Oliver Lodge's editor is a joke that affords me peculiar satisfaction. In the days when I used to play respectful tennis with him in Birmingham he had a great reputation for being able to make abstruse scientific subjects attractive and intelligible to the layman. And so I reflected that while pure science was not within my editorial mandate, the literature of science was, and the Royal Society of Literature has been fortunate in inducing a great scientist to take part in its deliberations. There are eminent historians who regard Sir John Fortescue as chief among living exponents of their craft. If I do not know enough to express an opinion about that, I know enough to know that everything he writes makes authority engaging, and I knew that if he could be persuaded he was just the man to write the paper that I wanted upon the sporting literature of the 'sixties. I suggested Surtees, but Sir John declined, saying that Surtees was too early. He dropped a hint that if it had been Whyte-Melville it might have been another matter. Naturally, Whyte-Melville it was, and surely a vanished phase of English society never had a tenderer or a more challenging epitaph.

SIR HENRY TAYLOR

By *Lascelles Abercrombie*

The history of literature inevitably presents itself as a series of *periods*, which are not merely chronological partitions, but rather characteristic stages in the process of literature. Literary history, indeed, cannot be content simply to describe the sequence of literary events; it is not the sequence of things, but the connexion of things, that makes history. The chronology of literature, however, is sometimes at odds with the periods which literary history displays. The year 1850, for instance, might justly be called the very heyday of the Victorian period; not merely by chronology, but because in that year were published those two perfect specimens of Victorianism, *In Memoriam* and *David Copperfield*. But in that same year there also entered into the process of English literature *The Prelude* and *Death's Jest Book*. Right in the midst of Victorianism chronology records the appearance of two books as alien as anything possibly could be from whatever may be meant by Victorianism. Nothing could better exhibit the artifice of literary periods. For, though it may be interesting to know when a book was written, the date that counts in history is the date of publication; it is then that a book begins, properly speaking, to be literature. The entry into English literature of the greatest poem of the pre-Victorian period was a Victorian event; and the real importance of that most un-Victorian poet, Beddoes, commences in the year of *In Memoriam*.

It may perhaps be objected that *The Prelude* and *Death's Jest Book* were both unnaturally delayed in their publication; but that does not alter the actual position, which is, that in chronological fact one period is thoroughly telescoped into another. And if we come down ten years or so, into the 'sixties, we find another instance of this, equally striking though far less important, against which no such objection can be made. Sir Henry Taylor was a man born to confound, so far as in him lay, the periods of literary history. His first book was published in 1827; and both by its date and by its nature (it is an unstageable poetic drama), appears to belong to that brief epilogue to the Romantic movement which, roughly speaking, fills the gap between Byron and Tennyson: Taylor's *Isaac Comnenus* would seem to group itself naturally enough with Beddoes' *Bride's Tragedy* and Darley's *Sylvia*. And for thirty-five years Taylor went on producing, at long intervals, the same kind of poem; never without Victorian applause, but never with any real assimilation to Victorianism. A survey of English literature in the 'sixties could hardly omit this placidly but stubbornly un-Victorian figure. That indeed might be said of the three previous, and perhaps of the two following, decades. But he is peculiarly noticeable in the 'sixties: in 1862 the last of his dramatic poems was published, and in 1864 he summed up his whole poetic achievement, and definitely put his claim to a reputable place in English literature, by publishing his collected poems in three volumes.

So there, in the 'sixties, he most unmistakably stands: chronologically *in* the period, but certainly not *of* it.

Sir Henry Taylor's most remarkable achievement was not in literature: it is the magnificent countenance of his old age, which may be seen in the frontispiece to his very engaging *Autobiography*. That, however, belongs to a time twenty years later than the 'sixties; and to a time thirty years earlier than his collected poems belongs what is, I suppose, his most enduring achievement; and this at any rate arises out of literature. In the notes to *Philip Van Artevelde* he says: "The history of Jacques Van Artevelde, the father, is more generally known to the English reader than that of Philip, the son". I will not speak for the history; but as for the name, it is Philip Van Artevelde, not Jacques, that is now known to the English. And that is entirely Sir Henry Taylor's doing. I do not know how far his dramatic poem is still read; but at least the name of its hero has passed into the tradition of English literature. That is something to have achieved. And of course it means that the poem itself made, at one time, a great and by no means transient impression. But it seems that, from the very beginning of its vogue, its title had a singular power of catching the public ear. As soon as the poem was published, Lansdowne House and Holland House welcomed its author to their literary routs: but they did not welcome him as Henry Taylor; in those exalted circles he went by the name of Philip Van Artevelde; one hostess even addressed her invitation to "Philip Van Artevelde, Esq."

What sort of a poet was this Henry Taylor? The catalogue of his work is soon told. In 1827 he published

Isaac Comnenus; in 1834 his masterpiece, *Philip Van
Artevelde*; in 1842 *Edwin the Fair*; in 1850 *The Virgin
Widow* (afterwards called *A Sicilian Summer*); and in
1862 *St Clement's Eve*. All these are dramatic poems.
The collection of 1864 includes some lyrical and occasional pieces; but they are quite negligible. There is also
a narrative poem—*The Eve of the Conquest*—which is not
without merit; though perhaps its chief interest is, that it
has some faint resemblance to Tennyson's use of the
epic idyl, and, but for its date, might have been thought
to show his influence. There is, besides, a considerable
body of prose. *The Statesman* (1836) got him into some
trouble (since he was a Civil Servant) by its ironical
account of the way to succeed as a politician. The irony
is somewhat muffled by verbiage; and if it were stript
bare would seem pretty mild nowadays: our politicians
succeed by methods Henry Taylor's most extravagant
fantasy had never dreamt of. Two volumes of essays,
Notes from Life and *Notes from Books*—Henry Taylor, as
a Civil Servant, had pleasant opportunity to reflect on
both—also come well before the 'sixties. And his most
considerable prose work, the *Autobiography*, an important document for social and political history, falls
twenty years later. Readable though the *Autobiography*
is, and often delightful for its simple candour, it is to his
poetry that Sir Henry Taylor owes his place in English
literature: that is to say, to the figure which, with his
three volumes of collected poems, he definitely assumes
in the 'sixties. It is, then, his place as a poet that I shall
consider; and his place as a poet is the place which may
be allowed to his dramatic poems.

And that, some critics will say, is no place at all. The dramatic poem is a mistake; and mistakes cannot be allowed in poetry. I shall not spend much time over this. The notion is, of course, that the form which poetry takes in the theatre has no artistic validity outside the theatre. It may be noted that the argument against the dramatic poem would, if pushed home, become an argument against reading plays; obviously, when we read a play, it makes no difference to our enjoyment whether it has or has not been acted. Sit in an armchair and read *Prometheus Bound*, and it thereby becomes as certainly a dramatic poem as *Prometheus Unbound*. And since people enjoy reading plays, it seems a forlorn business to argue that they ought not to do so. But apart from this, the theoretical condemnation of the dramatic poem is itself doubly mistaken. The poet who uses dramatic form for what he intends to be taken simply as reading matter is doing nothing exceptional. All poetry takes its form from some original occasion or method of performance. If lyrical and narrative poetry are allowed to exist independent of the musician and the rhapsode, there seems no reason why dramatic poetry should not exist independent of the actor. But in any case (and here is the second mistake) to lay down *a priori* what is allowed and what is disallowed in poetry, shows a remarkable misconception of the critic's function. Judge by results: that is the only valid rule in criticism. And ever since Plato it has been plain that there are peculiar advantages to be gained by putting reading matter into dramatic form.

Henry Taylor, then, if it suited his inclination and his

purpose, needs no justification for writing dramatic poems. It certainly suited his inclination; in that, he simply followed all the rest of the Romantics, from Blake down to his contemporaries, Darley and Beddoes. They all wrote dramatic poems; and all for the same reason, which may be summed up in one word—Shakespeare. Taylor seems never to have questioned his inclination to write dramatic poems: for him, it was just the natural thing to do. But it may be doubted whether it always suited his purpose. At any rate, he often writes as though he had no very clear idea what the peculiar advantages of dramatic form are. Much of what he had to say would have been much better said as narrative; and, though on the whole his purpose fell in pretty well with the form he had chosen, it also on the whole failed to gain all that it should have done from being cast in that form. But this was the nemesis of the Romantic attitude to Shakespeare; and that it was more conspicuous in him than in the rest of the Romantics was due to the fact that he was not, as the others were, protected by the poetic instinct which could partially avert it. For Taylor's adoption of the Elizabethan method of drama was purely romantic; that is to say, he adopted it without really understanding it. He did not see that Elizabethan dramatic technique was exactly conditioned by the Elizabethan stage; since he had no notion what that stage was like. For him, as for the other Romantics, Shakespeare's technique was perfect freedom. All you had to do was to compose a series of dialogues, explaining their occasion by stage directions. Thus any purpose could be thrown into dramatic form. It was quite unnecessary to ask whether the purpose itself was dramatic; it became dramatic by being written as drama. But of course the justification of dramatic form in reading matter is the production of an imaginative effect analogous with the effect of a play in the theatre. Not understanding what the effect of an Elizabethan play would be in the theatre for which it was composed, Henry Taylor worked out his dramatic poems, in what he took to be the Elizabethan style, without any regard for an analogous effect in his reading matter. It suited him well enough to make his characters live entirely by their self-revelation; it did not suit him by any means so well to make the action of his poems exist entirely by being embodied in the dialogue of such characters.

In this misconception of the form he adopted, Taylor goes with the Romantics: though, as I have said, the other Romantics were saved by their poetic instinct, so far as the justification of their dramatic poems as reading matter is concerned. But in other respects Taylor belongs no more to Romanticism than he does to Victorianism. He had a profound admiration for Wordsworth and Coleridge, and delighted to invoke their authority for his principles: but these were merely the external principles of poetry, the scaffolding of poetic construction. There is nothing of Wordsworth or Coleridge in what he built by means of these principles. He reflected much on man and nature: but without anything like Wordsworth's pantheism or Coleridge's transcendentalism. As for Byron and Shelley, he repudiated them altogether. The one was all passion, the other all imagination: both had fatally neglected "the immortal and intellectual part" of poetry. This, as we learn from the preface to *Philip Van Artevelde*, is what he undertook to supply. But not without the other ingredients. "I would have no man depress his imagination," he says: "but I would have him raise his reason to be its equipoise." This is sound doctrine enough; equally sound is his warning against the conscious endeavour to write beautifully. Mrs Shelley had said of her husband's work: "every line and word he wrote is instinct with peculiar beauty". To which Taylor replies: "let no man sit down to write with the purpose of making every line and word beautiful and peculiar. The only effect of such an endeavour will be to corrupt his judgment and confound his understanding". This, in his opinion, was what had happened to Shelley; but of course Mary Shelley had said nothing whatever about Shelley sitting down to write *with the purpose* of making every line beautiful: she merely said that every line *was* beautiful. But this is typical of the whole of that remarkable document, the preface to *Philip Van Artevelde*. It is a capital instance of the possibility that a man may have all the right ideas about poetry, and yet be a hopelessly bad critic. The difference between literary theory and literary criticism has seldom been more plainly exhibited.

The preface is, however, an invaluable comment on Taylor's own poetry. We can read in it the very picture of his mind—a large, intelligent, self-possessed mind, which took itself seriously, and had good reason to do so; which could contemplate itself very coolly, but never thought of interrogating itself; which worked slowly, thoroughly, and equably, and always had plenty of time; whose temper was never crossed, whose purpose was never distracted, by gloom, by rapture, or by humour. The mind thus unconsciously self-portrayed in this preface can be plainly perceived at work throughout the whole series of the dramatic poems. Indeed, two of his main characters, Isaac Comnenus and Philip Van Artevelde, he endowed with some qualities that are evidently his own. They are both men of action, vigorous and decisive in their outer lives, but with the power of holding their inner selves aloof and in reserve, noting their own behaviour, and the affairs in which they find themselves engaged, with a detached interest and a keen, dispassionate speculation. That is how Henry Taylor himself went through life. He was not a man of action. He was a very useful official in the Colonial Office, whose domestic experiences were nothing re-markable. But that was his attitude; in these two characters it is transposed into the key of a life of action. He had the power of looking on, of watching with an impersonal speculative interest the way the world dealt with him, and he dealt with the world. This comes out very strongly in the *Autobiography*. No doubt the reminiscent mood would encourage it; but the whole tone of the book is that of a man whose habitual con-sciousness has been in that style. Thus, his family was anxious for him to get married; so was he. He heads a chapter with the words "Diligent endeavours of friends to find me a wife", and opens it thus:

I have spoken of the distress which was suffered by my father and mother and Miss Fenwick through the overthrow of my hopes in April, 1838. And mixed with the sorrow was the fear either that I might not marry at all, or that I might be a long time in finding my way to a wife.

They and other of my friends had for some years been anxious to see me safely married, believing that I would not be happy in single life; and also, perhaps, believing that, through some sudden captivation, some inadvertency of commitment, I might very possibly one day or another make a marriage in which I would be less happy still.

That is a curiously impersonal way to speak of one's most intimate affairs; but readers of *Isaac Comnenus* and *Philip Van Artevelde* will recognise the attitude.

In the two heroes of these poems, perhaps the most curious appearance which this detached, impersonal attitude makes is their repudiation of the emotion of surprise or wonder. Comnenus declines to be surprised by any turn events may take. When he, the rebel, is most surprisingly, as one might think, visited by the Princess Theodora, she says

> Thou well mayst wonder, and I think thou dost,
> Albeit thou show'st it not;

to which he replies

> Not much; not much;
> Ten years are gone since I have felt surprise
> Save at my own existence and the stars.

But Philip Van Artevelde's refusal to wonder at things is quite unqualified:

> Treading the steps of common life with eyes
> Of curious inquisition, some will stare
> At each discovery of nature's ways,

As it were new to find that God contrives.
The contrary were marvellous to me,
And till I find it I shall marvel not.

Watts-Dunton, in one of those phrases which are designed to take the place of thinking, used to speak of the Romantic movement as "the renaissance of wonder". The description is sufficiently true to remind us that Sir Henry Taylor's hero, thus steadily and philosophically refusing to wonder at things, does not belong to Romanticism. And it is entirely characteristic of this hero that, at a climax of his emotional affairs, he should entertain his lady with a nice account of his intellectual habits—that he should see himself, at that moment, as part of the interesting process of life which he has noted in the world. The lady is indeed a romantic figure, as such ladies usually are. She is the high-minded, high-spirited courtesan whose sincere love comforts Philip in the dark conclusion of his career; and who, of course, has only become a courtesan through misfortune—a psychological misfortune, the story of which is rather subtly told in an intermezzo between the two parts of the drama, in a strain of lyrical narrative meant, perhaps, to be like Coleridge, but much more like Walter Scott. Taylor had, in fact, ventured to do something which a Romantic poet could hardly have endured to do. In the first part of the drama, when Philip's powers and fortunes are in the ascendant, he is nobly encouraged by Adriana, whom he loves in a very exalted fashion, though gravely and without transport; and it is a main factor in the tragedy of the second part that, immediately after his triumph, his first love dies. He is left alone, with only her memory to support him, in the losing battle of the second part, in which, for all his heroism, he gradually slides downhill to the perdition of all his hopes. At least, he is left alone until Elena arrives, and then, quite unromantically, but very exactly as things go in the world, he falls in love again. And love, which once blest his youthful aspiration with an ideal marriage, now consoles his middle-aged decline with a *liaison*. It says much for Henry Taylor's art that this second affair is as interesting and attractive as the first; and that, I think, is largely due to the way it reveals Philip's curious attitude to himself and to his concerns. Physical passion, one might suppose, would be a main element in his second love; and passion is certainly implied. But Philip can detach himself from the physical event, and, at a crucial moment of his relationship with Elena, compare his emotions with his early speculations in natural history. This is the sort of speech with which love inspires him: it is worth quoting not only as a psychological curiosity, but as a specimen of Taylor's poetic quality:

> Then I considered life in all its forms;
> Of vegetables first, next zoöphytes,
> The tribe that dwells upon the confine strange
> 'Twixt plants and fish; some are there from their mouth
> Spit out their progeny; and some that breed
> By suckers from their base or tubercles,
> Sea-hedgehog, madrepore, sea-ruff, or pad,
> Fungus, or sponge, or that gelatinous fish
> That taken from its element at once
> Stinks, melts, and dies a fluid;—So from these,
> Through many a tribe of less equivocal life,

Dividual or insect, up I ranged,
From sentient to percipient—small advance—
Next to intelligent, to rational next,
So to half-spiritual human-kind,
And what is more, is more than man may know.
Last came the troublesome question, what am I?
A blade, a seedling of this growth of life
Wherewith the outside of the earth is cover'd;
A comprehensive atom, all the world
In act of thought embracing; in the world
A grain scarce filling a particular place!
Thus travell'd I the region up and down
Wherein the soul is circumscribed below;
And unto what conclusion?

In any form of dramatic composition, we must always
beware how we discover the author in the characters he
invents. But I do not think any reader of the *Autobiography* could fail to recognise, in its consistent revelation of the author's disposition and mental attitude,
something very similar to the character of Philip Van
Artevelde.

No poet, perhaps, was ever more precisely conscious
of his purpose than Henry Taylor. The motto of
Philip Van Artevelde puts it exactly: *Dramatica poesis est
veluti Historia spectabilis.* *Historia spectabilis*—that, in
its most literal sense, in a far more literal sense than
Bacon ever intended, is the nature of Taylor's dramatic
poetry: and to present us with *Historia spectabilis* was a
work entirely suited both to his talents and his temperament. Apart from his minor pieces, the one exception is
that unfortunate fantasy *The Virgin Widow*, in which he

becomes, to me, perfectly unreadable; and of which I shall therefore say nothing.

His purpose, then, was not simply, or even primarily, to write dramatic poems: it was to dramatise history, to make history come to life. He had, I think, a genuine sense of history; certainly, it was his intention to exhibit with essential truth that which had actually happened. For him, the important thing in his subjects was that they *had* actually happened. To take purely artistic liberties with history would have been to defeat his real purpose. I am incompetent to judge how far his *Historia spectabilis* may be scientifically accurate. He has some verbal inaccuracies which are plain enough, apart from some odd scansions of proper names and foreign words (his *Eléna* was noted by his contemporaries). *Edwin the Fair* is a title which history would not very readily accept; the real name, Edwy, Taylor thinks was a pet-name, and takes as evidence of the king's popularity. He speaks, with strange indifference to grammar, of the witenagemot as "the witena". But broadly, his history seems sound enough, and may be a good deal sounder than I know. The truth that matters, however, lies as much in the epithet *spectabilis* as in the substantive *historia*. As far as the latter is concerned, perhaps we do not need to feel assured of more than this, in order to be affected as Henry Taylor intended: that at a certain time and place, capital events of a certain character happened, and went in a certain direction. Why they should have had just that character—why they should have gone in just that direction—these are the matters which, if they are made really understandable, will make *historia* truly *spectabilis*. This means, in effect, that Henry Taylor's business was to show the truth of history as the exponent of human nature. He had the experience which would enable him to do so; for he knew both men and affairs. The permanent official's half-exasperated, half-amused experience with politicians, for example, comes out in Philip Van Artevelde's description of the men to whom he had to entrust his difficult negotiations:

Than Lois de Vaux there's no man sooner sees
Whatever at a glance is visible;
What is not, that he sees not, soon nor late.
Quick witted is he, versatile, seizing points,
But never solving questions; vain he is—
It is his pride to see things on all sides,
Which best to do he sets them on their corners.
Present before him arguments by scores
Bearing diversely on the affair in hand,
He'll see them all successively distinctly,
Yet never two of them can see together,
Or gather, blend, and balance what he sees
To make up one account; a mind it is
Accessible to reason's subtlest rays,
And many enter there, but none converge;
It is an army with no general,
An arch without a key-stone.—Then the other,
Good Martin Blondel-Vatre—he is rich
In nothing else but difficulties and doubts;
You shall be told the evil of your scheme,
But not the scheme that's better; he forgets
That policy, expecting not clear gain,
Deals ever in alternatives; he's wise

In negatives, is skilful at erasures,
Expert in stepping backwards, an adept
At auguring eclipses; but admit
His apprehensions, and demand, What then?
And you shall find you've turned the blank leaf over.

The fine intelligence, that has the task of *making history*, can only make it through such instruments as these: that is one reason why history goes the way it does.

But Henry Taylor had not only the right experience to draw on for dramatising history; he had a very considerable power of psychological imagination; and it is chiefly by virtue of this that his history becomes *spectabilis*. This power, indeed, was by far the largest part of his poetical endowment; as we may see by turning to the shorter pieces in which it had no scope. He had a respectable command of versification and diction; but never the thrilling rhythm, never the magic phrase. Yet he has some good images; and what is specially to his credit, can make striking use of common things; as when Wulfstan (whose character of inefficient wisdom was suggested by Coleridge), speaking to his text that "love changes with the changing life of man", contrasts the freedom of its growth in youth with what happens when love plants itself in later years:

In middle age—a garden through whose soil
The roots of neighbouring forest trees have crept—
It strikes on stringy customs bedded deep,
Perhaps on alien passions.

Sometimes, too, his imagination can do the office

of description, as in this vignette of landscape in
Flanders:

> the tedious tract
> Of naked moorland, and the long flat road
> And slow straight stream, for ever side by side
> Like poverty and crime.

On the whole, though it is too often in the conventional dialect of verse-writing, his language is sufficiently interesting to deserve the name of poetry. But characterisation was his real business: provided, that is to say, he kept within the limits of his appointed purpose, and used his psychological imagination for dramatising history. When he went outside these limits, as in *The Virgin Widow*, his talents forsook him. Yet, in spite of that strange aberration (which occupied him four years), he knew well enough that, even if he stuck to history, he must take care to choose the right kind of history: he knew that his talents were fastidious. Once, when he was, as he says, "in search of a subject", Lord Aberdeen suggested the conquest of Naples by Charles of Anjou. But, adds Taylor, "I rejected it as too romantic, thinking that I should stand more firmly upon plainer ground". Indeed, what really suited him was *political* history. When some problem in the politics of a period offered itself to his experienced inquisition as something which might be explained, or at least set out, in terms of psychology, then his special talent did admirably. What, for example, was the secret of Dunstan's power? Why did he succeed and King Edwy fail? What did all those tales of St Dunstan and the Devil really mean? His psychological imagination gets to work; and we have

ARTHUR HUGH CLOUGH

By *Humbert Wolfe*

Arthur Hugh Clough—born 1819 and died 1861—is the perfect paradox. If he is regarded superficially—and it is very difficult to regard him in any other way —he is the complete middle Victorian. His birth, his education, his friends, his career might have been dictated to the VIth Form at Rugby by Dr Arnold as suitable for incrustation in the prose of Cicero or Vergilian verse. He left (or so it seemed) nothing undone that was required of a Victorian. He was born of a decent mercantile family, and if his father committed the slight irregularity of taking him from Liverpool to South Carolina in his fifth year, his mother saw to it that he remained completely insulated. He did not remain long enough to suffer the derangement of large horizons, and was soon back in England to enter into the spiritual dominion of Dr Arnold. At school he was so supremely his headmaster's favourite pupil that at times he appeared not only a prig but a model to all prigs—a satire on prigs savage enough, though too well-mannered, to have been written by Swift. Constantly quoted is a sentence from one of his letters, composed it would seem by some ironic fiend: "I verily believe my whole being is soaked through with the wishing and hoping and striving to do the school good". Faithfully tracing the path assigned he went as a scholar to Balliol, and there or later as Fellow of Oriel he encountered such wholly suitable companions as Jowett, Tait, Church, Thomas and Matthew Arnold (who were, of course, old Rugby friends), Shairp, Conington, Palgrave and Arthur Stanley. But still more appropriately he encountered the indispensable comrade of all serious Victorian youth—doubt. It is not clear at what point he stood in the Tractarian controversy. He was (it seems) accused of Newmanism—an accusation which he rebutted without heat. But whatever his doctrinal inclination both his moral and spiritual reflections were exactly what an inspired parodist would have invented. As to himself, he writes in 1841:

> How often sit I, poring o'er
>   My strange distorted youth,
> Seeking in vain, in all my store,
>   One feeling based on truth;
>
> Excitements come, and act and speech
>   Flow freely forth;—but no,
> Nor they, nor ought beside can reach
>   The buried world below.

While a few years later he was writing of his Maker:

> Do only Thou in that dim shrine,
> Unknown or known, remain, divine;
> There, or if not, at least in eyes
> That scan the fact that round them lies,
> The hand to sway, the judgment guide,
> In sight and sense Thyself divide:
> Be Thou but there,—in soul and heart,
> I will not ask to feel Thou art.

some of the initial honours showered on the novelist. But Clough, though he found friendship on every hand, found little else, and was glad to return a year later to a humble post in the Education Office found for him by Carlyle, to marry his Miss Smith, and to become the admirable father of three children. He died suddenly in Italy, when working on his last book *Mari Magno* and was buried—*O fortunate nimium*—outside Florence in the Protestant Cemetery that looks to Fiesole.

It would be difficult to conceive, if this be the true inward version of Clough's life and spirit, a destiny more suitable to the text-books, and one more perfectly fitted to be that of the poet of the tenacious times of Queen Victoria. But before we accept this as truth we must ask ourselves two things. How did it happen that a figure so lukewarm created even violent emotion in the breasts of some of the greatest and most sensitive souls of his time? And secondly how did this creature, carefully adjusted to a preconceived notion of his period, come to write that decisive little satire *A Decalogue* and still more *Dipsychus*, that utterly un-Victorian and completely neglected rendering of *Faust*? When we have weighed the answers to these two questions we shall, I think, be driven to conclude that behind the Clough of Rugby, Balliol and Oriel, behind the man who was the superficial prey of the major dubieties of his time, there lived and died, almost unknown, a dark splendour which was stamped with the hall-mark of passion, clean hatred, and a sense of withering distaste for shams as burning as Swift's and only muffled by the point of time in which he wrote.

Let us therefore consider first the testimony of his friends upon the ambiguous object of their worship. Take first Carlyle, whom he much frequented, and whose doctrines are alleged deeply to have concerned him. The not too forthcoming Scotsman wrote of him to Froude after his death thus: "A mind more vivid, more veracious, mildly radiant, I have seldom met with, and in a character so honest, modest, kindly. I expected great things of him". I ask you particularly to mark the last sentence, to which I shall revert in a moment. Shairp, in a poem written fourteen years after his death, wrote thus:

Foremost one stood with forehead high and broad—
   Sculptor ne'er moulded grander dome of thought—
Beneath it, eyes dark-lustred rolled and glowed,
   Deep wells of feeling where the full soul wrought;
Yet lithe of limb, and strong as shepherd boy,
He roamed the wastes and drank the mountain-joy
   To cool a heart too cruelly distraught.

Here again, apart from the profound admiration that the lines disclose, the significant point is the qualification of the "deep wells of feeling where the full soul wrought", by the reference in the last line to the distracted heart. Bagehot wrote of him after his death (and perhaps he comes nearest to the truth of any of them): "He was equal to his own precept:

Seek seeker, in thyself: submit to find
In the stones bread, and life in the blank mind.

To offer petty praise and posthumous compliments to a stoic of this temper is like bringing sugar-plums for St Simeon Stylites". I leave Matthew Arnold for the instant and cross the Atlantic to call Lowell, Longfellow, Emerson and Charles Norton to the witness-box. Lowell was a stout friend to Clough. He was his companion on the voyage to America when University Hall was abandoned, and he published *The Bothie* in the *Atlantic Monthly* from February to May 1858, paying what Clough considered "a handsome sum" for it. He wrote of this not very distinguished novel in hexameters: "I do not know a poem more impregnated with the Nineteenth Century, or fuller of tender force, and shy delicate humour". (Here again I ask you to note the epithet "shy".) Indeed, he made no doubt that Clough was a man of genius, saying: "Clough will be thought a hundred years hence to have been the truest expression in verse of the moral and intellectual tendencies, the doubt and struggle towards settled conviction of the period in which he lived". Longfellow is recorded to have said of him: "I like him exceedingly; with his gentleness and his bewildered look and his half-closed eyes" (again observe the "bewildered look"), while Norton was moved to claim "his life was a success such as scarcely one man in a generation achieves". Emerson, who truly loved him and of whom in one aspect Clough was a disciple, said no less of him than that he was "a new and better Carlyle". Finally we have Matthew Arnold—that great poet who, with his formidable father, is in my view largely responsible, though, of course, unconsciously, for Clough's withdrawal into himself. After Clough's death Matthew Arnold wrote: "That is a loss which I shall feel more and more", and then continues sadly musing, "People were beginning to say about Clough that he never would do anything now, and, in short, to pass him over. I foresee that there will now be a change, and attention will be fixed on what there was of extraordinary promise and interest in him when young, and of unique, and imposing even as he grew older without fulfilling people's expectation". Here I beg you to dwell on that air of wistful condescension which Arnold could not put on one side. That "promise", those "expectations"—what were they, and how in fact were they disappointed? A partial, and to me wholly misleading, though beautiful, answer is afforded in two of the last three verses of that marvellous threnody *Thyrsis*:

> Thou too, O Thyrsis, on like quest wast bound;
>   Thou wanderedst with me for a little hour!
>   Men gave thee nothing; but this happy quest,
> If men esteem'd thee feeble, gave thee power,
>   If men procured thee trouble, gave thee rest.
>   And this rude Cumner ground,
> Its fir-topped Hurst, its farms, its quiet fields,
>   Here cam'st thou in thy jocund youthful time,
>   Here was thine height of strength, thy golden prime!
> And still the haunt beloved a virtue yields.
>
> What though the music of thy rustic flute
>   Kept not for long its happy, country tone;
>   Lost it too soon, and learnt a stormy note
> Of men contention-tost, of men who groan,
>   Which task'd thy pipe too sore, and tired thy throat—
>   It fail'd and thou wast mute!
> Yet hadst thou always visions of our light,
>   And long with men of care thou couldst not stay,
>   And soon thy foot resumed its wandering way,
> Left human haunt, and on alone till night!

This is the last evidence that I shall call, and I shall hope to show that it clinches all the rest.

But clinches in what way? What, if we sum up, is the net effect of all these tributes? In the first place we perceive that Clough radiantly moved great spirits not only in the hey-day of his early youth—the golden prime of *Thyrsis*. He met Longfellow, Norton and Lowell in the middle 'thirties, and their witness is no less ringing than that of the friends of early manhood. He carried about with him—even when he seemed a failure in men's eyes, when his pipe was "task'd too sore" and his throat "tired"—some indwelling beauty and strength which, as the French say, imposed itself. We may conclude from this unanimity that, whether he realised expectations or not, there was to the end something in Clough that both excited and eluded. As to this again there is no doubt. In every case there is the insistence on his promise. Carlyle "expected great things of him" and Matthew Arnold reverts constantly to people's "expectation". Dr Arnold found in him the perfect embodiment of his vision of what posterity should be, and looked confidently to him to prove to the world what a Rugby man could be. That is one side of the testimony. The other is even more striking. Carlyle speaks of his "modesty", Shairp, going further, mentions a heart "cruelly distraught". Bagehot finds him a stoic, Longfellow recorded his "bewildered look and his half-closed eyes", and Matthew Arnold, rounding it all off, writes of the "happy quest" which when men "gave him nothing, gave him power". It is plain, therefore, that here Clough had his secret. It is, I think, equally plain that none of his friends and contemporaries plumbed it. Perhaps the passage of three-quarters of that century, of which Lowell spoke, will help us to make a reasonable guess.

I have briefly indicated the domination which Dr Arnold exercised over at least the outward expression of his pupil's mind. All that immense prestige, searching affection, and unrelenting purpose could achieve in moulding a boy's spirit was accomplished by the headmaster. He took upon himself the dangerous prerogative of God, and sought not merely to make Clough in his own image, but to breathe the breath of life into him. Arnold sent Clough out to Oxford as his individual creation, but when he despatched Matthew thither a year or two later he saw to it that his influence should remain vital, insistent and diurnal. There has been controversy as to what Clough meant when he said of himself at Oxford (in partial explanation of his failure in Schools) that he was "like a straw drawn up by the draught from a chimney". It has been supposed, as I suggested above, that it has a reference to his preoccupation with the religious controversy of the moment. Not a little support for this view can be found in his religious poems, full as they are of current perplexities. But my own belief is that the struggle, which was absorbing and was finally to destroy Clough's originality, was a much more personal one. It was in my view the agony of the innate satirical genius of Clough seeking in vain to rid itself of the swaddling-clothes of Arnoldism, and of all the honourable and clogging pieties of the period. Clough was not, as I think, desperately deciding whether to range himself with Newman or with Pusey. He was not drawn by one or the other. His instinct—defeated by circumstance—was to escape from both, and in that escape to free himself from the Arnold constriction, which in his inmost heart he was afraid to recognise as such, and which therefore closed gradually about him till it squeezed out life itself.

Though many critics have recognised the crippling nature of the influence of the two Arnolds, nobody has (as far as I know) yet stated Clough's tragedy in quite such definite terms. It is necessary, therefore, to defend the thesis in some detail. Let us look at one or two phrases in *Thyrsis* again for a moment, and then consider how wildly insensitive they are if related to the expressed Clough, and yet how unconsciously true if they refer to the inner Clough whom I am seeking to extricate. Matthew Arnold writes of Clough in his undergraduate and post-graduate days at Oriel as ranging over Cumner in his jocund youthful time—in his golden prime. Where either in his poems of the period, his letters, or the comments of his friends are we to find this jocundity, this visionary gold? While still at school, aged seventeen, we find this jocund spirit writing on the occasion of *An evening walk in Spring*:

> That they can soon and surely tell
> When aught has gone amiss within,
> When the mind is not sound and well
> Nor the soul free from taint of sin.

Not, you will concede, an uproariously jocund reflection on such an occasion for the most brilliant

Rugbeian of his day. Again when he is twenty we find
this reveller in youth writing:

> So I went wrong,
> Grievously wrong, but folly crushed itself,
> And vanity o'er-toppling fell, and time
> And healthy discipline and some neglect,
> Labour and solitary hours revived
> Somewhat, at least, of that original frame.

A year later Clough continues his "happy country tone"
with

> Come back again, old heart! Ah me!
> Methinks in those thy coward fears
> There might, perchance, a courage be
> That fails in these the manlier years.

In 1841 he continues his careless youthful raptures with
a series of sonnets blithely entitled *Blank Misgivings of a
Creature moving about in worlds realized.* While Clough
was thus performing on his rustic flute in public, in
private he was writing letters informed with a certain
drab despair, as when he said after signing the Thirty-
Nine Articles (with certain internal reservations): "My
own justification to myself is simply that I can feel faith
in what is being carried on by my generation, and that
I am content to be an operative—to dress intellectual
leather, cut it out to pattern, and stitch it and cobble it
into boots and shoes for the benefit of the work which is
being guided by wiser heads".

All these expressions have been seriously (and, as I
think, pompously) construed into a confession of extreme spiritual anguish. W. G. Ward, his friend, seeing
the thing as did all the others, and thereby actually

helping to the very conclusion which he prayed to avert, said: "What was before all to have been desired for him was that during his undergraduate career he should have given himself up thoroughly to his classical and mathematical studies, and kept himself from plunging prematurely into the theological controversies then so rife at Oxford...". It was indeed to have been desired that he should not have been distracted from his University studies, and from something even more important—the possession of his own soul—by controversies. But was the controversy, as has been generally supposed, a theological one? I believe not, and for the following reasons.

Matthew Arnold, as we have seen, testifies to his youthful jocundity—a testimony categorically contradicted by all that we have in writing. Either then Arnold was talking conventionally of the assumed universal happiness of youth—still Nature's priest—or he was unconsciously laying his finger on the real secret of Clough's trouble. Might it not be, indeed must it not have been, that there was in Clough a laughing cavalier who was to find himself drawn not by the sympathetic hand of Franz Hals but by the melancholy pencil of some mid-Victorian worthy? Is it not likely (as we shall see in a minute) that the "vivid, mildly radiant and ingenious" mind of which Carlyle wrote was conscious of a growing and inevitable suffocation?

Let us from this angle consider two significant aspects of his poetry. We have in the first place the passionate regret with which he turns from youth, and the friends of his youth. Of all his early poems only those in this key have any real merit—a fact which Matthew Arnold was too good a critic to miss and yet too close to Clough, and too much himself to understand. *Parting* contains the verse implicit with all his secret longing for the irretrievable:

> O tell me, friends, while yet ye hear,—
> May it not be, some coming year,
> These ancient paths that here divide
> Shall yet again run side by side,
> And you from there, and I from here,
> All on a sudden reappear?
> O tell me, friends, while yet ye hear!

But alas! it was but little that his friends were hearing, and that all distorted. And next in *Qua cursum ventus* his inner self—the jocund, the hopeful, the destined to no consummation—does for an instant fling off the bonds of tradition, discipline and defeat, to cry in the two splendid verses that Matthew Arnold rightly celebrated:

> But O blithe breeze! and O great seas,
>   Though ne'er, that earliest parting past,
> On your wide plain they join again,
>   Together lead them home at last.
>
> One port, methought, alike they sought,
>   One purpose hold where'er they fare—
> O bounding breeze, O rushing seas!
>   At last, at last, unite them there!

Vain hope, vain cry, for the spirit within and the spirit without were never to be united, precisely because Clough guessed but did not dare to acknowledge even to himself what these two spirits were.

We have at least one point established. Clough

bitterly regrets the youth he is leaving, and yet his own account of that youth is so sombre as to suggest that no reasonable soul could ever wish to have it back again. He must, therefore, since he was neither dishonest nor wholly self-blinded, have been reaching back to the true Clough—Matthew Arnold's jocund spirit who could and did see life in reasonable proportion as a home for men and women and not for lost causes missing one another in a self-righteous fog.

This view is supported if not proved (and, indeed, to claim proof is beside my aim) by *The Bothie of Tober-Na-Vuolich*—written in September 1848, after taking his decision to throw up his Fellowship, and first published in November of that year by Macpherson at Oxford. *The Bothie* was a surprise to all who expected of Clough a pseudo-philosophical poem explaining the religious doubts which had led him to take so vital a decision. But ought it to have been a surprise? It is true that in 1845 he had written the much-discussed *Qui laborat orat*, which contained among other verses the lines:

> If well-assured 'tis but profanely bold
> In thought's abstractest forms to seem to see,
> It dare not dare the dread communion hold
> In ways unworthy Thee.
>
> O not unowned, thou shalt unnamed forgive,
> In worldly walks the prayerless heart prepare;
> And if in work its life it seem to live,
> Shalt make that work be prayer.

Here, it is urged, is full justification for the view that it was religion and religious doubt that was possessing and distracting his soul. How then account for the

sharp clarity of *Duty*, written at the end of 1847 or the
beginning of 1848, which reveals in a flash the satirist
beating his hands in vain against the muffled iron doors
of Victorian insensibility:

> 'Tis the coward acquiescence
>   In a destiny's behest,
> To a shade by terror made,
>   Sacrificing, aye, the essence
>   Of all that's truest, noblest, best:
>
> 'Tis the blind non-recognition
>   Or of goodness, truth or beauty,
> Save by precept and submission;
>   Moral blank, and moral void,
>   Life at very birth destroyed.

Which of these two is Clough's inmost soul speaking?
The gentle submission to the moral blank and void
of the earlier Arnold-dictated poem, or the outright
savagery of a desperate warrior, like Cuchullain "taking
arms against a sea of troubles", and by opposing being
ended, swamped, drowned and finally pickled in brine
by them. I do not believe that there can be two answers
to that question.

If, therefore, we are right in assuming that Clough
resigned his Fellowship only superficially to escape Holy
Orders, but actually—though perhaps only half-con-
sciously—to escape the trammels of what he would himself never have called Arnoldism, we at any rate need not
be surprised at the nature of *The Bothie*. So far from
being a religious meditation, it is an almost rollicking
account of a reading-party in the Highlands with a very
cheerful and human love-story running through it. We

need not delay ourselves too long with the hexameter-form in which it was written. Clough himself indicated that he had been affected by Longfellow's *Evangeline*, and Matthew Arnold—who called the poem serio-comic—spoke of its admirable Homeric qualities and even suggested that "Dangerous Corrievreckan... Where roads are unknown to Loch Nevish" had the true Homeric ring, For my part I should have thought that if one thing were certain it is that no sustained poem can be written in English hexameters any more than a man with his feet hobbled can hope to beat a champion sprinter in a hundred yards race. Nor am I sure that Clough really thought that great poetry could be written in hexameters. *The Bothie* was not intended to be great, and perhaps not even to be poetry. It was rather an immense sigh of relief, a schoolboy shout on escaping from school into the air. He would confound all that damnable priggish expectation—which was his life's bane—by writing a rapid, good-humoured story, and to crown all he would write it in the roughest, merriest form which should set them all guessing. For, if this were seriously intended as a poem and not as an explosion of high spirits, how are we, as a matter of form, even to begin to explain lines such as:

Philip shall write us a book, a Treatise upon *The Laws of Architectural Beauty in Application to Women*;

and still more unpronounceably:

Wherefore in Badenoch drear, in lofty Lochaber, Locheil, and
Knoydart, Moydart, Morrer, Ardgower and Ardnamurchan.

It appears to me, at least, that Clough chose the metre as the most obviously outrageous that lay to his hand, and that he was humming cheerfully to himself as he wrote:

> Each for himself is still the rule;
> We learn it when we go to school—
> The devil take the hindmost, O!
>
> And when the schoolboys grow to men,
> In life they learn it o'er again—
> The devil take the hindmost, O!

It must not, of course, be supposed that *The Bothie* does not occasionally strike off genuine poetic sparks in spite of the heavy handicap to which Clough with, as I think, deliberate malice, subjected himself—as, for example:

It was on Saturday eve, in the gorgeous bright October,
Then when brackens are changed, and heather blooms are faded,
And amid russet of heather and fern green trees are bonnie;
Alders are green, and oaks; the rowan scarlet and yellow;
One great glory of broad gold pieces appears the aspen,
And the jewels of gold that were hung in the hair of the birch-tree,
Pendulous, here and there, her coronet, necklace and ear-rings,
Cover her now, o'er and o'er; she is weary and scatters them from her.

But occasional poetic beauty is not the main business here. Clough is rejoicing first in freedom, and second in his new-found ability to tell a straightforward story with vigour and interest—a power which he was to exhibit again in *Amours de Voyage* and in the unfinished *Mari Magno*. The real essence of the poem is the implicit and sometimes overt criticism of existing tradition. There is

some schoolboyish enunciation of the theory that a
woman's place is the home (odd on the lips of the brother
of Newnham's first Head). But the truer note breaks out
in such an episode as the radical Hewson's speech at the
Highland sports dinner given by Sir Hector, the Chief-
tain. After certain ambiguous tributes to the community
between English and Scots, cemented by bows, bills and
claymores, he deprecates the honour of replying for the
Oxford party thus:

I have, however, less claim than others perhaps to this honour,
For, let me say, I am neither game-keeper, nor game-preserver.

It is the voice of defiant and satiric criticism which was
to speak clearer and louder in *Dipsychus* and then after
The Decalogue for ever to hold its peace.

But how are we to reconcile the cheerful humours of
the reading-party and the amiable love-affair of Philip
and Elspie with Matthew Arnold's complaint that only
too soon Clough's "happy country tone" was exchanged for a "stormy note"? We have seen instances
of that happy country note emitted while Clough was
enduring the confinement of Oxford. Now having
shaken free with almost irrepressible spirits he is giving
vent to "the stormy note". Is not the inevitable inference that Matthew Arnold was bitterly lamenting not
that Clough had lost his own way but that he had lost
Arnold's? Was he not secretly finding this extravagant
fun as beneath the high seriousness of the Rugby tradition, and viewing Clough in consequence with a quite
undeserved and mistaken compassion? Was it not rather
the truth that Clough, if only for a little while, had

escaped from the stormy note of his leaden prime to
exult in the country tone of his early middle years? And
is it not more than probable, if he had been as heartily
encouraged by his friends and his period to be a humanist
and a satirist as he was to be don and a mild worshipper
of the established order, *The Bothie* would have been
only the first step in the ultimate enfranchise of a genius
almost as extravagantly full of the fun of life as G. K.
Chesterton himself?

For my part I believe that the answer is "yes". Nor do
I base this only on the evidence of *The Bothie*. I observe
that, leaving *Dipsychus* on one side, the three most considerable poems in the matter of scope that Clough
attempted were all swift, direct, story-telling, and in no
way disturbed by introspection or self-accusation. It is
true that Clough prefaces the first of these poems with
two dingy quotations—dingy, that is, in their attitude to
the world—

> O you are sick of self-love, Malvolio,
> And taste with a distempered appetite!

and
> Il doutait de tout, même de l'amour.

These quotations might have prepared the reader for
something very different from a second spirited adven-
ture in hexameters. Claude—the indecisive hero—who
finds so little to please him in Rome and later so much to
please him in Georgina Trevellyn, is by no means a
young Werther. He suffers neither from world-pain
nor excessive self-depreciation. His trouble is a much
simpler and much less precious one. He simply cannot
make up his mind whether he wants his Georgina

enough to surrender the delights of freedom. He is no
fool, this Claude. On the contrary, he is no little of an
observer and an ironic observer. He writes of Italy as
he sees it:

This, their choicest of prey, this Italy; here you see them,—
Here, with emasculate pupils, and gimcrack churches of Gesu,
Pseudo-learning and lies, confessional-boxes and postures,—
Here, with metallic beliefs and regimental devotions,—
Here, overcrusting with slime, perverting, defacing, debasing,
Michel Angelo's Dome, that had hung the Pantheon in
    heaven,
Raphael's Joys and Graces, and thy clear stars, Galileo!

And as his inconclusive love-affair moves on its languid
way he compensates for his failure as a lover by an ever-
increasing sharpness of satiric comment—comment that
cumulatively is before *Dipsychus* the most serious
satirical performance of the middle century.

Here, for example, is a most luminous attack on the
father of Protestantism:

Luther, they say, was unwise; like a half-taught German, he
    could not
See that old follies were passing most tranquilly out of
    remembrance;
He must forsooth make a fuss and distend his huge Witten-
    berg lungs, and
Bring back Theology once yet again in a flood upon Europe:

which is followed by this reflection on decent middle-
class social climbers:

Ah, what a shame, indeed, to abuse these most worthy
    people!

Ah, what a sin to have sneered at their innocent rustic
    pretensions !
Is it not laudable really, this reverent worship of station ?
Is it not fitting that wealth should tender this homage to
    culture ?
Is it not touching to witness these efforts, if little availing,
Painfully made, to perform the old ritual service of manners ?

While here is as stout a comment on the fancied glamour
of war as the most impenitent pacifist of us all could
desire:

Dulce it is, and decorum, no doubt, for the country to
    fall,—to
Offer one's blood an oblation to Freedom, and die for the
    Cause; yet
Still, individual culture is also something, and no man
Finds quite distinct the assurance that he of all others is
    called on.

Sweet it may be and decorous, perhaps, for the country to
    die; but
On the whole, we conclude the Romans won't do it, and I
    sha'n't.

Or later after the battle between the French and the
Romans for the possession of the Eternal City:

                 Death may
Sometimes be noble; but life, at the best, will appear an
    illusion.
While the great pain is upon us, it is great; when it is over,
Why, it is over. The smoke of the sacrifice rises to heaven,
Of a sweet savour, no doubt, to Somebody; but on the altar,
Lo, there is nothing remaining but ashes and dirt and ill
    odour.

From which we proceed to a bitter valuation of the
origins of marriage thus:

Juxtaposition, in fine; and what is juxtaposition?
Look you, we travel along in the railway carriage or steamer,
And, pour passer le temps, till the tedious journey be ended,
Lay aside paper or book, to talk with the girl that is next one;
And, pour passer le temps, with the terminus all but in
    prospect,
Talk of eternal ties and marriages made in heaven.

Ah, ye feminine souls, so loving and so exacting,
Since we cannot escape, must we even submit to deceive you?
Since so cruel is truth, sincerity shocks and revolts you,
Will you have us, your slaves to lie to you, flatter—and
    leave you.

I beg you to ponder for a moment upon these extracts
typical of the penetrating, clear-headed, if slightly
petulant, attitude of the whole work. I then ask you to
remember that the book is not only an active and even
exciting account of a frustrated love-affair, but finds
occasion to offer brilliant little pictures of the siege of
Rome, of Roman scenery, of pictures and contemporary
Italian life. Then I would have you wonder whither is
fled Shairp's "mind distraught", what has happened to
"the intellectual perplexity which" W. G. Ward felt
"preyed heavily on his spirits, and grievously interfered
with his studies", how has Longfellow's "bewildered
look" changed to a glance so keenly sure, and, above all,
what of the "sorely tasked pipe and tired throat".
Surely some conspiracy of blindness—product no
doubt of the age—darkened his friends, who sought with
persistent, and, to me ridiculous, sympathy to find in one

who might and should have taken his place among the great English satirists, a dreamer, a sensitive plant not fit for the daily commerce of wind and rain, above all, an exquisite, shadowy Pierrot of a scholar-gipsy skulking in his long sleeves always in the dark outside the window of the impossible beloved.

It irked him, writes Matthew Arnold,

> It irk'd him to be here, he could not rest.
> He loved each simple joy the country yields,
> He loved his mates; but yet he could not keep,
> For that a shadow lour'd on the fields,
> Here with the shepherds and the silly sheep.
> · Some life of men unblest
> He knew, which made him droop, and fill'd his head.
> He went; his piping took a troubled sound
> Of storms that rage outside our happy ground;
> He could not wait their passing.

Always, you see, the same faint beauty, and always this insistence on the change from youthful jocundity to the "troubled sound". You have had examples of the earlier mood, and you have heard the later. Which is troubled, and which speaks the true Clough, who of all men ever created should have prayed to be saved from his friends?

Yet even in their despite and in despite of the attitude they continuously thrust upon him, his native genius for satire made a last if not wholly successful bid to express the true Clough in *Dipsychus*. Let us, before we examine the poem, remember that though it was the third of his first three long poems, it was written in 1850 by a man of thirty-one—not very old to have arrived at

so acute a comprehension of the contradictions of life,
and not very old, alas! to have bidden farewell to the
genius that was actually not to manifest itself again till
the year of death which found him writing the Chau-
cerian *Mari Magno*.

The spirit of *Dipsychus*—as I have called it, the mid-
Victorian *Faust*—is admirably conveyed in *The Latest
Decalogue*—a poem probably written not much later, in
which is one of the most convincing pieces of short
satire in the language:

> Thou shalt have one God only; who
> Would be at the expense of two?
> No graven images may be
> Worshipped, except the currency:
> Swear not at all; for, for thy curse
> Thine enemy is none the worse:
> At church on Sunday to attend
> Will serve to keep the world thy friend:
> Honour thy parents; that is, all
> From whom advancement may befall;
> Thou shalt not kill; but needst not strive
> Officiously to keep alive:
> Do not adultery commit;
> Advantage rarely comes of it:
> Thou shalt not steal; an empty feat,
> When it's so lucrative to cheat:
> Bear not false witness; let the lie
> Have time on its own wings to fly:
> Thou shalt not covet, but tradition
> Approves all forms of competition.

Dipsychus begins in the Piazza at Venice with a conversation (sustained throughout the poem) between the

doubter and the Tempter. The scene ends with the
Tempter observing:

> And see that fellow singing yonder;
> Singing, ye gods, and dancing too—
> Tooraloo, tooraloo, tooraloo, loo—
> Fiddledi, diddledi, diddle di di;
> Figaro sù, Figaro giù—
> Figaro quà, Figaro là!
> How he likes doing it—Ha ha!

To which Dipsychus replies:

> While these do what? Ah, heaven! too true, at Venice
> Christ is not risen either.

Dipsychus later in the public garden has his moment of
doubt when he cries:

> Why did I ever one brief moment's space
> But parley with this filthy Belial?
>   Was it the fear
> Of being behind the world, which is the wicked?

Thence Dipsychus is lured into Society. He speaks of it
most Juvenal thus:

>   At the best,
> With pallid hotbed courtesies to forestall
> The green and vernal spontaneity,
> And waste the priceless moments of the man
> In regulating manner.

But the Tempter rounds off the scene cheerfully with:

> 'Tis sad to what democracy is leading—
> Give me your Eighteenth Century for high breeding,
> Though I can put up gladly with the present,
> And quite can think our modern parties pleasant.

One shouldn't analyse the thing too nearly:
The main effect is admirable clearly.
"Good manners", said our great aunts, "next to piety":
And so, my friend, hurrah for good society!

This is followed by a scene in which Dipsychus refuses to fight a duel with a Croat officer who has insulted him, on the ground that so small a thing is not worth the peril of life, and is thus mocked by his Spirit:

Post haste, to attend—you're ripe and rank for't—
The great peace-meeting up at Frankfort.

(A little "Hudibras" this, wouldn't you say?)

Joy to the Croat! Take our lives,
Sweet friends and please respect our wives;
Joy to the Croat! Some fine day,
He'll see the error of his way,
No doubt, and will repent and pray.
At any rate he'll open his eyes,
If not before, at the Last Assize.

Then an excursion to the Lido on which in exchange for an outburst from Dipsychus which contains among other savage lines these:

Ye men of valour and of worth,
Ye mighty men of arms come forth,
And work your will, for that is just;
And in your impulse put your trust,
Beneath your feet the fools are dust.
Alas, alas! O grief and wrong,
The good are weak, the wicked strong;
And O my God, how long, how long!
Ding, there is no God; dong:

the Tempter chants:

> "There is no God," the wicked saith,
>   "And truly its a blessing,
> For what He might have done with us
>   It's better only guessing":

ending with

> But country folks who live beneath
>   The shadow of the steeple;
> The parson and the parson's wife,
>   And mostly married people;
>
> Youths green and happy in first love,
>   So thankful for illusion;
> And men caught out in what the world
>   Calls guilt, in first confusion;
>
> And almost everyone when age,
>   Disease, or sorrows strike him,
> Inclines to think there is a God,
>   Or something very like Him.

From this we have one of the two ravishing songs of the book, which show how gallant and how jocund an ear is the possession of this distraught shadow:

> Afloat; we move. Delicious! Ah,
> What else is like the gondola?
> This level floor of liquid glass
> Begins beneath us swift to pass.
> It goes as though it went alone
> By some impulsion of its own.
> (How lightly it moves, how softly! Ah,
> Were all things like the gondola!)

And the second follows almost immediately beginning with:

> As I sat at the café, I said to myself,
> They may talk as they please about what they call pelf,
> They may sneer as they like about eating and drinking,
> But help it I cannot, I cannot help thinking,
>> How pleasant it is to have money, heigh ho!
>> How pleasant it is to have money.

After this Dipsychus discusses his future career with the fiend who cries:

> If not the Church, why then the Law.
> By Jove, we'll teach you how to draw!
> Besides, the best of the concern is
> I'm hand and glove with the attorneys.
> With them and me to help, don't doubt
> But in due season you'll come out;
> Leave Kelly, Cockburn, in the lurch,
> But yet, do think about the Church.

To which succeeds the undiluted Faust motif in the examination of his soul by Dipsychus, ending rather in the accent of the melancholy Dane:

>   Oh, how would then
> These pitiful rebellions of the flesh,
> These caterwaulings of the effeminate heart,
> These hurts of self-imagined dignity,
> Pass like the seaweed from about the bows
> Of a great vessel speeding straight to sea!
> Yes, if we could have that; but I suppose
> We shall not have it, and therefore I submit!

To which the Tempter replies:

> Submit, submit!
> For tell me then, in earth's great laws
> Have you found any saving clause,
> Exemption special granted you
> From doing what the rest must do?
> Of common sense who made you quit,
> And told you, you'd no need of it,
> Nor to submit.

The struggle between the Soul and Satan continues with a Gustav Doré chorus of angels intervening, ending with the submission of Dipsychus thus:

> So your poor bargain take, my man,
> And make the best of it you can.

To which Satan replies:

> With reservations! Oh, how treasonable!
> When I had let you off so reasonable.

And with a final spurt of bitter humour the devil, in being challenged to reveal his identity, says he cares little whether he be called Mephistophiles, Belial, or what not, but suggests as a convenient title either Cosmocrator, or Cosmarchon, adding:

> Cosmarchon's shorter, but sounds odd:
> One wouldn't like, even if a true devil,
> To be taken for a vulgar Jew devil.

We need not devote too much attention to the *Poems of Love and Duty* and religious poems. For here we have, as I suggest, the Clough *malgré lui*, the honest doubter of *In Memoriam*, because honest doubt is the rôle assigned to him by his melancholy-loving associates. Nor need we explore *Mari Magno*, the happy return to his true

D

medium of story-telling in verse, which, though excellent
and native stuff, shows but little advance on *The Bothie*
and the *Amours de Voyage*. Its interest is only to demon-
strate the tragic fact that in spite of everything Clough,
as he really was, remained alive and capable of self-
expression to the end.

But if we consider *The Bothie*, *Amours de Voyage* and
Dipsychus dispassionately it seems to me that we have
overwhelming proof that in Clough a great natural
satirist and story-teller was smothered not by his own
doubts but by the doubts thrust upon him by his friends.
Born in a happier time, a less superficially introspective
time, he would, I believe, have found a place beside
Dryden and Byron as one of the greatest of the English
in the satiric mode. All the circumstances of his life and
time combined to defeat this—Dr Arnold, the false
expectations of his friends, the hatred of his age for clear
Attic laughter, and above all its immense appetite for
morbid self-analysis. He was in truth Dipsychus, but the
Tempter against whom he was struggling, and to whom
in the end he submitted, was not the spirit of Evil, but
the spirit of Prussian jack-booted Good. Again and again
his valiant spirit made desperately gay sorties outside the
walls of the besieged city. But in vain. For there were
traitors within the gate, who lifted their eyebrows at his
gallant adventures into the open. Till in the end he
reconciled himself to the starvation diet of the invested
city of his soul, and lived the life of the professional
martyr assigned to him by the temper of the times. But
for all that he had flung down his glove more than once,
and Time, as Lowell prophesied, is picking it up for him.

THE EARLY NOVELS OF
WILKIE COLLINS

By *Walter de la Mare*

Like other human beings, a novelist is sole tenant of his House of Life. Its rooms may be few or many, its cellar dank or sweet, its acreage wide, its views ample or restricted, its gables and attics high up among the four winds of heaven, or not so; but *un*like most men, he shares that house with a concourse of strangers—his readers. Again and again, as his several novels are published, he "shows them over", though in so doing he need nowhere appear in his own person, as does poet, essayist, critic or philosopher. Instead, he masquerades in many disguises—his characters; each one of whom, none the less, whatever its origin, cannot but be, in some respects, compounded of his own mind, experience and personality. This, if self-expression is a benefit to human nature, may be of substantial advantage to him, since few of us are so simple as to possess only one "I". Apart from mask and domino, however, he may also deliberately rearrange some of the furniture of his house, set aside one or two rooms mainly for show, and keep shut up and locked the more private and, possibly, even the most interesting.

This being so, even a few pages of autobiography, a few letters, or the brief and quiet reminiscences of a friend, may richly aid our understanding of him; and without danger of intrusion. Indeed, of the foremost Victorian novelists—Dickens, Thackeray, Trollope, George Eliot, Lytton, Charles Reade—we have abundant (and perhaps even a superfluity of) direct knowledge. Wilkie Collins is an exception. He remains a little remote from them all—a somewhat enigmatical figure. As yet he has not even been accorded a niche in the "English Men of Letters" series.

Yet of the conspicuous novels published in the three years, 1859–61—and an abundant and enviable harvest it was—*The Virginians, A Tale of Two Cities, Adam Bede, The Mill on the Floss, Evan Harrington, Framley Parsonage, Orley Farm, The Cloister and the Hearth, Great Expectations, Silas Marner* and *The Woman in White*, the title of the last-mentioned is so familiar that one is apt not to notice its meaning (i.e. that she was not in *Black*), and *No Name*, of 1862, is in some respects a better novel. It has a more supple plot and is less melodramatic.

Fiction has always been looked down upon by the superior as the Cinderella of literature. Even as recently as 1894, with Wilkie Collins himself for text, Swinburne could rail at the neglect and belittlement of the novelists of his time. Kings and democracies, he fulminated, had always been notorious for base ingratitude—the serpent's tooth. But "readers and spectators", from Shakespeare's day even to his own, had been no less culpable.

A man, (he continued) who has amused our leisure, relieved our weariness, delighted our fancy, enthralled our attention, and refreshed our sympathies, cannot claim a place of equal honour in our grateful estimation with the dullest or the most perverse of historians who ever falsified or stupefied

history, or metaphysicians who ever "darkened counsel" and
wasted time and wearied attention by the profitless lucubra-
tions of pseudosophy. To create is nothing: to comment is
much. The commentary may be utterly hollow and rotten,
the creation thoroughly solid and alive; the one is nothing
less than criticism, the other nothing more than fiction. "Une
âne qui ressemble à monsieur Nisard" takes precedence, in
the judgment of his kind, of the men on whose works, in-
ventive or creative, it is the business of a Nisard to pass
judgment and to bray.

The pungency of this attack has evaporated. The
pedantic ass still brays, perhaps, but he munches up the
plentiful thistles of fiction with the rest, and nowadays
wins perhaps even less of a hearing than he deserves.

Swinburne's essay, however, is concerned with Collins
as a writer, not with Collins as a man. He was born in
New Cavendish Street in the summer of 1824. There was
authorship in his ancestry, his grandfather, a picture
dealer, having endeavoured to prove himself a poet; but
there was more paint, and this on both sides of his family.
At fourteen he left his private school and travelled with
his father in Italy. There he remained for two years, and
on his return home was articled to a firm of tea-merchants.
He began to write—possibly in his teens, certainly in his
early twenties: *Antonina* being the first and the least
characteristic of about thirty books in all, only three of
which are not fiction. It is an historical romance of the
Bulwer Lytton pattern—full of violence, both of events
and style, and culminating in the sack of Rome by the
Goths. Its characters have that effect of an ornate un-
reality which seems to be so difficult to avoid when

human beings—doubtless much "like you and me"—
are contemplated through a veil of many centuries:

"Slay on! Slay on!" answered the raving voice [of the
insane Ulpius] from within. "Slay, till not a Christian is
left! Victory! Serapis! See, they drop from our walls!—
they writhe bleeding on the earth beneath us! There is no
worship but the worship of the gods! Slay! Slay on!"...

"Light!" cried the priest. "His damnation be on his own
head! Anathema! Maranatha! Let him die accursed!"

A touch here and there in this almost unreadable
romance may hint at the author of *The Woman in White*,
but only a critical seer could have foretold the later novels
after reading *Antonina*.

Its happiest feature is that while it was still in manuscript it gave his proud father so much pleasure that
Wilkie was thereupon released from Tea. His name was
entered at Lincoln's Inn, and he was called to the Bar in
1851. Still more fortunately, *Antonina* was succeeded by
nothing of its precise genre. Meanwhile Collins had
begun to paint, and in 1849 he exhibited a landscape in
the Academy.

His father had died two years before, and in 1848 his
son published *Memoirs of the Life of William Collins*. This
is a remarkable book not only for the reason that it was
written when he was only in his twenty-fourth year, but
for its endearing loyalty and affection, its modesty, insight, judgment, dignity, and quiet and sedate style.
There is no observable trace of filial flattery (or of filial
prejudice), and all is straightforward. "No man ever
lived", Wilkie Collins said of his father, "who less

affected mystery in his Art"; he was never ambitious to be the "Colossus of a clique". Like father, like son.

Even in the earliest pages of the *Memoirs*, the craftsmanship of the future novelist definitely shows itself:

Had Hastings in 1816, been what Hastings is in 1848, the fashionable loiterers who now throng that once unassuming little "watering-place", would have felt no small astonishment when they set their listless feet on the beach, yawned at the library window, or cantered drowsily along the sea-ward rides, in beholding, at all hours from earliest morning to latest evening, and in all places, from the deck of the fishing boat, to the base of the cliff, the same solitary figure, laden, day after day, with the same sketching materials, and drawing object after object, through all difficulties and disappointments, with the same deep abstraction and the same unwearied industry.

The "solitary figure" is that of William Collins in distant retrospect; but the passage might well be the opening of one of his son's novels.

That father's earlier years had been a struggle against poverty. When he was a boy, his mother was left so poor after her husband's death—all his possessions having been sold up to pay his creditors—that they sat down to dinner together with an old packing-case for a table. Things soon bettered, however, and in a few years his career was assured. He devoted himself to his art; and even on his deathbed, in 1847, made a water-colour sketch of some objects at the foot of it which had reminded his fading eyes of an old derelict ferry-boat moored at an abandoned quay. In 1811, when he was only twenty-three, commissions were coming in, and he could venture to address to the Secretary of the Royal Academy a protest at the "degrading situation" in which one of his pictures had been hung in the exhibition at Somerset House—in the fireplace. There, not only its beautiful gilt but even its canvas was in danger from the hoofs of the devotee. Might he protect it with a wooden framework? The reply, dated May Day, was hardly less mild than the remonstrance:

I cannot help expressing some surprise that you should consider the situation of your picture degrading, knowing as I do, that the Committee of Arrangement thought it complimentary, and that, low as it is, many members of the Academy would have been content to have it.

Three years after this protest he was elected an Associate; within six he was a full R.A. No fewer than one hundred and twenty-five of his canvases were welcomed to the august walls, and the majority of them to the "line". "As Happy as a King" was one of the most popular; its title shows his general choice of subject; and to judge from the only example of his pictures I have seen, their naturalness and simplicity are still as fresh and pleasing to the mind as are their colours to the eye.

Unfortunately William Collins hated letter-writing, though he took great pains with it. Apart from vivid glimpses of George Morland, Wilkie and Scott, references to famous contemporaries in the *Memoirs* are therefore tantalising in their brevity: "Dined with Raeburn"; "Wordsworth read to me"; "Your hints about Coleridge I did not fail attending to". Read what? What hints? Alas, though this last-mentioned "profound and philosophic poet" would sit by his friend's easel pouring forth "mystic speculations into his attentive ear", not one of them is recorded. None the less, literature was in the family, one of its treasured traditions being that on the father's side it was of the same stock as that of the author of the *Ode to Evening*. For this rather nebulous reason William Collins was wedded free of charge—and by a Scottish minister.

The *Memoirs* are seldom merely anecdotal; they are the quiet and veracious record of the life of a man who manifestly deserved every ounce of loving admiration his son accorded him—of a father whose companionship must have been a priceless blessing to such a son. Full, however, though they are of life, humanity, scene, comment and criticism, there are few clear impressions of their young author. All that we see of him is a faint reflection in the looking-glass behind the pious, ardent and lovable image of his father; sharing with him a gondola in the very middle of the Grand Canal on market day, while he placidly paints on—Beppo, their gondolier on such occasions, having once been in service as cook to Lord Byron—or visiting with him the masterpieces in the picture galleries. Of himself there is, directly, little.

Rambles Beyond Railways, published in 1851, is a mild and, as its title suggests, rambling account of a walking-tour in Cornwall; and here there are more personal glimpses. To explain the fact, for example, that during his exploration of the copper-mine at Botallack, in miner's overalls four sizes too large for him, his gigantic guide gently lifted him by the slack of his trousers over a yawning gulf, he confesses that he was only 5 ft. 6 in. in height, and very near-sighted. There is also a lithograph by the artist-friend who accompanied him on his travels which depicts a personage (evidently intended to represent the author) in a very tall hat, and standing in imminent jeopardy beneath the monoliths of the Cheese Wring. But it bears no discernible resemblance to Millais' familiar spectacled portrait: the bulging studious forehead, the rounded chin sunk between the points of the wide collar, the elbows resting on the arms of the chair, the ringed fingers of the left hand precisely disposed on those of the right.

Wilkie Collins had chosen Cornwall for his rambles "because with Kamschatka it was then the most untrodden ground" that he could select, and his gossip about places and people, the politics, customs and industries of the county is lively and observant, touched with humour and usually jocular in tone. Here and there he becomes serious. At the Holy Well of St Clare with its ruinous oratory he laments the abandonment of the pious usage of a past age—the ceremonies of an English Church

whose innocent and reverent custom it was to connect closer together the beauty of nature and the beauty of religion, by such means as the consecration of a spring, or the erection of a roadside cross. There has been something of sacrifice as well as of glory, in the effort by which we, in our time, have freed ourselves from what was superstitious and ignorant in the faith of the times of old—it has cost us the loss of much of the better part of that faith, which was not superstitious, and of more which was not ignorance....

The eye of the painter is everywhere active, and occasionally, as in the *Memoirs*, a passage occurs which is not only characteristic of his fiction, but also of the rhythms and cadences of his prose. Here, for example, in the dim light of three tallow dips, he is sitting deep in the copper-mine, a hundred and twenty feet below sea level and four hundred yards from the shore, with but three feet of richly metalled rock between him and the Atlantic; and he listens:

After listening for a few moments, a distant, unearthly noise becomes faintly audible—a long, low, mysterious moaning, that never changes, that is *felt* on the air as well as *heard* by it—a sound that might proceed from some incalculable distance:—from some far invisible height—a sound unlike anything that is heard on the upper ground, in the free air of heaven—a sound so sublimely mournful and still, so ghostly and impressive when listened to in the subterranean recesses of the earth, that we continue instinctively to hold our peace, as if enchanted by it, and think not of communicating to each other the strange awe and astonishment which it has inspired in us both from the very first.

Cornwall, not then flattered as "the English Riviera" but no less lovely for that; still wild and desolate; its people, as he found them, courteous and hospitable, though strangers or "foreigners" were still "rare and mysterious curiosities"—Cornwall with its narrow gulfs of emerald greenery, its solemn cliffs begemmed with wild flowers, and its glass-clear snow-foamed sea, more than once reappears in the novels; but not then as mere scenery. It fed his imagination, as its hemlock and bugloss and sea-poppy are nourished by its sands.

In 1850, when *Antonina* was published, Wilkie Collins met Dickens, then in his fortieth year and already famous as the author of eight of his principal novels. Collins was then only twenty-six, but they soon became, as they remained to the end, the closest of friends, a friendship of "inestimable value" to Collins, though perhaps the literary influences involved in it were not wholly advantageous on either side. Both were ardent amateur actors. Collins took the part of a valet in Lytton's *Not So Bad as We Seem*, and with Dickens, Tenniel, Mark Lemon and Augustus Egg appeared in a farce entitled *Mr Nightingale's Diary*. He became a constant contributor to *Household Words*, and later to *All the Year Round*. His short story, *A Terribly Strange Bed*, a twin to which will be found in one of Conrad's collections of stories, appeared in 1852. And not only was *The Dead Secret* of 1857 published serially in *Household Words*, but while still in his twenties he collaborated with Dickens in some of his Christmas numbers.

Of the letters that passed between them we have only Dickens's, since, horrified by some recent use which had been made of private correspondence, early in 1855 Dickens made a bonfire in his meadow at Gad's Hill, and burned, it is said, every letter he possessed. Excellent, then, though Dickens's share of the correspondence is for its own sake, we gain from it only oblique glimpses of its recipient—effervescing pages of unstinted praise for the work of his young rival: "an excellent story, charmingly written, and showing everywhere an amount of pains and study in respect of the art of doing such things that I see mighty seldom"; and a fleeting picture of the great man weeping in a railway carriage "as much as the author could possibly desire" over his young

friend's *The Diary of Anne Redway*—a tale no less remarkable for its sustained pathos than as a revelation of
how the author of *The Moonstone* could (in rehearsal, as
it were) woefully fumble a criminal clue. In yet another
letter Dickens suggests no fewer than twenty-seven
titles, including *Below the Surface, Secret Springs* and *The
Turning Point*, for the novel which Collins himself afterwards called—and even more invitingly—*No Name*.
There are confessions: that, as Editor, Dickens has been
pruning and preening Mrs Gaskell's proofs, and at the
same time defying her to deny that they are the better for
it; and that if he were called into the witness box in a
case concerning one of Charles Reade's novels—the indictment being that, like the first "state" of *Basil*, owing
as Collins said to "prurient misrepresentations", it had
shocked Mrs Grundy—he would have felt during cross-
examination so insecure in his sentiments that he would
have been compelled to resort to his wits. Even as early
as 1852 he commiserates Wilkie Collins on his ill-health,
and with such a tit-for-tat as an almost lyrical outburst
concerning the state of "an old afflicted KIDNEY" of his
own—"once the torment of my childhood".

Most interesting are fragments of discussion on the
aims, difficulties and sorrows of authorship:

These are the ways of Providence, of which ways all art is
but a little imitation;
and

Will you rattle your head and see if there is not a pebble in
it which we could wander away and play at marbles with?...
My blankness is inconceivable—indescribable—my misery
amazing.

And last, in a letter written from the Lord Warden Hotel, Dover, there is an invitation to yet another pooling of inkpots for yet another Christmas story:

Sir (as Dr Johnson would have said), if it be not irrational in a man to count his feathered bipeds before they are hatched, we will conjointly astonish them next year. *Boswell*: Sir, I hardly understand you. *Johnson*: Sir, you never understand anything. *Boswell* (in a sprightly manner): Perhaps, sir, I am all the better for it. *Johnson* (savagely): Sir, I do not know but that you are. There is Lord Carlisle (smiling); he never understands anything and yet the dog's well enough. Then, sir, there is Forster; he understands many things, and yet the fellow is fretful. Again, sir, there is Dickens, with a facile way with him—like Davy, sir, like Davy—yet I am told that the man is lying at a hedge ale-house by the sea-shore in Kent, as long as they will trust him. *Boswell*: But there are no hedges by the sea in Kent, sir. *Johnson*: And why not, sir? *Boswell* (at a loss): I don't know, sir, unless—— *Johnson* (thundering): Let us have no unlesses, sir. If your father had never said "unless", he would never have begotten you, sir. *Boswell* (yielding): Sir, that is very true.

The method of the two friends when thus collaborating was to divide the story between them, each of them afterwards freely revising the other's share. Should the perfect result of such a method, like a fine Persian rug, be harmoniously all of a piece? If so, then their partnership was not a complete success. When in *No Thoroughfare* we read:

There is one among the many forms of despair—perhaps the most pitiable of all—which persists in disguising itself as Hope...

and in *No Name*:

"I have lived long enough in this world to know that the Sense of Propriety, in nine English women out of ten, makes no allowances and feels no pity."

the tone is true Collins. The complete opening chapter of *No Thoroughfare* indeed appears to be of a single authorship. Then, surely, the prospect changes—not necessarily for better or worse: it changes. The one writer, a sedulous and gifted craftsman, works with the pains and sobriety of a Dutch painter, every detail clear and precise. The other, a man of genius—though we know with what care Dickens also contrived, created and conducted his stories—usually *seems* to be following his nose, and exquisitely sensitive that unique organ was. He is an impressionist. Literary detective work based on internal evidence, however, and even in respect of problems less pregnant than the *Plays*, is perilous. Which of the novelists, for example, was responsible—not for:

I was no fitter company for her than I was for the angels; I well knew that she lay as high above my reach as the sky over my head...I suffered agony—agony. I suffered hard, and I suffered long. [Indeed my sufferings were] just as great as if I had been a gentleman...

but for:

They had had a late dinner, and were alone in an inn room there, overhanging the Rhine: at that place rapid and deep, swollen and loud. Vendale lounged upon a couch, and Obenreizer walked to and fro: now, stopping at the window, looking at the crooked reflections of the town lights in the dark water (and peradventure thinking, "If I could fling him into it!"); now, resuming his walk with his eyes upon the floor.

"Where shall I rob him, if I can? Where shall I murder him, if I must?" So, as he paced the room, ran the river, ran the river, ran the river.

Here one might swear to the "atmosphere", but what of that last little metrical rill of rhetoric? So again with *The Perils of Certain English Prisoners,* with its Charker, whose remarks are roughly three:

That's silver, that is. And silver a'nt gold. Is it, Gill?
I am right, and right a'nt left. Is it, Gill?
and
     I've got my death. And Death a'nt Life. Is it Gill?

This is a tale whose little details radiate in many directions—not only forwards and in the direction of *Treasure Island, Lost Endeavour, King Solomon's Mines* and *Nostromo,* but also of *Enoch Arden* and Mr Kipling—with its astute, waggish, treacherous South American native; its pompous Governor, whose only wear, apart from his gold lace coat, is red tape, and whose one object in life is to write reports; and its little bedizened monkey-like Portuguese "gentleman buccanier" with his guitar. Its Mrs Pordage, too, is at least distantly related to Mrs Wragge in *No Name,* a lady who in turn is not only (with a change of wardrobe) vaguely related to the Countess Fosco, but, by a celestial metamorphosis, became the White Queen in *Alice Through the Looking-Glass.* As for "the pretty children":

That seventh starlight night, as I have said, we made our camp, and got our supper, and set our watch, and the children fell asleep. It was solemn and beautiful in those wild and solitary parts, to see them, every night before they lay down, kneeling under the bright sky, saying their little prayers at women's laps. At that time we men all uncovered, and mostly kept at a distance. When the innocent creatures rose up, we murmured "Amen!" all together. For, though we had not heard what they said, we knew it must be good for us....

To Dickens, surely, must be attributed *their* paternity, for, while all such little innocents ("women's laps", "must be" and all) are public dangers in private authorship, Collins's children—his Louisa, Amelia and Robert, for example, in *The Dead Secret*, of 1857—a bare *Le Secret* in the French translation—who at the early age of eight have tasted both rod and birch—are free from any tinge of sentimentality and are wholesome flesh and blood; while Zo in particular, in *Heart and Science*, a greedy, tender-hearted, happy-go-lucky little dunce, is not only the saving grace of a poor book, but enraptured Swinburne. A little unexpectedly, perhaps, in view of his roundels on infancy and the milk-and-roses sequence of poems he indited to a small friend on holiday.

In spite of Collins's long and close friendship with Dickens, the references to him in Forster's *Life* are few and niggardly. One of them describes a trip to Cumberland which the two friends made in 1857 in search of "local colour" for *The Lazy Tour of Two Idle Apprentices*. It included the ascent of Carrick Fell. In the midst of it a dense fog descended on the explorers. They lost their way on the mountain slopes, and after hours of nocturnal groping, Wilkie fell into a rocky rivulet and sprained his ankle. It was at Doncaster soon after this excursion that Dickens bought a race-card, whereupon (without betting) he scribbled down at haphazard the names of what proved to be the three winners of the three chief races. It was thus he always squandered his gifts. But even *his* hospitable soul failed to welcome the racing riff-raff.

There is also a lively account of the wedding of Dickens's younger daughter, Kate, to Collins's younger brother, Charles Alston. This was a charmingly festive affair, embellished with floral arches, and punctuated by the village blacksmith who, in firing off a *feu de joie* with two midget cannon, all but deprived the bride of her father. To the bridegroom, a writer and an artist of unusual gifts, Forster pays a true and generous tribute:

> No man disappointed so many reasonable hopes with so little fault or failure of his own....His difficulty always was to please himself....An inferior mind would have been more successful in both the arts he followed.

This emphasises, however, his neglect of Wilkie Collins, who dismissed the famous biography as "The Life of John Forster, with Occasional Anecdotes of Charles Dickens"; his own copy of it, it is said, being littered with indignant annotations and corrections. Finally,

> I don't come to see you because I don't want to bother you. Perhaps you may be glad to see me by-and-bye. Who knows? Affectionately always, Charles Dickens.

It was Dickens's last letter to his old friend. And, "who knows?"

The only other book of Collins's that is not fiction is a collection of occasional papers entitled *My Miscellanies* of 1863. Apart from concise accounts of three notorious criminal cases in France of the eighteenth century, these are in the main satirical, ironical or jocular in tone.

One of the last variety concerns a monthly nurse, a Mrs Bullwinkle, fictitious name for an actual personage, and nicknamed the Cormorant. In the four weeks of her ministry she devoured, we are told, two hundred and forty-six meals, inclusive of "snacks". She is worthy of mention as an example of the difficulties encountered even by the most "realistic" of novelists in keeping pace with life.

A similar paper specifies a list of enquiries sent to the editor of a popular magazine of the 'fifties from a British public greedy, then as now, for free—and easy—information. A copious supply of this indeed was the sole primary intention of Alfred Harmsworth's first independent venture into journalism—his weekly *Answers to Correspondents*. Collins's list includes entreaties for recipes for the making of ginger-bread, crumpets and black varnish; remedies for warts, nervousness and knock-knees; for guidance on the pronunciation of *picturesque*, on the meaning of *Esquire* and of *I.H.S.*, and on the weight of a new-born infant; whether, too, a modest widow should discourage "attentions" from a married man; whether *Mazeppa* was written by Lord Byron, and *Robinson Crusoe* by Defoe; whether a history of Greece is an ancient history, and whether the name of David's mother is mentioned in the Holy Scriptures. How many such appeals were inspired by the editorial office-boy he does not compute. As for the answers: "All months are lucky to marry in, when your union is hallowed by love"—seems to be a fairly comprehensive one.

The most substantial of the essays are an appeal for

68   Walter de la Mare

more *original* fiction and a dirge—one now of many
stanzas!—on the dismal state of the English theatre. This,
he said, was due in part to imported French plays and to
burlesques, appetising enough for "the fast young farmer
from the country or for a convivial lawyer's clerk" and
"gloated on by a nightly audience whose ignorant insensibility nothing can shock"; and in part to the fact
that whereas in France the best plays of his day were the
work of the good novelists—"they are clever, they have
invention, they can write"—Balzac, Hugo, Soulié,
Dumas; in England the novelist had no practical incentive to work for the stage, since he could expect from it by
comparison with fiction no adequate reward.[1] As for the

[1] And Collins's views on this question are by no means the less interesting because (whatever their merits) he himself successfully adapted
some of his own novels for the theatre. In Mr and Mrs Bancroft's *On and
Off the Stage* many references are made to the production of his plays. Of
Man and Wife, "magnificently acted", in 1873, 136 performances were
given. As a preliminary he had read the play to the assembled company:
"This he did with great effect and nervous force, giving all concerned
a clear insight into his view of the characters; and, indeed, acting the old
Scotch waiter with rare ability, to roars of laughter."
    In 1874 Collins in turn pays a tribute to Mrs Bancroft's Lady Teazle:
"I don't know when I have seen anything so fine as her playing of the
great scene with Joseph; the truth and beauty of it, the marvellous play
of expression in her face, the quiet and beautiful dignity of her repentance,
are beyond all praise...."
    The New Magdalen, at the Olympic, was also "a great success", though
a production of *The Moonstone*, in which it was proposed that Mr and
Mrs Kendal should act for the first time with the Bancrofts, was finally
decided against for the reason that it was too melodramatic in its treatment for the Prince of Wales's Theatre.
    That Wilkie Collins warmly welcomed and gladly took advantage of
suggestions from the producers of his plays is attested also by Sir Arthur
Pinero in a letter from which he has very graciously permitted me to
quote. He too speaks of Collins's unfailing kindness towards those who
can best realise the blessing it can confer:
"I was then an actor in the 'stock' company of the Alexandra Theatre,
Liverpool, and Collins came to Liverpool to produce at that theatre in

actors: "Show me a school of dramatists", he adds, "and I will show you a school of actors soon afterwards".

Yet another essay in the *Miscellanies* is a plea on behalf of Everyman, cowed at times as he must be by the tyranny

a tentative way his dramatic version of 'Armadale' entitled 'Miss Gwilt' ....I was cast for the small but important part of Mr Darch, an elderly solicitor, and in the course of the rehearsals Collins was extremely kind to me;...I remember his appearances at rehearsal very clearly. He used to sit, his manuscript before him, at a small table near the footlights, and there he made such additions and alterations as Miss Ada Cavendish [who was financing the production] deemed necessary. He did this with the utmost readiness and amiability, influenced perhaps by her habit of calling him 'Wilkie', a familiar mode of address which, I recollect, surprised and shocked me not a little.

"My next meeting with Collins was in connection with...an ill-fated drama of his which was done at the Adelphi Theatre. I forget the name of it....At the first performance, I found myself standing beside the author at the back of the dress-circle. We exchanged greetings, and I noticed that, expecting a call at the fall of the curtain, he wore a large camellia in his button-hole. Everything went wrong. The audience, amused by some awkwardly phrased expressions, tittered; then, as the play advanced, broke into unrestrained laughter; and finally, enraged by an indignant protest from one of the actors, hooted the thing unmercifully....I never saw him again....

"His goodness to me, so flattering from an eminent man to a mere youth, was ever in my mind, and to this day I feel grateful to him."

The "ill-fated drama" was entitled *Rank and Riches*, and G. W. Anson, who played the "bird doctor" in it, after shaking his fist at the audience, shouted through the uproar that they were "a lot of damned cads"— a generalization that was never forgiven him.

Collins always maintained that the gifts essential in the novelist are those best fitted for the drama; and since his day practice has proved his point; though the failures of Henry James and Joseph Conrad lie heavily on the other side of the account. For most novelists indeed the situation at present resembles that of "Henry ——" who thus expressed his feelings to the managers of the Prince of Wales's Theatre in 1877:

"Honnered Lady,—i was borne in allen Street and i am now pottman at the swan with 2 neks i have no art to continue in my persision so i writ to arsk you to putt me on the bords of your theatre i am a borne actor for I citch myself makeing speaches out of plays in the middle of the nite if you will give me the charnce I will do my duty well and be a creditt to your theater if you see your way to give me the charnce i must arsk you to say nothink of it to my famly yours truly humble servent—Henry ——".

of the Art-critic. The art of painting, Collins maintained, is the one which "least requires a course of critical training, before it can be approached on familiar terms". It scandalised him to see his admirable fellow countrymen in the mute ecstatic posture of the young lady of *The Soul's Awakening* before Michaelangelo's *Last Judgment* or Raphael's *Transfiguration*, merely because this expert or that had intimidated them into believing that they "didn't even know what they liked". Like his artist in *After Dark*, this son of a painter was "rather of a revolutionary spirit in matters of art, and bold enough to think that the old masters have their faults as well as their beauties". The faces of the Holy Family, in a certain valuable Correggio, he maintained, "not only failed to display the right purity and tenderness of expression, but absolutely failed to present any expression at all". It was a child in the folk-tale who discovered that the king had no clothes on; and whatever the merits of the pictures in question may be—there is a sensitive and profound tribute to Tintoretto's *Crucifixion* in the *Memoirs*—it is probable that a natural taste, or at any rate a natural honesty, can be as easily ruined by a pretence of admiration as the instinctive delight of the young in what is good for them may be checked or corrupted by an enforced diet of what is bad.

Like the *Memoirs* and the *Rambles*, the *Miscellanies* are of interest now chiefly because they reveal, though very scantily, the novelist's personal views and opinions. But yet again, of definite self-portraiture there is little. Concerning himself, his experiences in this world, his deeper feelings and convictions, he is unusually reticent.

From 1863 onwards Collins continued to live quietly with his mother until her death in 1868, and after a visit to America in 1874, where he gave a series of public readings, chiefly of *The Frozen Deep*, he returned to London, removing occasionally in a narrow orbit from house to house, and last to Wimpole Street, where he died on September 23, 1889. He was buried in Kensal Green Cemetery, his funeral being attended by Sir Arthur Pinero, Hall Caine, Holman Hunt, Oscar Wilde and Edmund Gosse.

He had many excellent friends, could be good company himself and enjoyed good company in others.[1] None the less, it is said that he was driven into privacy by "the miseries incidental to his becoming famous", and there is a reference in the *Dictionary of National Biography* to "intimacies formed as a young man" which "led to his being harassed, after he became famous, in a manner which proved very prejudicial to his peace of mind". Constant ill-health affects the mind, though not in all ways adversely, as well as the body. But since he himself maintained in a preface to *Poor Miss Finch* that the conditions of human happiness are independent of bodily affliction, and that such affliction may even take its place among the ingredients of happiness, this alone can hardly account for the decline in his powers. Apart too from obvious technical defects, his actual presence—that secret company—so supple, engrossed and delighted in his best work, has become unmistakably tart and uninterested in

[1] A detailed and personal study of the novelist will be found in the opening chapters of *Wilkie Collins, Le Fanu and Others* by Mr S. M. Ellis, which was published some little time after this brief paper was written.

such a novel as *Heart and Science* of 1883—with its shallow treatment of the one half of its title, and its splenetic but by no means pointless attack on the zealots of the other.[1] Its Dr Benjulia is but just real enough to show the extent to which he has been caricatured.

This "most inartistic moral indignation", to which Mr Hugh Walpole has referred in his paper in *The Eighteen-Seventies*, may account in part for the comparative failure of Collins's later novels. But though "over-production"—he wrote twenty-three novels in thirty-six years—is a questionable charge, that of "scamped work" must be remorsefully admitted. There is no question either of the decline in his literary reputation. In an appreciation of "the breadth and power of his genius" which appeared in the *Contemporary Review* in 1888, Harry Quilter lamented that "it is but rarely we hear the name of Wilkie Collins mentioned in England nowadays, that we read a word in his praise". Two years afterwards Andrew Lang is bewailing the fact that he has been compelled as a reviewer to read in the lump novels

[1] "... See the lively modern parasites that infest Science, eager to invite your attention to their little crawling selves. Follow scientific enquiry, rushing into print to proclaim its own importance, and to declare any human being, who ventures to doubt or differ, a fanatic or a fool. Respect the leaders of public opinion, writing notices of professors, who have made discoveries not yet tried by time, not yet universally accepted even by their brethren, in terms which would be exaggerated if they were applied to Newton or to Bacon....Absorb your mind in controversies and discussions, in which Mr Always Right and Mr Never Wrong exhibit the natural tendency of man to believe in himself, in the most rampant stage of development that the world has yet seen. And when you have done all this, doubt not that you have made a good use of your time. You have discovered what the gentle wisdom of Faraday saw and deplored, when he warned the science of his day in words which should live for ever: 'The first and last step in the education of the judgment is—Humility'."

which he might, one by one, have enjoyed at leisure. He has high praise for *The Woman in White* and *The Moonstone*; but otherwise the bouquet of his appreciation is faint. He deplores Collins's humour and his treatment of the supernatural; and he questions his "facts". And he left Collins's "intermittent brilliance" to his biographer, "if he is to have a biographer", to explain.

Apart from Quilter and Lang, we have one critic declaring that Collins's art was crippled by his habit of moralising, and another that he was totally incapable of seeing "when he was and was not almost brutally coarse", while yet a third describes him as "one of the most fearless and honest fictionists who ever fed the public's sensation hunger while seeking to influence the public's serious sentiments".

> Lives of great men all remind us
> We can make our lives sublime.

It was a favourite theme of Longfellow. And yet one may at the same time welcome and deplore the fact that so little is known (outside his fiction) of Collins the man. We can sit by our friend's easel and indulge in mystic speculations the more freely perhaps for this very reason. In one respect, moreover, and this a crucial one, he has been unusually candid and confiding. For almost without exception he appended prefaces to his earlier novels —now explanatory, now challenging, now grateful, and, occasionally, apologetic. And though for the most part these prefaces keep to generalities, they are of singular interest.

In that, for example, to the second and revised edition

of *Basil*—which first appeared when he was twenty-eight—he states that the main event of the story had been founded on a fact within his own personal experience. It is for this reason, perhaps, that one episode in it is of a tragic horror and actualisation that he never excelled. "The more of the Actual", he continues, "I could garner up as a text to speak from, the more certain I might feel of the genuineness and value of the Ideal which was sure to spring out of it....Is not the noblest poetry of prose fiction the poetry of everyday truth?" In this conviction he had sacrificed "the usual conventionalities of sentimental fiction"—Basil, for example, first meets Margaret, by whom he is instantly infatuated, in an omnibus—a less luxurious vehicle then than it is now. Since, then, Collins argues, his scenes and events are "ordinary", they should appeal to "sources of interest within the reader's own experience", and his attention being thus secured, an appeal was possible *beyond* that experience, which might "fix his interests, excite his suspense, occupy his deeper feelings, or stir his nobler thoughts". He claims, too, the novelist's right to admit misery and crime into his fiction, though not in such a way as to win sympathy for characters definitely evil.

As for those persons who believe that the novelist's vocation is merely to amuse them, who shrink from "honest and serious reference" to subjects they themselves think of in private and talk of in public, who discover the improper where nothing improper is intended, "whose innocence is in the word, and not in the thought; whose morality stops at the tongue"—as for *them*, runs his challenge, let this be taken as his final repudiation of them. They would be treated in future with the silence of contempt. And no doubt they continued to read him in hope of further "discoveries".

As with *Basil* so with many of the later novels. The views expressed in their prefaces—whether or not they are wholly sound, and whether or not Collins's actual practice fully confirmed his aims—are well worth study. They explain clearly what he set out to do, though they fall far short of intimating what he actually achieved. They reveal his sustained interest in fiction as an art, his eagerness in experimentation, his moral independence (within certain limits), and the endless thought and care he bestowed on story and characterisation. And last, and repeatedly, they express his desire to please, to keep, and to conciliate his "readers".

He does not, however, tell us how much this very natural desire affected his work, either in the conceiving or the doing of it. To try solely to please is one thing—to hope to have pleased, quite another. Nor does he confess what kind of readers he had in mind, though we know what kind of readers he despised—the prude, the prig, the snob, the humbug; though his scorn even of these was no obstacle to his keen enjoyment in depicting them in his books. Fools, too:

Examples may be found every day of a fool who is no coward; examples may be found occasionally of a fool who is not cunning—but it may reasonably be doubted whether there is a producible instance anywhere of a fool who is not cruel.

His confidence that his readers would be interested in his aims and methods is testimony at any rate to the intelligence of these readers, and suggests that we need not be unintermittently derisive of our Victorian grand-mothers! And whatever limitations this audience imposed on him in his choice of theme or his treatment of it, one thing is evident, that in all his best work he pleased himself. No preface declares that he had ever fallen short of this aim.

Nor does he anywhere, I believe, make a distinction between story and plot in his fiction. And here, quite another kind of aesthetic sacrifice comes into view. It is as a master of plot at any rate—whatever its constituents, love, law, mystery, crime—that he remains unexcelled. His plots vary as much in complexity, which may be a merit, as they vary in the degree to which his characters are in service to them, which in itself is a defect. Whether simple, however, as in *Basil* and *The Dead Secret*, or involved, as in *Armadale* and *No Name*, it is not the mere plot that is most impressive, nor even that the events in it succeed one another in a rational and coherent order, but rather the assiduity with which it is re-complicated. It is usually less intricate than he makes it appear to be, though for sheer "ingenuity", ran Charles Reade's tribute, "give me dear old Wilkie Collins against the world!" His hope was to induce in his reader's mind two things; first, a condition of acute suspense; and next, a sustained desire to have it satisfied. And even when the "Secret" is not dead but as open as the skies, he intends us to await with bated breath *his* confiding of it. The doctor in *The Moonstone*[1] prescribes sedative reading for

[1] At how small a flame may the imagination take fire! Wilkie Collins called his story *The Moonstone* because it was actually suggested to him by

his patient—*Pamela, The Man of Feeling, Lorenzo de Medici*: since these works possess "the one great merit of enchaining nobody's interest and exciting nobody's brain". Precisely the reverse of this was Collins's aim.

Move by move, first on this side then on that, this literary Capablanca's novels—a nebulous "reader" his opponent—resemble a game of chess. So also does *Hamlet*. If Hamlet himself (or his author) but could or would make up his mind, the game might be finished in three or four moves: "fool's mate", though that might be. So too in *The Woman in White*. Unveil that flitting mysterious female in the first chapter, and all is over. *Stories* cannot be done with as easily as that. Nor, however long drawn out, need they come to a sudden and possibly explosive end; leaving little more than vacancy and darkness behind them. *Their* light may continue to shine on in our minds, and their characters continue to live there, company in our solitude, and company perhaps of a continuous influence. A plot on the other hand resembles a puzzle or a mathematical problem. As soon as the solution is made clear, it ceases to interest us.

It would, however, be as unfair to judge Wilkie Collins as a novelist solely by means of brief synopses of

a moonstone in the possession of Charles Reade. This had been the gift of a brother, Edward Reade, who brought it from India—though it had not been extracted from the head of the Moon god. Indeed there could hardly be a worse name for the wildly scintillating diamond which is described in Chapter IX. The actual gem itself, which is now in the possession of Mrs Reade of Ipsden, and which she very magnanimously entrusted into my hand for a moment, has a soft milky luminousness, and, viewed sideways, resembles the pupil of an eye—such an eye indeed as have the horses of the chariots of the moon!

his plots as to summarise the "carnal, bloody and un-natural" tragedy of *Hamlet Prince of Denmark* as:

Preliminary fratricide	1
Deaths connived at	2
Deaths violent but merited	3
Suicides	1
Murders	2
Grand total	9

It is, moreover, neither plot nor story in a novel that is of primary importance, whatever graces and incentives each may add, but the powers of mind and imagination expended on their unfolding. And Collins's finer qualities are often encumbered rather than aided by the purely intellectual difficulties—his triumphs over which none the less as sheer intellectual feats are likely to be under-estimated—that he consistently set himself.

His assertion that the telling of a story is bound to entail the lively presentation of character is no less valid even if it be admitted that in many of the world's best stories the characters are little more than embodied abstractions—in nearly all folk-tales, and epics, and in *The Pilgrim's Progress*, for example. By "characters" in general Collins meant gentle, sturdy, or rank growths of common humanity, not exotic souls and essences; though with due distillation we may all of us perhaps be so sublimated. But whatever value he set on them, in the playing out of his literary chess he was content to use even his best and brightest too much as mere pieces. As such they interest, excite, mystify, amuse and engross us. But they never positively possess us—storm the very citadels of mind and heart. He refuses to allow them their full freedom. They have their being more for his sake than for their own; and though their average not only in life-likeness but in sheer intelligence may surpass that of Dickens's, how many of Collins's characters have become household words?

He delights in the device of contrast; not only of the humorous with the tragic, of sentiment with cynicism; but of old with young, genteel with "humble", astute with stupid, charms of the body with faculties of the mind. There is a simple and gratuitous example of this in so early a story as *Mad Monkton*: the austere and formidable Father Superior of the "Convent" on one side, the old sacristan, whose sole solace in life is snuff, on the other. So too the easy-going dissolute elder-brother in *Basil*, and the icy melodramatised Mannion; the suave and pitiless Pickwickian prince of rascality, Count Fosco, and his merely villainous understudy, Sir Percival Glyde. It is with characters as such—sentient bricks and mortar —that he steadily erects his plots.

No Name, for example, presents us in its first chapter with an idyllic Victorian family circle—and Collins is never more at home than when at home. It consists of a prosperous, middle-aged and devoted mother and father. They have, for friend and foil, an old sardonic recluse, and also two daughters, the elder reserved and resigned, the younger wild, spirited, resolute, and, when driven to extremes, unscrupulous. Their trials over— they attain at last the same (provisional) haven, a happy marriage. A selfish woman of wit and few principles, Mrs Lecount, is set over against a selfish wag with no less

wit and even fewer principles, Captain Wragge; and
both of them, by fair means and foul—in Captain
Wragge's case, by the invention of a Pill and a system of
advertising it—secure at last a competence, and triumph.
There are two honourable and devoted English gentlemen, preordained husbands for the sisters. There is half-
witted Mrs Wragge, strongly resembling, in our physical
contacts with her, the impact of a Victorian feather-bed,
and there is an indomitable and matter-of-fact family
governess. And last, there is a weak and silly young man
with nothing but a pretty face to commend him, who is
set over against a weak and fatuous imbecile with nothing
but his wealth to commend *him*. And since of all things
living, apart from the prudes and prigs, Collins scorned
most a fool, it is these two alone who win no reward but
ignominy. The contrasts here it will be noticed—and it
is a tribute—are mainly of intelligence: only silliness fails.

Of all human beings young men perhaps are the most
difficult in fiction to bring to life, and for the most part,
Collins's young men are inclined by nature to be not
only weak and insipid, but less than quite real. Not so his
young women. A few are as fair but never quite so
brainless as Dora; a few, Basil's angelic sister for instance,
are as colourless as Agnes. The rest are of two kinds. The
first, apart from their physical charms—always of figure
and carriage and usually of face—are not only of substantial flesh and blood, but have brains, hearts, and
character. They are men's women. They were made to be
wooed; he sees to it that they are won. They are sharply
and clearly aware of what they want, they mean to get
it. Some of them dare all in the attempt; on the one side,

Magdalen and Rachel, on the other Margaret (in *Basil*) and Miss Gwilt—a forger at the age of twelve, an adventuress as base as she is fascinating at thirty-five—scornful, witty, audacious, clear-headed, and—with soul still breathing in the charnel-house of her mind—as devilish in her hatred as she is self-oblivious in her love.

"There I was", she confides to her Diary, "alone with him, talking in the most innocent, easy, familiar manner, and having it in my mind all the time, to brush his life out of my way, when the moment comes, as I might brush a stain off my gown. It made my blood leap, and my cheeks flush. I caught myself laughing once or twice much louder than I ought—and long before we got to London I thought it desirable to put my face in hiding by pulling down my veil."

She is first cousin, on the melodramatic side, to Alice Arden of Feversham:

What! groanest thou? Nay, then give me the weapon! Take *this* for hindering Mosbie's love and mine!

But Miss Gwilt would never have repented the "this" and would have defied her maker's last mechanical chapter, if she could.

As much to Collins's taste, and as vividly realised, are his strong-minded and incorruptible young women, of whom no mere man, even if the opportunity were given him, could count himself worthy: Marian Halcombe, for example, who was not only a match (though, to his regret, in but one sense of the term) for that old reprobate Fosco, but the idol of Edward Fitzgerald. Miss Garth, too, candid, faithful, self-sacrificing spinster, who in a more consolatory world would have found her destined mate upon the Bench. But though no Collins character, so far as I can recall, reaches that particular pinnacle, his fiction is rich in the professions. Both the clergymen, for example, in his earlier novels are excellent; the younger in *The Dead Secret* is a true-blue, domesticated, country parson; the elder and more patriarchal in *Armadale*, Mr Decimus Brock, is no less deeply pious than he is sagacious and discreet. Indeed, the last of Mr Brock's letters in *Armadale* is not only wholly in keeping with his piety and goodness, it has the ring of a profound and personal conviction.

..."Nothing that is done in unquestioning submission to the wisdom of the Almighty, is done wrong. No evil exists, out of which, in obedience to His laws, Good may not come. Be true to what Christ tells you is true. Encourage in yourself, be the circumstances what they may, all that is loving, all that is grateful, all that is patient, all that is forgiving, towards your fellow-men. And humbly and trustfully leave the rest to the God who made you, and to the Saviour who loved you better than his own life.

This is the faith in which I have lived, by the Divine help and mercy, from my youth upward. I ask you earnestly, I ask you confidently, to make it your faith too. It is the mainspring of all the good I have ever done, of all the happiness I have ever known; it lightens my darkness, it sustains my hope; it comforts and quiets me, lying here, to live or die, I know not which."...

But while for every churchman in the novels there must be three doctors, they bristle with the Law and abound in lawyers. Honest, or less honest, they are the pillars of Collins's State. Their formidable, practised, rational, but by no means always unsympathetic, minds, their precision and pungency, add an invaluable stability to their setting.

"Be good enough to remember, Augustus", he rejoined, "that My Room is not a Court of Law. A bad joke is not invariably followed by 'roars of laughter' *here*. Let Mr Bashwood come in."

They give not only legality but *order* to the plot, curb the emotional, stimulate the depressed, act, like ice and bromide, on the wits of the excited, and in the last resort form an impregnable palisade against the onslaughts of villainy.

As for the pawns in his game—here the metaphor falters; since in chess all pawns are, in theory, equally valuable and those of one colour look precisely alike, whereas Collins's pawns—which in general remain pawns, though he frequently sketches in in one novel a character he "crowns" in a later—are as richly various as they are deftly used. Unlike Miss Gwilt, for example— "How I hate the coarse ways of the lower orders!"—he shows a peculiar interest in servants of every rank and order: from Mr Boxious's masterly errand-boy in *After Dark* (who has a substantial second cousin in *Pickwick*), and the susceptible little housemaid in *Basil*; up to Mr Betteredge, in *The Moonstone*, prince of stewards, with his "late lamented", his tittle-tattle daughter Penelope, and his *Robinson Crusoe*. Above all Collins indulges himself in hapless young women in service who languish under some cloud of illicit passion or remorse—his Louisa, his Sarah Leeson, his Rosanna Spearman of the Shivering Sands. Who that ever met this scarred and romantic young woman could forget her? And who, alas, even in these days, would venture to give her a "place"?

"People in high life", wrote Mr Betteredge, in his "report" to his mistress, "have all the luxuries to themselves —among others, the luxury of indulging their feelings. People in low life have no such privilege. Necessity, which spares our betters, has no pity on *us*. We learn to put our feelings back into ourselves, and to jog on with our duties as patiently as may be. I don't complain of this—I only notice it."

Collins had not only noticed it, he had made those hidden feelings his own. With "people in high life" he was less closely concerned, and of the Nobility, who so profusely adorn the fiction of his day, there is the merest gilding. When too Allan Armadale confesses to three defects inexcusable in a country gentleman—he had never been to a university, he is unable to make speeches, and can enjoy a ride on horseback without galloping after a wretched stinking fox or a poor distracted little hare—we are confident that he has his author's sympathy. Basil's haughty father, on the other hand, whose blood was of so deep a Norman blue that a coronet was of as little importance to him as a kind heart, is perhaps a sacrifice on the altar of Victorian realism:

"Basil!" he cried, "in God's name, answer me at once! What is Mr Sherwin's daughter to *you*?"

"She is my wife!"

I heard no answer—not a word, not even a sigh....Over his upturned face there had passed a ghastly change, as indescribable in its awfulness as the change of death.

This shock is due not to the fact that Miss Sherwin's father is a negro, a criminal or an atheist, but that he is a linen-draper. In general, Collins remains loyal to that backbone of England, its middle and (whichever end of the backbone this may be) its upper middle class.

Heredity, however, is a frequent element in his novels, and money, with or without love for company, is their dominant incentive, his plots frequently depending on either or both. And of how much denser a metal is *his* money than, say, Thackeray's or Henry James's or even Jane Austen's, five of whose novels none the less as spontaneously begin with a little discourse on this theme as they end with a peal of long-anticipated wedding bells.

As for his skill in the concise *description* of character— though in a hapless moment he is capable of such prose as "the ex-usher's hair was grown again on his shaven skull, and his dress showed the renovating influence of the accession of pecuniary means..."—it is already mature in *After Dark*: Lomaque, for example,

was poor, quick-witted, secret, not scrupulous. He was a good patriot, he had good patriot friends, plenty of ambition, a subtle, cat-like courage, nothing to dread—and he went to Paris....

On the other hand, Mr Welwyn

was a thoroughly common-place man, with no great virtues and no great vices in him. He had a little heart, a feeble mind, an amiable temper, a tall figure, and a handsome face....

And again:

The French woman arrived punctual to the appointed day—

glib and curt, smiling and flippant, tight of face and supple
of figure. Her name was Mademoiselle Virginie, and her
family had inhumanly deserted her....

Could meaning be packed tighter? Dress, too: how
charmingly, in the following fragment, it enhances the
wearer of it, even to the little blue buttons—

A bright laughing face, prettily framed round by a black
veil, passed over the head, and tied under the chin—a
travelling-dress of a nankeen colour, studded with blue
buttons, and trimmed with white braid—a light brown cloak
over it—little neatly-gloved hands, which seized in an instant
on one of mine and on one of Owen's—two dark blue eyes
which seemed to look us both through and through in a
moment—a clear, full, merrily-confident voice—a look and
manner gaily and gracefully self-possessed: such were the
characteristics of our fair guest which first struck me at the
moment when she left the postchaise and possessed herself
of my hand.

And how startlingly is one's inward eye greeted by the
mere colours of—

Her light-checked silk dress with its pretty trimming of
cherry-coloured ribbon, lay quite still over the bosom
beneath it.

In all this he is not only attentive but sensitive. When
too at times he combines in a paragraph characterisation,
dress, emotional spectator and a complete symbol-in-
little of the story that follows—in this case *Basil*—his
rivals are few:

The fair summer evening was tending towards twilight;
the sun stood fiery and low in a cloudless horizon; the last

loveliness of the last quietest daylight hour was fading on the violet sky, as I entered the square. I approached the house. She was at the window—it was thrown wide open. A bird-cage hung rather high up, against the shutter-panel. She was standing opposite to it, making a plaything for the poor captive canary of a piece of sugar, which she rapidly offered and drew back again, now at one bar of the cage, and now at another. The bird hopped and fluttered up and down in his prison after the sugar, chirping as if he enjoyed playing *his* part of the game with his mistress. How lovely she looked! Her dark hair, drawn back over each cheek so as just to leave the lower part of the ear visible, was gathered up into a thick simple knot behind, without ornament of any sort. She wore a plain white dress fastening round the neck, and descending over the bosom in numberless little wavy plaits. The cage hung just high enough to oblige her to look up to it. She was laughing with all the glee of a child; darting the piece of sugar about incessantly from place to place. Every moment, her head and neck assumed some new and lovely turn—every moment her figure naturally fell into the position which showed its pliant symmetry best....

After a lapse of some minutes, the canary touched the sugar with his beak. "There, Minnie!" she cried laughingly, "you have caught the runaway sugar, and now you shall keep it!" For a moment more, she stood quietly looking at the cage; then raising herself on tip-toe, pouted her lips caressingly to the bird, and disappeared in the interior of the room. The sun went down; the twilight shadows fell over the dreary square; the gas lamps were lighted far and near; people who had been out for a breath of fresh air in the fields, came straggling past me by ones and twos, on their way home—and still I lingered near the house, hoping she might come to the window again; but she did not re-appear....

What is most conspicuous, then, in Collins's plots is the presence of a vigilant, active and powerful mind. Such a mind in fact as would be no less helpful in the fiction of our own day. Nothing escapes his attention. His grasp never relaxes. Whatever "readers" he had in view, he positively squanders his pains on them. This is observable in little matters as in great. In order that Miss Gwilt shall discover she is being followed, he makes her alight from a cab, *and*, in order to gloss the coincidence, he at once adds that she was disgusted with its horrid close smell: "(Somebody had been smoking in it, I suppose)". So too, on a larger scale, in *Armadale*. No psycho-analyst could disdain the ingenuity with which a doctor—worthier far of Harley Street than of the Isle of Man—explains how Allan Armadale's diffuse and broken dream on the wreck of the French timber-ship, *La Grâce de Dieu*, may have been woven together in his "sub-consciousness" out of trivial experiences during the day gone by. But Collins's sole aim in this analysis is that his story shall be able to carry the extravagant weight of that dream's coming true in every particular in the chapters that follow. He exults indeed in the improbable and in the fringes of actuality, but lavishes his pains and skill in attempting to prove them otherwise. And even though this self-imposed handicap reveals the conscientiousness of the craftsman rather perhaps than that of the artist, it is a rich testimony to him as a novelist.

"I shall make this a remarkable document", Count Fosco declares, after arranging on his writing table "several quires of paper and a bundle of quill pens" before setting to work on his confession: "Habits of literary composition are perfectly familiar to me. One of the rarest of all the intellectual accomplishments that a man can possess is the grand faculty of arranging his ideas. Immense privilege! I possess it. Do you?" The direct enquiry is a little disconcerting; but whatever our answer may be, the accomplishment *is* unusual, and Collins possessed it in marked measure. A little before this, Walter Hartright has paid a grudging tribute to Fosco's "extraordinary mixture of prompt decision, far-sighted cunning, and mountebank bravado". Tone down the last of these terms a little and they too apply equally well to the novelist himself.

Again: "What are we, I ask", Fosco continues, and though he knows it not, he is already *en route* to the icy marble slab in the Morgue—

"What are we but puppets in a show box? O omnipotent Destiny, pull our strings gently! Dance us mercifully off our miserable little stage! The preceding lines, rightly understood, express an entire system of philosophy. It is mine."

As novelist, it may have been Collins's; but what a lively and promiscuous property-boxful of humanity is his for all that! There might well be a roomy annexe to the national wax-works in the Marylebone Road devoted solely to groups of our chief novelists' characters—Fielding's, Richardson's, Sterne's and the rest. However rich that array, no admirer of Collins would mistake his particular "stand". In number—and at a rough computation they would be four to five hundred strong—in variety, in romanticalness, and—whatsoever their age, sex, calling, station, intelligence or moral qualities—in their pronounced family likeness also, they would bear comparison with their neighbours. The best of them are triumphantly in the round; a rather large number remind us of an adjacent "chamber", though they may have merited no place in it; and those in the background are somewhat stuffless in effect. They owe no more to mere eccentricities of dress, looks and habits than Dickens's; they are many of them as close to actuality as Thackeray's; and yet, somehow, because they were puppets, danced carelessly off their maker's stage, they seem to suffer less than either novelist's in this imaginary conversion from the medium of words into the medium of wax.

His "famous formula" for the practising novelist intent on his readers was: "Make 'em laugh" (as Dickens did); "make 'em cry" (as both Dickens and Thackeray did); and last, "make 'em wait". But of downright laughter as distinguished from an inward sardonic smile, an amused chuckle, or a far halloo of applause, there is little in his fiction. There is humour, but it is apt to be rather crude, and more seldom than it might be, *good* humour. Compassionate too though he was of the weak, the persecuted, the oppressed, the beclouded, he does not often exact from us the tribute of a tear. Occasionally— for one of his readers, at any rate—he does better than merely make him cry. Here and there, there is a cadence in his prose—"'Is there a fatality that follows men in the dark?'"; "'Even my wickedness has one merit—it has not prospered'"—which, however faintly, echoes even Emily Brontë herself. And again:

"You know what odd fancies take possession of me sometimes", I said. "Shall I tell you the fancy that has taken possession of me now?..."

"Are there lonely hours", she went on, still never looking away from the corner, still not seeming to hear him, "when you are sometimes frightened without knowing why— frightened all over in an instant, from head to foot?...I have felt that, even in the summer. I have been out of doors, alone on a wide heath, in the heat and brightness of noon, and have felt as if chilly fingers were touching me....It says in the New Testament that the dead came out of their graves, and went into the holy city. The dead! Have they rested, rested always, rested for ever, since that time?...I am nothing to myself... I suppose I have lost something. What is it? Heart? Conscience? I don't know. Do you?" She scattered the last fragments of grass to the winds; and, turning her back...let her head droop till her cheek touched the turf bank. "It feels soft and friendly", she said, nestling to it with a hopeless tenderness...."It doesn't cast me off. Mother Earth! The only mother I have left!"

As for "making 'em wait", the suspense on which Collins insisted can be of more than one kind, and his kind is seldom the outcome of mere curiosity. Skill and ingenuity contrive and direct his stories, but the varying states of mind in which they involve us are a more subtle enticement. Since he cannot be content with the ordinary in life, it must be given the appearance of the strange, the bizarre. He may cite reasons for introducing the deaf-mute, Madonna, into *Hide and Seek*, but such reasons alone would hardly account for the presence of no fewer than three blind characters in his earlier novels. And it is not only unusual physical conditions that attract him, but the spiritually cowed and oppressed, the victims of

strange and obscure obsessions, forlorn souls burdened
with "secrets", cringing wrecks of humanity. The
haunted and the less than sane frequent his pages. What,
then—if we are so inclined—engrosses us in his fiction
is in much the curiosity to get an answer to a riddle, but,
in still more, the desire to remain under his spell.

Apart, too, from his tart, benign or matter-of-fact old
lawyers, his misanthropes,[1] his satirical observers of mankind, and his wideawake rogues and rascals, his chief
characters, even the young and the virtuous, are the prey
of forebodings. Their lives are festooned with shifting
drifts of mystery. They dread the pitfalls awaiting innocence, a morrow full of menace:

"There are times, Lenny," she said, "when all one's
happiness in the present depends upon one's certainty of the
future."

And again:

"A strange end," thought Magdalen, pondering over her
discovery as she stole upstairs to her own sleeping-room—
"a strange end to a strange day!"

Yet, more often than not, these threatening disasters
fail to arrive. Two at least of his earlier novels, again,
begin with death-bed scenes, and in the opening chapter

    [1] Mr Clare, for example, in *No Name*:
"When the boys went to school, Mr Clare said 'good-bye' to them—
and 'thank God' to himself....His favourite poets were Horace and
Pope; his chosen philosophers, Hobbes and Voltaire. He took his
exercise and his fresh air under protest; and always walked the same
distance to a yard, on the ugliest high-road in the neighbourhood....He
could digest radishes, and sleep after green tea. His views of human
nature were the views of Diogenes, tempered by La Rochefoucault; his
personal habits were slovenly in the last degree; and his favourite boast
was that he had outlived all human prejudices".

of *Armadale* a complete generation is "mown down" by
the motionless spectre who in Collins's world lurks unnaturally near. He delights in scenes of solitude—gloomy
woods, stagnant waters; and the most characteristic of
his chapters are haunted with the dark; not, as with
Bunyan, a darkness feared and detested, or one that gives
the moon and stars a deep serene wherein to shine, but a
darkness for its own sake, resembling a drug of the imagination. All this may affect us as do lingering dreams and
nightmares, though his dreams seldom have "heavenly
meanings", and his "supernatural", both in quality and
degree, is as far from Le Fanu's as his humour is from
Dickens's.

"It doesn't matter", she answered quietly, out of the
darkness. "I am strong enough to suffer, and live. Other
girls, in my place, would have been happier—they would
have suffered, and died. It doesn't matter; it will be all the
same a hundred years hence...."
She rose and paced the room with the noiseless, vigilant
grace of a wild creature of the forest in its cage. "How can
I reach him, in the dark", she said to herself....
The tears gushed into her eyes. She passionately dried
them...and turned her back on the looking-glass. "No
more of myself", she thought; "no more of my mad,
miserable self for to-day!"...Shrinking from the fast darken-
ing future...she looked impatiently about the room.

This is Magdalen's darkness. But here is Miss Garth,
talking of Magdalen's far less mysterious sister:

"*You*'re one of the impenetrable sort. Give me Magdalen,
with all her perversities; I can see daylight through her.
You're as dark as night."

And this is Captain Wragge—on the theme of another order of darkness dear to his author's fancy:

"Mrs Wragge is not deaf", explained the captain. "She's only a little slow. Constitutionally torpid—if I may use the expression.... Shout at her—and her mind comes up to time. Speak to her—and she drifts miles away from you directly... Mrs Wragge!"

Indeed, in these novels, however gay and radiant the English sunshine may be, however clear the bird song and spring-like the young women in their muslins and their shawls; somewhere—as a sidling glance over the shoulder will prove—there waits a hearse, with its mutes and its mourners and its swish-tailed horses; and night is coming on! But it is not *the* night. Towards *Finis* there will come a call for candles; or, possibly, gas; and all will be well.

And as with Collins's portrayal of human nature, so with his Nature itself. His brief descriptions of scene, so admirably woven in with plot and situation, reveal both how close and temperamental an observer he was and the pictorial skill which was his heritage from both sides of his family. But scene is rarely *mere* scene in his stories, seldom purely objective. Even when, apart from his favourite devices of diary and letter, it enters into his direct narrative, it is described through one of his characters in a state of rapture or suspense, of fear or dread or despair or anguish:

The heat-mist still hid the horizon. Nearer, the oily, colourless surface of the water was just visible, heaving slowly from time to time in one vast monotonous wave that rolled itself out smoothly and endlessly till it was lost in the white obscurity of the mist. Close on the shore, the noisy surf was hushed. No sound came from the beach except at long, wearily long intervals, when a quick thump, and a still splash, just audible and no more, announced the fall of one tiny, mimic wave upon the parching sand....

And again:

It was a dull, airless evening. Eastward was the gray majesty of the sea, hushed in breathless calm; the horizon line invisibly melting into the monotonous misty sky; the idle ships shadowy and still on the idle water. Southward, the high ridge of the sea dyke, and the grim, massive circle of a martello tower reared high on its mound of grass, closed the view darkly on all that lay beyond. Westward, a lurid streak of sunset glowed red in the dreary heaven—blackened the fringing trees on the far borders of the great inland marsh—and turned its little gleaming water-pools to pools of blood. Nearer to the eye the sullen flow of the tidal river Alde, ebbed noiseless from the muddy banks; and nearer still, lonely and unprosperous by the bleak water-side, lay the lost little port of Slaughden, with its forlorn wharfs and warehouses of decaying wood, and its few scattered coasting vessels deserted on the oozy river-shore. No fall of waves was heard on the beach; no trickling of waters bubbled audibly from the idle stream. Now and then, the cry of a sea-bird rose from the region of the marsh; and, at intervals, from farm-houses far in the inland waste, the faint winding of horns to call the cattle home, travelled mournfully through the evening calm.

This as mere picture is admirable, and how sensitive are the cadences and echoes of its prose. But how much more effective it is as fiction, even if a little diffuse, for being the reflex and symbol of a mood, a condition of mind—and of *our* momentary condition of mind.

Nature is the looking-glass of humanity, reflecting our mutable appearances on the long journey; and it is thus Collins silvers in the pervasive "atmosphere" of his earlier novels—their stealthy gloom and stagnancy, the tinge of hallucination, the loading of the dice. He pinned his faith as a novelist to the "actual". But his actual, when most his own, resembles that of a cheerful sunlit morning—the flutter of birds, the sound of distant voices —when, slowly and furtively, there seeps in upon every object within it the gloom and the hush, the sullen ominousness, the leaden lull of an advancing eclipse; it is the actuality of a summer evening lit suddenly by the wide refulgent flicker of distant lightning. Quiet and blue his sea may lie, but lo!—high in the heavens—a remote, serene drift of warning clouds. Surest of transitory ordeals for the beloved among his characters is that of being the prey of omens and the sadness of the unknown—of an inescapable destiny that is, as it were, the other side of the fabric of remorse. Further he will not venture. With the inmost secrets of the self and of the imagination he is not —openly—concerned.

Incidental to this are his favourite "properties": hidden letters, mislaid wills, disguises, strange disappearances, private detectives, spyings and eavesdroppings; portents and the subterranean workings of Chance; physical disfigurements, secret passions, tears and swooning and "brain fever"; infatuations, jealousies, hypochondria, sleep-walkings, delirium and the tomb. As a catalogue it is absurd, the machinery of melodrama.

But in judicious doses how telling! These are his spices, his flavourings, his appetisers; they give savour and pungency to his wide knowledge of the world at large, and his consuming interest in it. An interest not merely in human beings in all their variety—their clothes, furniture, houses, habits, oddities, the workings of their hearts and brains and (almost) all that is theirs; but in trade, science, medicine, law; in landscape and sea-faring, in literature, art, the drama, and music. How delicate a surprise it is in his company to chance in neighbouring pages on passing references to Keats's "cold hill-side", to Allan Cunningham's "a wet sheet and a flowing sea"; and, again and again, to the pure gaiety and loveliness of the music of Mozart.

An absorbed detachment in the brooding face is the chief mark of Millais's portrait of the novelist; it is the face of a recluse and a day-dreamer. What precise effect on his work was produced by the drug which as far back at least as 1851 he was compelled to take in relief of long periods of pain and insomnia is a question for the specialist, not for the critic. But reference to it in his tales is frequent:

Who was the man who invented laudanum? [Miss Gwilt confides to her candid diary]. I thank him from the bottom of my heart, whoever he was...I have had six delicious hours of oblivion.... "Drops", you are a darling. If I love nothing else, I love you.

And in an earlier story:

It was marked in large letters, "Laudanum—Poison". My heart gave a jump.... "Poison, dear, if you take it all," says

Mary, looking at me very tenderly; "and a night's rest, if you only take a little".

But no drug accounts for the triumph of "the sensation novel". It was itself one of the drowsy syrups in an age of Industry, and already in active service when *Basil* was published. As early as 1862 *Mr Punch* summarised the dire effects of the species as:

Harrowing the Mind, making the Flesh creep, causing the Hair to stand on End, giving Shocks to the Nervous System; destroying the Conventional Moralities, and generally unfitting the Public for the Prosaic Avocations of life.

The tone here—apart from the sense—of this hoary old moralist, and it is amusing that his capitals should have failed him at "life", is reminiscent of an acquaintance whom Dickens referred to in a letter to a friend:

I dined with an old General yesterday, who went perfectly mad at dinner about the *Times*—exudations taking place from his mouth—while he denied all its statements—that were partly foam, and partly turbot with white sauce....

Ruskin was also a moralist. He listed the ten deaths in *Bleak House*; arraigned Hugo, Thackeray, George Eliot and even Scott; but he also admirably defined the essential of an ideal fiction. Bad novels in large doses, he maintained, render the ordinary course of life uninteresting. The judgment reminds one of other dangers of his age: "Workers having carious teeth were found to be subject to the insidious phosphorus necrosis, which began as a masquerade of toothache and ended as a sort of leprosy of the jaw". But whence springs the fountain of human interest and what causes its flow and ebb? Unfortunately, for many of us, and whether self or circumstance be to blame, the ordinary course of life *is* uninteresting. And worse devices than good "sensation" fiction are conceivable for taking us out of—and decoying us into—ourselves. There are, too, many degrees of sensationalism, as there are of naturalism or sub-naturalism or impressionism; and the Victorian variety, whatever its defects may be, had its virtues. It will still help its readers to see and feel, to understand one another, and (if that is the best way with them), to forget for the while their troubles. Assuredly in the *writing* of his novels, Collins, as he confessed, forgot *his*—lapped as he was in the condition of the worm in the cocoon spun out of its own entrails; ink his nectar, solitude his paradise, the most exhausting earthly toil at once his joy, his despair, his anodyne and his incentive.

Moreover, the human mind, like the human body, is capable in part of secreting its own antidotes to poisons that may silt their way in. And among, not perhaps the poisons, but the arid diets of the mind are the literature that is lifelessly dry, the books that are merely intended to be edifying, the merely de-animating tractates of science, the "clever", shallow, destructive satires, the commercialised politics, the false hymns, the mock poetry, the "pseudosophy". "And who indeed can be the wiser for reading books about subjects quite out of the way, incomprehensible, and most wretchedly written?" It may in fact be the books which we read as we suppose "for our own good", but without any real vital fountaining interest in them, that do the mind as much harm as books can. How much harm exactly that may be is a difficult question.

As Collins said himself, "Not one man in ten thousand living in the midst of reality has discovered that he is also living in the midst of romance". He attempted to woo the nine hundred and ninety-nine into that conviction. Apart from imposed restrictions, he decanted mortal existence pretty much as he found it, adding a few drops of his own heady and peculiar elixir; and in spite of their dark air of the sinister, silvered with gleams of the extravagant and the grotesque, his novels are rooted in fairly solid earth—middle-class England in the mid-nineteenth century.

The reading or re-reading, moreover, of eleven of his books, and the dipping again and again into old favourites, has not prevented one almost lifelong admirer from facing what surely (in *Mr Punch's* phrase) must be classed among the "Prosaic Avocations of life"—the compounding of a lecture. Indeed, to find nothing to praise in what delighted critics so diverse in gifts and outlook as Dickens, Swinburne and Fitzgerald, would be a scarcely enviable feat of fastidiousness. They ardently admired Collins's best and were unfeignedly grateful for it. So admirable indeed is that "best", not only in its craftsmanship but in its abundant charity and hospitality, that one can hardly avoid speculating not so much how far it falls short in aim, in scope and in fineness of the great fiction of the world, but of what Collins himself in other circumstances might have attempted. Greater things than these, it hints, were not beyond his reach. If this be so, that he fell short of *his* best may be due in part to the fact that he was too closely and professedly intent on pleasing his public; since such an intentness may be in the nature of a veil rather than a bridge between writer and reader.

Apart from the promise of *Basil*, no other of his earlier novels seems to have been *wholly* true—either to the novelist himself, to his creations, or to that profounder humanity of which they afford so many glimpses but seldom a sustained view.

Exit PLANCHÉ—*Enter* GILBERT

By *Harley Granville-Barker*

The extravaganza of the 'sixties must have been very jolly nonsense at its best; and the first—and last—thing to remember about it is that it pretended to be no more. But while the jollity has long been silenced, the nonsense is on record. Messrs Samuel French Limited (who deal nowadays in far superior wares) can still dig you out a score or so of the sixpenny pamphlets of "Thomas Hailes Lacy's Acting Edition"; and, to the serious literary eye, these jingles and puns of Burnand's, or Brough's, or Byron's (H. J.!) do verily shame the print. Well, how would an unvarnished report of last year's Christmas party read? "At this point the Lord Chief Justice, assuming a pink paper cap with purple streamers, crowed like a cock, while the Right Reverend the Bishop of Blanchester, not to be outdone, gave, amid loud applause, his celebrated imitation of a hen laying an egg."

If in that lost, loved London of gas lamps aureate in fog, of clacketing hansoms and ladies' gowns that swept the muddy streets, your fancy was for an evening's relaxation of this sort you would go by first choice to the Royal Strand Theatre. (Most of the theatres seem to have been "Royal" in those days; it was generally no more, I think, than a compliment they paid themselves.) It stood—and was still standing in the "noughts" of this century—midway between the two churches. A Tube station took its place. That seems to have gone too (and what, by the way, has happened to the Tube ?). To the last there were hanging in its remoter corridors some fly-blown frames filled with faded *carte-de-visite* photographs of the heroes and heroines of the old burlesques, taken in the studios of the London Stereoscopic Company, Regent Street; of the heroines chiefly. Strange little figures! They had passed already from the dowdy to the quaint; they are in the realm of the picturesque, even of the romantic now. Ada Swanborough, Pattie Oliver, Lydia Thompson, Amy Sheridan, Lottie Venne— Marie Wilton herself! One could have gone there (but this was in 1859) with Charles Dickens to see her as the boy Pippo in *The Maid and the Magpie* burlesque. He sent a note to Forster telling him by no means to miss it. "I have never seen such a curious thing and the girl's talent is unchallengeable. I call her the cleverest girl I have ever seen on the stage in my time, and the most singularly original." She illuminated the "Royal Strand" till 1865, when she borrowed a thousand pounds from her brother-in-law and, with Byron for a partner, took the dirty little theatre in Tottenham Street. A large slice of the money must have gone to-wards cleaning and decorating it, to hanging lace curtains in the boxes (she tacked them up herself on the opening day) and antimacassars over the stalls. The most "stirring event of the season", says the *Illustrated London News*, was the production of *La! Sonnambula; or the Supper, the Sleeper and the Merry Swiss Boy.*[1] Thereafter things went

---

[1] It may be worth while to put on record the decoration—the *I.L.N.* describes it at length—of a smart mid-Victorian theatre. "The front of

well enough, yet not too well. If she had still her best to give, Byron's was hack work, and was deteriorating at that, and the tide of taste for his particular sort of nonsense was already past the flood. In a happy—and generous—moment, he introduced T. W. Robertson to the combination. In a yet happier one Miss Marie Wilton became Mrs Bancroft, and the rest of that story is theatrical history.

· But the Strand kept the flag flying bravely[1] for another five years or so. There was burlesque at the Royalty Theatre too. Burnand was its chief provider; in 1866 he provided a *Black Ey'd Susan*, in which Miss Pattie Oliver charmed London, and a Mr Charles Wyndham, fresh from army surgeon's service with the Northerners in America, supported her. It was to be found, on occasion, at the Queen's in Long Acre (opened in 1867: and there is the façade still and the entrance hall, hardly changed, at the corner of Endell Street), where Miss Henrietta Hodson, who became Mrs Henry Labouchère, reigned. In 1868 Robert Reece wrote for her *The Stranger;*

the boxes presents an ogee with white and gold trellis picked out with blue; and the ceiling is divided into six panels, with gold stars and blue centre. The arch of the proscenium is framed with white enamelled scrolls, the panels in blue and Prince of Wales's feathers in white relief forming the centre. A niche with an ornamental stand of flowers graces each side of the proscenium—an arrangement, we understand, due to the taste of Miss Wilton. There are four commodious rows of stalls, consisting of fifty-four in number, all spring stuffed, and cushioned, and covered with blue leather and white enamelled studs. The box seats, entirely new, are similarly stuffed and covered; and the whole circle, brilliantly illuminated, is lined with rosebud chintz." By this, though, I think I may be wrong about the antimacassars, which will have belonged to the Olympic of Madame Vestris' day.

[1] Or should one say "the sacred lamp burning"? No; I fancy that phrase was John Hollingshead's invention for the Gaiety of the 'seventies.

stranger than ever; and the programme announces, "The piece produced under the direction of Mr H. Irving and the author". Very good nonsense *The Stranger; stranger than ever* is! If we are to have puns, shall we better the one which heralds the hero's entrance (to music *tremoloso*) upon the happy village scene?

> When comes he here?
>   Anon—his wand'ring feet
> Will shortly lead him to the accustomed seat.
> Each evening you may see him sitting so,
> Under that *linden when the sun is low!*
> On close inspection, too, you'll also see
> His noble *eye, sir, rolling rapidly*

—that is, if we have not quite forgotten our Campbell, as 1868 presumably had not.

Easter-time would find burlesque added to the bills of most of the smaller theatres; an old custom, this, soon to end. Christmas, more certainly, would see them occupied, and prominently, by Fairy Extravaganzas, Classical Burlesques, New and Original Burlesque Pantomimes, Operatic Extravaganzas—there was doubtless a nicety about the nomenclature, which now asks very sharp discerning! And at the St James's on December 29, 1866, we have *Dulcamara, or the Little Duck and the Great Quack*, by W. S. Gilbert, the first stage venture of Bab of the Ballads. A critic compared it favourably with Planché's work, and Lady Gilbert—still for a few months to remain Miss Lucy Blois Turner—can remember how delighted they both were by that.

PLANCHÉ

Planché was a much respected veteran. He was now seventy years old and had written and helped to write some 57 extravaganzas (the name his own adopting), not to mention a hundred or more farces, comedies, melodramas, and librettos for operas besides. He wrote the libretto for Weber's *Oberon,* and one of the disappointments of his life was over Mendelssohn's final recalcitrance (after much making of agreements and evasively polite correspondence) to set to work seriously upon a score for *The Burghers of Calais*—great work that it was to be! By 1872 he can confess to at least a share in 176 plays of one sort or another; 62 of them all his own, the rest collaborations and "liftings", mainly from the French. As to these last, conscience still waited upon international copyright; the early Victorian dramatist held the freebooter's licence handed down from the Elizabethan. Planché, being introduced to Scribe at the Garrick Club with the bland recommendation "*Encore un qui vous a pillé*", capped it in compliment by "*Impossible de faire même du nouveau sans piller Monsieur Scribe*". And Scribe smiled politely. Not that there was much profit in the thefts. Thomas Dibdin was reputed to be the "author" of 800 dramatic pieces, no less; but when he died in 1841 at the age of seventy, he had been glad enough of a subscription of £50 a year to keep him from poverty in his decline. Planché himself lived modestly enough and was prodigiously industrious. His 176 plays apart, he was an antiquary of renown, wrote a standard history of British Costume (it was he who persuaded Charles Kemble to stage *King John* with historical accuracy, and so started a movement which has only just run its once salutary course), was attached to the Herald's Office, and, at seventy-six, completing his memoirs, could boast that he was still working as hard as he had ever done during the last fifty years. Yet a Civil List pension of £100 a year was a matter of importance to him. Nor did the receivers—the managers —do much better than the thieves; the theatre was in a wretched state financially. Nobody profited in fact, least of all the public.

Planché, unlike others, readily acknowledged his debt to France, even for the work which was most his own, the extravaganzas. He took the idea, and even the material for the first of them (the first written; its production was long delayed) from a *Folie Féerie, Riquet à la Houppe*, which he saw in Paris in 1821. English burlesque at this time was in an even more deplorable state than play-writing in general. The worst would not find its way into print; one can only hope even now that the best is not exemplified by a concoction entitled *Othello Travestie*, credited to a certain "Maurice G. Dowling, Esq.", which Mr Lacy thought it worth while to publish. With Othello a gibbering nigger, whose speech to the Senate is set to the tune of *Yankee Doodle* and begins

> Potent, grave and rev'rend sir,
> Very noble massa . . .

—a Desdemona following him to the tune of *Bonnie Laddie* with

> I'll tell you why I loved the Black;
> *Too ral*, etc.

'Cause ev'ry night I had a knack,
  Too ral, etc.
Of list'ning to his tales bewitchin',
My hair while curling in the kitchen.
  Too ral, etc.

—and far worse to follow yet, the scene of her murder (a "comic" murder!) being really too nauseatingly vulgar for quotation; with this for a standard no wonder Planché found his fairy tale unwelcome! Not till he encountered Madame Vestris did he get his chance.

She had her faults, had Madame Vestris; but she was a woman of courage, commonsense, and—timeliest of qualities!—of great good taste. What she did for English drama, at a time when it was more than usually difficult to do anything whatever for that rapscallion art, when you had, managerially, either to be "legitimate" and face almost certain loss in the vast barns of Drury Lane and Covent Garden, or evade the law elsewhere by peppering your plays with songs and dances and pretending they were not plays at all, has been too tardily remembered. She found in Planché's delicate simplicities excellent material for the colour and spice of her acting and singing and dancing: she was accomplished in all three, and had enough vitality besides for the inspiring of the actors around her. We may guess, indeed, that she re-fortified his dilution of the French spirit to something even above its original strength. Between the two of them, at any rate, they seem to have produced a civilised entertainment in this kind. And for fifteen years to come, till, game to the last, she left the theatre to die, Planché, with little interruption, wrote Christmas and Easter plays

for her, the Christmas play often lasting till Easter, and
the Easter play sometimes seeing the summer through.
Here, as such things go, was an achievement to be proud
of; and it is worth commemoration.[1]

Simplicity, delicacy and what one can best call innocence; these are the Planché hall-mark. One may add
taste and tact, and exact judgment also—he knows
when to stop. In no kind of writing do such qualities
count for more; there is no substance in it, manner is
everything—its good manners, in fact. The trick of his
method is old enough, it is, indeed, classic; he makes the
sublime not, let us remark, ridiculous, not by any means
grotesque, but easy and familiar; and, because he is
Planché, pleasantly, good-naturedly familiar. Take the
very first page of *Olympic Revels*. Jupiter, Neptune,
Hercules and Plutus are playing whist, and Jupiter loses his
temper with their chatter . . .

I'll play no more; and next time, I insist,
When you joke—joke; when you play whist—play whist!
    All. Finish the rubber.
    Jupiter.   I will not, I say.

[1] To be accurate, they did not begin with a transformed French fairy
tale, but with "A Mythological Allegorical Burletta" as the title page
has it "borrowed from the English of George Colman, the younger, the
Heads being taken from that gentleman's tale of the Sun Poker". It was
from this that *Olympic Revels or Prometheus and Pandora*, first performed
at the Olympic Theatre, January 3, 1831, took its being. *Riquet with
the Tuft* did not see the light till December 26, 1836. But they had both
been lying in Planché's drawer since some time in the 'twenties ("see the
light" is the pertinent phrase, then). Both pieces are of a pattern—
though *Riquet* has prose passages, and before and after Planché preferred
to abide by verse—and both equally reflect admiration for the French
model. Be it added that for both, since Planché was busy as usual with
other things, George Dance was called in to collaborate. But his contribution, however useful, cannot have been very significant.

Turn up the table; take the cards away.
Let's have some music. Hermes, where's Apollo?
   Mercury. Gone to the Glee-club at the Cat and Swallow.
   Jupiter. Deuce take the fellow; where is Bacchus now?
   Mercury. He's at the Punch Bowl, drunk as David's sow.
   Jupiter. Where's Mars?
   Mercury.   He's gone to drill.
   Jupiter.   Where's Juno, pray?
   Mercury. She's in the laundry, sir; it's washing day.
   Jupiter. The sky's deserted! Isn't Momus there?
   Mercury. No, sir; he's eating fire at Troy fair.
   Jupiter. Where's Esculapius?
   Mercury.   Priam's rather queer,
And he's gone down to bleed him, sir.
   Jupiter.   Oh dear!
Then I'll to sleep; bid Somnus step this way.
   Mercury. Lord, sir—he's yawning o'er the last new play.

It is by no means so easy to do as it may look; it asks
neatness, economy and precision, and the rhymes must
fall pat. Mercury is despatched to Vulcan to discover
whether Pandora, intended for the undoing of Prometheus, is not completed yet. He re-enters:

   Jupiter. Returned—Well-flown! How fares the lame old
      tinker?
   Mercury. Why, sir, his leg appears a little better.
But, for particulars, please read this letter.
   Jupiter (taking letter by the corner and holding it up).
How dare he send me such a dirty note?
He might have washed his hands before he wrote.
(Reads.) "Vulcan's respects, regrets to make Jove wait—
The thunderbolt will not be done till eight.

The lady all his time has been demolishing,
But she's just finished now, except the polishing;
Will bring her home himself as soon as done;
Mount Etna—post meridian—half-past one."
The polishing! He works confounded slow;
Zounds, I bespoke her full three weeks ago.
No thunder! Well, then I must do without it
Till eight, that's all that I can say about it.

He treats his fairy stories in much the same way,
though here, of course, the transposition is less from
dignity to impudence than from the marvellous to the
matter-of-fact; the trick, rather, is to treat the marvellous
in terms of the matter-of-fact. He boasted that he never
distorted the stories themselves, and that this was a strong
factor in his success with them. It is as true as such a
boast need be. With the tragic tales there are difficulties.
But he resolves the end of *Blue Beard; or the Fatal
Curiosity* (one of the best of the series) into the key of
the ridiculous very skilfully by suddenly calling on the
audience to help. Fleurette, the unlucky twentieth wife,
is about to pay the penalty of her curiosity; for, though
Sister Anne has sighted the rescuing horseman, Baron
Abomélique (no "three tailed bashaw", says Planché,
but, as he should be, a French nobleman of the fifteenth
century) has his sword drawn already. Then there is a
loud knocking at the door, and O'Shac O'Back,[1] the
head valet, enters to announce:

O'Shac: Lieutenants Bras-de-fer and Longue Epée.
Abomélique. Tell 'em I'm not at home,

---

[1] John Brougham, for whom the part was written, was a popular
actor of Irish characters—hence, and why not, O'Shac O'Back!—and a

O'Shac: They've found you out.

Abomélique. Say I'm at dinner, then, you stupid lout!

O'Shac: I told 'em you were waiting for your *chop*;
And so they said they'd in upon you drop,
And take pot luck!

Abomélique (seizing Fleurette). My vengeance lose I won't.
So thus I score up twenty!

> *As he is about to strike, Joli-Cœur, Bras-de-fer and Longue Epée rush in.*

Joli-Cœur.   No, you don't *(seizes his arm).*
Head up, Fleurette!

> *Bras-de-fer, Longue Epée.* There, take that, you old wizard.
> (*Passing their swords through Abomélique, who falls.*)

O'Shac: Thunder and turf, they've run him through the
        gizzard!

Joli-Cœur. Dost pity him?

O'Shac: Who, I sir? No, sir; never!
But there's a quarter's wages gone for ever.

> *Abomélique sits up.*

Abomélique. Kind-hearted soul, your shaken nerves com-
        pose,
They have but run me through my wedding clothes.

Fleurette. Perhaps it's better so, and for this reason;
We humbly hope to run you through the season....

Vestris, who played Fleurette, was famous for her "way
with the audience".

dramatist too; Boucicault's collaborator, for one thing, in the long
famous *London Assurance*. One of the pleasantest features of the prefaces
to the little plays, written when he was over eighty, is the tribute which
he never forgets to pay to the actors who had served him well forty or
fifty years, it may be, before.

Thence to the formal and traditional "apology":

O'Shac: . . . we have, all 'gainst common sense,
To-night committed a most grave offence.
Abomélique. If 'tis a *grave* one, then we must submit;
But if we've once to laughter moved the pit,
We plead that here uncommon nonsense revels
And strives to kill with laughter all blue devils. . . .
Fleurette. Our Blue Beard's not a great Bashaw of three
     tails,
But a French gentleman of one—the details
Dished up, *à l'Olympique*, by the same cooks,
Who for so long have been in your good books.
Smile on us still, nor let our Blue Beard be
A "Fatal Curiosity" to me.

He has, by the way, turned Shakespeare to liberal
account for the working up of the "situation"; Blue-
beard's vociferous demands for the fatal key with the
blood on it (blue blood!) being set to the very words—
ever so slightly caricatured—of Othello's for the handkerchief. But this sort of thing was common form both
with Planché and his followers into the Eighteen-
Seventies, and had been, I fancy, with his ascendants too
for a generation or so. Quotations from Shakespeare
are always peppered thick; though with the Patent
theatres and their repertory fading to an ever fainter
memory you could be less and less certain that your
audiences would "catch on" promptly enough.

PARODYING SHAKESPEARE

There are a dozen ways of turning the Bard to account.
You can drop in a well-known line neatly and surprisingly—and quite congruously; as when in *The New*

Planet[1] the gods of Olympus behold a panorama of London by night:

Mars.   There's the Horse Guards!
Pallas.   And there's the Athenaeum!
My statue crowns its portico so wide,
   The new Planet.   I hope the wisdom is not all outside.
   Ceres.   And there's Mark Lane, where rogues in grain are rank,
   The Earth.   How sweet the moonlight sleeps upon the Bank!

The very delicacy of the pun will win a quiet smile. And there is this also to be said, incidentally, about Planché; he was as content to write for the reward of a smile as a guffaw, a rare virtue in the comic writer.

You can parody the purpose of some familiar passage, as in *Once Upon a Time There were Two Kings*, for the reception of the victorious Prince Brutus; when an officer enters with

                  Sire, the royal fleet's in sight.
   The King.   Run to the ramparts—bid as quick as light
The cannonier to fire the cannon there;
And let the cannon bid the trumpet blare,
And let the trumpet to the kettle shout,
The kettle to the ophicleide without,
The ophicleide inform the pipes and drums
That they should play "The Conquering Hero Comes".

This, at a play's opening, makes you feel pleasantly at home.

Or you can burlesque an entire situation, as in the second scene of *The Good Woman in the Wood*, "a room in the palace of King Bruin"; when with a

---

[1] *I.e.* Neptune; the play was written a few months after its discovery.

*March and flourish—Enter King, Queen, Prince, Court and
    Guards.*

  King Bruin. Though yet of our late brother, who has been
So long defunct, the memory's so green
That we have subjects who dare still look blue
When that grave subject is alluded to;
This is to give you all a gentle hint
Not to presume at acts of ours to squint
Through spectacles of any hue but those
Made by our order of "Couleur de Rose",
And sold, to suit all ages and conditions,
By "Wink and Company", the Court opticians....
But now, our cousin Sylvan, and step-son.
  Prince (aside). A little more than *cozened*, I am done
Unutterably brown, if all be true....

  Shakespeare himself surely—though he took his puns
seriously—would have enjoyed the joke.
  Or (as thirty lines later) you can echo tragedy in mock
heroics with topical seasoning added; when the King
beckons the captive Princess Carpellona to him with

Approach, fair Princess, and dismiss your fear;
Say, can you love our son, Prince Brutus, here?
  Princess. Love Brutus!
  King.   Well enough to wed him.
  Princess.   I?
  King. Many would jump to do so.
  Princess.   -   Jump! Oh my!
Rather than marry Brutus, bid me jump
From off yon tower into the ocean plump;
Or walk through Smithfield on a market morn
And take the air upon a bullock's horn;

8-2

Or print a kiss on the unmuzzled mug
Of the black bear that eat the lady's pug;
Or the big boa-constrictor's cage inhabit
Who took a blanket for a large Welsh rabbit;
Or in a boneyard with some knacker dwell
And madly play upon the bones, like Pell;
Things that to hear them told have made me freeze—
And I'd much sooner do it, if you please.
    King (*to Prince Brutus*). As far as maiden delicacy may
Permit a timid maid her mind to say,
I think from what she hints we may discern
Your passion does not meet with much return.

—which again, quite apart from the neatness of the last
two couplets, is well enough; when Mr Pell's reputation
as "Bones" to the "Ethiopian Serenaders" is at its
height, and the python's exploit at the Zoo fresh in
memory. There will also doubtless be immediate point
in the dangers of Smithfield market and the catastrophe
of the bear and the pug; and if there is, besides, some
popular Juliet of the moment to imitate, so much the
better.

    There is such parody as in the speech beginning

        O, who can feed upon a hot-cross bun
        By merely thinking on a penny ice....

This is of coarser fibre. I came across it years ago and it
found, for no good reason, a sticking place in my mind.
It is probably by Talfourd or Byron, just possibly by
Brough or Reece. An expert critic could of course
identify the style quite positively; even as nowadays we
can say (some of us) that such a line, no matter in whose
ostensible play we find it, is by Chapman or Heywood,

Marlowe or Middleton. But I am not among the experts, in this category or that. Charles Kean, however, had revived *Richard II* in 1857; this may indicate a date.

From 1860 onwards the more recondite allusions will be far less sure of recognition; and the constant refuge in variations upon "To be or not to be" and "O my prophetic soul, my Uncle" does become terribly boring. It is still the thing, though, to scatter a few of the rarer quotations—perhaps as a sort of compliment to the culture of the audience! Byron can find use for

> And hang a calf skin on those recreant limbs!

—but he is careful to rub in its origin in the next line. Burnand, in a riotous burlesque of *Der Freischutz*, indulges first in the sad banality of introducing his operatic tenor with

> O, that this too too solid flesh would melt
> And make me somewhat easier in the belt!
> Or were this grosser part dissolved to dew,
> What would the butcher and the baker do?...

But he goes on to some quite delicate glancings at the Cassio-Iago dialogue upon reputation; not to rely greatly on their recognition however. Yet in general, if decreasingly, this burlesque was written for—written at, would be the better phrase—an, in this sense, educated audience. There would have been no risking otherwise the Princess's joke (in *The Sleeping Beauty*), as she thinks over her cloistered education, about the door through which she must not pass:

> The lock upon the door at the first landing,
> The only Locke upon my understanding.

Nor should we find at the race meeting in Talfourd's
Atalanta King Schoeneus of Scyros in his chariot, with
a picnic basket near labelled ΓΟΡΤΝΥΜ 'ΑΝΔ ΜΑΣΟΝ.

"ARISTOPHANIC" COMEDY; A DIGRESSION

Planché's first failure came when he set out—though
with all modesty, with extreme diffidence indeed—to
emulate Aristophanes. For the Haymarket Theatre in
1846 he tried his hand at a very free adaptation of *The
Birds* "to the modern and local circumstances requisite
to interest and amuse London playgoers of the nineteenth
century". But the thing is distressingly milk-and-watery.
It lacks salt, it lacks bite; now his respect for the great man
makes him timid, now he throws him over altogether in
his anxiety to give the public something of its customary
fare. Most decidedly this is not his game. But he liked
to look back on it in his old age as a "*succès d'estime* if not
d'argent", to claim it for a "hazardous experiment but...
worth making for the sake of art and the true interests of
the British stage". Three years later he tried the steep
and narrow path again, trusting this time to the form he
had made his own, with *The Seven Champions of Chris-
tendom*. This was announced as "a comic fantastic spectacle" but "in fact", he tells us in the later preface, it was
"a dramatic political allegory. A *Revue*, not of theatrical
and other novelties...but of the state of Europe at a
critical period, when some of the most momentous
events, burning questions, and gravest social grievances
were agitating every nation on the Continent, as well as
our own". This time the failure was satisfactorily dis-
guised as a popular success—as, with the practised

dramatist, such failures sometimes may be. For now
Planché takes out an insurance policy, so to speak, in
ballet and song and scenery. When it comes, though, to the
momentous events and burning questions, a few pious
platitudes must suffice. We may still applaud his good
intentions and what he felt to be his courage, not to
mention the Haymarket management's; he is courteously
careful "to do justice to the memory of Madame Vestris
by showing how far she was above that class of com-
mercial managers (to use Boucicault's felicitous designa-
tion of them[1]) who care little for the character of the
pieces they produce if they will only draw houses. Her
venture was greater than mine, for a *fiasco* at Easter would
have been the ruin of the season". It was a pathetic
ambition one fears (as he later records it), "to lay the
foundations of an Aristophanic drama, which the greatest
minds would not consider it derogatory to contribute
to "[2]—so far did he miscalculate his own capacities, his
audience, and circumstances in general. One circumstance in particular: the existence of the Lord Chamberlain! How did Planché see an English Aristophanes
getting on with that Olympian functionary? But in
the preface to *The Birds* (written in 1879) he remarks
upon "the recent successes of *The Palace of Truth* and
still more of *Pygmalion* upon these very boards" as
evidence that "there *is* a public who can enjoy good
writing and good acting unassisted by magnificent scenery
and undegraded by breakdowns". Gilbert was the one

---

[1] Boucicault should be put on record as the originator, then, of this
now much-worn phrase; Boucicault of all people!
[2] An article in *Temple Bar*, Nov. 1861.

man among his successors the nonsense mongers that had
proved himself capable of coming out from the ruck.
There, if anywhere, was his Aristophanes; and there—
though somewhat hyperbolically perhaps—the title did
in fact fall.

Gilbert had the very qualities which Planché lacked.
In the writing of drama and plain comedy he ran to conventional sentiment according to the fashion of his time.
But from the beginning his farce had an edge to it; and
when it came to topicalities, he could sting. Burlesque
was already in decline when he began to make his way;
as we shall see, it punned and rioted itself to death. He
tried the satiric play freed from both music and foolery,
and that did well enough, yet not too well. He experimented boldly and was the hardest of hard workers.
Then he encountered Sullivan, whose influence was towards the romantic and the picturesque. The trend here is
plain; from *Trial by Jury*, through *Patience, H.M.S. Pinafore*
and *Iolanthe* to *The Yeoman of the Guard* and the *Gon-
doliers*. But when after a rift they re-associate we have,
it is interesting to note, *Utopia Limited*, which is in
intention, which might well have been in fact, very
barbedly Aristophanic indeed.

The secret history of his relations with the Censorship
would be amusing, if it were secret enough to include
Gilbert's own private speculations as to how far he might
go, and a recounting of the distressed conferences between Reader and Comptroller and the Lord High
Executioner himself that must from time to time have
taken place in the little offices under York House to decide whether in this particular case (whatever the case

might be) they hadn't better on the whole, for just this once, "let it go". No one is more timorous than your despot when it comes to dealing with popularity. And Gilbert had quickly become popular; he had a tongue and a temper moreover, and the press was open to him. It was all very well to drop on Shelley, who was dead, or on Ibsen, who was a foreigner (with no one to take his part except a bunch of unfashionable intellectuals) and it was easy enough by a note dated *St James's Palace* to whip most theatre-managers to heel. But to meddle with the twin pillar of Savoy Opera, then at the height of its success—that might be very awkward. No wonder that in his evidence before the Joint Committee of 1909 Sir William confessed that he at any rate had had no trouble with the Censorship for years.

It is on record that he had eight lines cut from one of his first burlesques, and that from another the exclamation "Sakerament" was deleted because "the sound conveys the idea of a very objectionable and profane exclamation"; that to *Randall's Thumb* the Reader appended a note "all oaths (which are rather numerous in this comedy) must be omitted"; and he liked to relate that in his version of *Great Expectations*, where Magwitch said to Pip, "Here you are in chambers fit for a Lord", the MS. was returned to the theatre with "Lord" struck out and "Heaven" substituted. But this sort of thing might happen to anyone. There is the more famous case of *The Happy Land*, suppressed entire, after production too, because of its overt caricatures of Gladstone, Lowe and Ayrton—though, as the Lord Chamberlain had muddled his share of the matter, there was a compromise,

changes were made, and the play continued.[1] It is not so
well remembered that five years later Gilbert helped to
rewrite an old pantomime of Byron's for a charity performance, and played Harlequin in it himself, that the
characters were made up as well-known politicians, and
that in this instance the Lord Chamberlain, apparently,
was somehow never given a say in the matter at all. *Trial
by Jury* seems to have passed without trouble. But there
must surely have been to-ings and fro-ings at St James's
when *H.M.S. Pinafore* was presented for a licence. Would
the public think that Sir Joseph Porter, K.C.B., First
Lord of the Admiralty, who confesses that

> I grew so rich that I was sent
> By a pocket borough into Parliament;
> I always voted at my party's call
> And I never thought of thinking for myself at all.
> I thought so little, they rewarded me
> By making me the Ruler of the Queen's Navee

was intended for Mr W. H. Smith, the actual incumbent
of that post? Would Mr W. H. Smith think so? In
Patience the caricatures of Whistler and Wilde extended
even to make-up and costume. This was allowable
enough; they were people of no particular importance.
But what happened—whatever did happen—when the
MS. of *Iolanthe* arrived? Was—not the mere Commons,
but the Second Estate of the Realm to be thus mocked?
Were audiences to be encouraged to laugh at

> And while the House of Peers withholds
> Its legislative hand,

[1] Gilbert was only indirectly responsible here. The play was a burlesque
of his own, *The Wicked World*. He sketched it out, and set his pseudonym
of F. Tomline to the playbill; but Gilbert à Beckett did the writing.

And noble statesmen do not itch
To interfere with matters which
They do not understand,
As bright will shine Great Britain's rays
As in King George's glorious days;

—with Mr Gladstone actually in office, what was more!
The Lord Chamberlain may have learnt besides that, to
make the whole affair still more absurd, the peers were
to wear their coronets and robes, and the Lord Chan-
cellor his.[1] Was nothing said? Was Mr D'Oyly Carte
not "sent for"? Was the Prince of Wales not acquainted
with the threatened outrage? Was the Queen not told?
The Reader certainly did not take the responsibility on
himself, nor the Comptroller, nor in this case probably
even the Lord Chamberlain. The Office does not keep
records of its internal proceedings, I fancy. It is as well.
The chronicle of the freedoms it first denies and then
allows, seen broadening down from precedent to precedent, would not be an admirable one. It is inconceivable
that on this occasion a very great deal was not twitter-
ingly said. In no other dramatist would such hardihood
have been tolerated for a moment; but Gilbert was now
Gilbert, entrenched in popularity, and nothing was
done.

Into *Utopia Limited* he even introduced the Lord
Chamberlain himself, correctly uniformed (there were
all the other Court functionaries too, for that matter);
nor did the satire spare him as guardian of the morals of
the stage or policeman to the reputations received at

[1] Or he may not. Gilbert and the management were under no
formal obligation to tell him.

Court. But the play was licensed! One wishes Planché
could have lived to see it, to hear the final ironic eulogy
of Party government, and the Utopian chorus:

> There's a little group of isles beyond the wave,
> So tiny, you might almost wonder where it is;
> That nation is the bravest of the brave,
> And cowards are the rarest of all rarities.
> The proudest nations kneel at her command;
> She terrifies all foreign-born rapscallions,
> And holds the peace of Europe in her hand,
> With half a score invincible battalions!
> > Such at least is the tale,
> > Which is borne on the gale
> From the island which dwells in the sea.
> > Let us hope, for her sake,
> > That she makes no mistake—
> That she's all she professes to be.

But by this Gilbert has long had the measure of the
Lord Chamberlain. He knows well enough what he
may and may not do—and is probably content now to
do what he may, and can do so well, in peace. And he
shows extraordinary tact, even in his shrewdest thrusts
at Court and Parliament, County Council, Law, High
Finance, and the rest. It is all strictly impersonal;
amusing, yet never very deadly. It is, indeed, chaff
rather than satire. And one must own that while the touch
is certain and the skill mature, something of the old zest
has gone out of it.

Other things than censorship, however, go to keep
the Aristophanic drama of shy growth in England. It
demands, to begin with, a homogeneous public, who will

all be "in the know", whatever the "know" of the moment may be, who should, moreover, all be mutually aware of each other's knowingness. When it comes to topical comedy the bonds of sympathy in the theatre must be triangular. If an actor stirs my deeper feelings I would as soon keep that to myself, but I like to know that my neighbour is enjoying the joke too.

From this point of view Planché, with the smaller, compacter body of playgoers of his time, had been better off; and it is wrong to suppose, I think, that the mid-Victorian age was too self-complacent to welcome anything more searching than jokes about the smells from the Serpentine, the long delay in putting Landseer's lions in place, or the terrible condition (material, not moral) of Leicester Square. It was no more nor less so probably than any "age" before or since. At no time has it been the general English disposition to rejoice in that keen self-awareness, which is, actively and passively, the fruitful mood for satire. Groups and cliques may cultivate the needed liveliness of mind, the interest in ideas, the discontent with the obvious. But they, in the theatre of to-day certainly, are lost among the heathen crowd. Satire upon themselves they will welcome, but to make the crowd laugh too, it must go inaptly armed with a bludgeon. Satire upon the crowd their liveliness is not averse from; but oases of superior smiles are not, in the theatre, a rich reward. England, it is said, has yet to become an intellectual democracy. If this final revolution is now painfully in progress, and if it is to imply some slight amount of levelling up to compensate for all the levelling down, a modern Aristophanes may yet have his chance—even in the modern theatre. And, as a field for satire, democracy will do!

Planché's theatre though, all else apart, had served strange gods too consciencelessly and long for it to have much power of command over its audiences. It was living, on the one hand, upon a debased tradition of "classic" acting, on the other by filching foreign goods. No wonder it stood hat in hand, pathetically anxious to please.

And hereabouts was Planché's own weakness, though he did not see it. The virtues of his work were neither specifically English nor his own, nor were his would-be improvements upon it any less artificial. The whole thing is a hotch-potch, however charming a hotch-potch. It is shallow rooted, with no urgency of growth in it. Novelty is soon needed, and the scene painter steps to the fore; sure sign of flagging life in drama. Then we find Planché complaining that he is "painted out of existence", and protesting publicly when he is accused of fostering spectacle, that he has been its most unwilling victim. He has trouble with his actors too. Buckstone, an incorrigible clown, was a poor exchange either as actor or manager for Vestris and Charles Mathews. He records—not very regretfully in retrospect—the total failure of a certain popular low comedian who had been especially engaged to liven one of his Christmas plays. Ten years before he had scored a success with *Fortunio*, under Macready's management at Drury Lane, largely because "no one went out of his way to be funny". Macready, himself, on that occasion had "energetically and judiciously" superintended the rehearsals. He

"thought highly of the piece, and entered into the true
spirit of it with a zest that was as surprising to his company as it was beneficial to the representation. He knew
everyone's part, and acted each in turn. . .". Poor
Macready, he got precious little fun out of life as a rule.
One can see him at it! Miss Helen Faucit, what was
more (Lady Martin to be, wife to the official biographer
of the Prince Consort), had sat upon the stage, watching
every rehearsal, enjoying them thoroughly.

But now a wave of vulgar foolery is rolling in again
upon the theatre. Well, says Planché (this is in 1861), if
we are to be plunged "into jungles of jingles and sloughs
of slang all I demand is not to be accused of having set
the example".

SIMPLE FOOLERY

His complaint is just; and one turns from the reading
of his dainty lines to samples, the best of their kind, of
the farragos of foolery concocted by Byron, Burnand,
Brough, Reece and the rest, the popular stuff of the
'fifties and 'sixties, with something of the sensation of
passing from a pleasant evening party, where the talk has
been, not so desperately brilliant, but kindly and amusing
enough, into the row and disorder of a village fair. But
the fair, with all its crudities, is very much alive.

The old Masks admitted to their dignified and delicate
splendours an anti-mask of buffoonery; there was value
for each in the contrast. What Planché's work lacked was
just this inherent robustness; the frail pattern of it was
therefore fated to be clowned, as well as painted out of
existence. For clowning and the sheer exuberance of

animal spirits will always make their claim, in England certainly; and they are a legitimate part of all theatrical tradition.

These burlesques and extravaganzas of the 'sixties were largely mere material for clowning. Their jingles and puns are clowning—a pun is literary clowning, exactly that. Someone must surely have written learnedly about the Pun; it discloses a complex of some sort, I suppose, if you dig deep enough. I will not, in my ignorance, make the attempt. Bergson, in *Le Rire*, dismisses the *calembour* in a couple of sentences. Whether that interesting work exhibits more profoundly the difference between the philosopher and the ordinary human being, or between the Frenchman and the Englishman is (for an Englishman) a question; but there seems to be, oddly enough, hardly a definition of comedy in it which cannot be made to serve with the slightest shifting for a definition of tragedy too; and plainly, whatever the author's sense of humour, he has none of simple fun. Now the pun is purely comic; it is that or nothing. Hence the reckless impudence of the true punster; if he is to fail he may as well be hung for a sheep as for a Lamb (I find I have written that last word with a capital letter, in piety I will let it stay).

It is the correct thing, of course, to be a little shame-faced about your punning. Planché, in the first few lines of his first burlesque, quotes Dr Johnson upon pocket-picking. But he punned modestly and with great dis-cretion. He can refer with a pretty mixture of shame and pride to "an atrocious pun in *The Golden Fleece*, which is, of course, more frequently quoted than such

as are worthier of recollection". Yet it is only—when
Medea and Jason are discussing Glauce—that Medea says

> Oh, don't name that creature;
> I heard her say, "If your wife bores you, beat her".
> *Jason.* You quite mistook her—the reverse meant she;
> Beta in Greek, you know, is *Letter B.*

Burnand (who closed his *Pirithoüs* with a character ex-
claiming, "I've quite done; Resting and thankful with the
last worst pun") would have thought that tame enough
for a Bishop's sermon. For him and his fellows the
worse a pun was the better, in a sense. And there is something to be said for this. All the actor's skill is then called
upon to make it tell. How some of them *were* made to
tell is a mystery to me. Doubtless the audience had well-
trained ears; it would be a point of pride with your confirmed burlesque-goer not to miss a single one. Still,
there should surely never be too continuous a strain. Mr
David James, playing King Francis in William Brough's
The Field of the Cloth of Gold, and lost in the forest, will
have no great difficulty with

> These fine old trees my view on all sides border;
> They're Foresters of the most Ancient Order.
> Still, for their king thus trapping there's no reason;
> And so *high trees,* I charge you with *high treason.*
> My royalty at least there's no mistaking;
> I've walked till every bone tells me I'm *a king.*
> I'll lie down 'neath these boughs, for I protest,
> Walking this *forest long,* I *long for rest.*
> Francis, full length extended 'neath these branches,
> Will be what's called "*extension of the Franchis*".

D

And there is, let us note in passing, much art in the cumulative effect of this. "Ancient Order of Foresters" is, of course, not a pun at all. *High trees—high treason* is a straight-forward one, the pun direct; till every bone tells me I'm *a king* is the "pun implied", for variety; *forest long—long for rest* is the pun reversed. But it is all a preparation for the sheer impudence of *extension of the Franchis*, which should strike us 'twixt wind and water, and the skilled actor will see that his audience does not laugh till then. For the tasting of the joke's full flavour the play's date must be remembered: 1868.[1]

King Henry has arrived, still in the agonies of sea-sickness; and it is this gives occasion for the famous

Henry.   Where's Suffolk?
Suffolk.   Here, my liege, in waiting.
Henry. My loving Suffolk, I feel *suffoc*-ating,
I am so ill!
Suffolk. Nay, Sire, cheer up, I pray;
You were so brave and jolly yesterday.
Henry. Yesterday all was fair—a glorious Sunday,
But this *sick transit* spoils the *glory o'Monday*.

No difficulty here either; even nowadays, with the

---

[1] Upon the page opposite, incidentally, we find a doggerel song which has something of a topical smack to-day. Tête de Veau, the Constable of Calais, is presenting King Henry with a petition:

Tête de Veau. My address, Sire, to work a charm I meant;
If you'll let me but read it I'll engage—
Darnley. The old story, of course; disarmament,
To comply with the spirit of the age.
Le Sieur de Boissy. But great nations were always fond of soldiers,
And you think now, so it to me appears,
France and England being friends, all necessity now ends,
For the Army, Navy, or the Volunteers.

classic quotation barred from Parliament, a punster
might venture on it. And Anne Boleyn will find her

> I'm grieved to state
> Queen Kate gets daily more *in-daily-cate*

simple enough. But the exchange between the Constable and Darnley,

> *Tête de Veau.*   I'm safe—I am the guest of France,
> While you an exile here are rated.
> *Darnley.*   Yes,
> It's not *exile-a-rating* I confess;

—must have been hard to drive home; nor was it (possibly)
very "*exile-a-rating*", even when driven. And here, perhaps, we happen on the secret. As with all foolery, there
should be something exhilarating about a pun.

The Field of the Cloth of Gold is "last period" Brough,
and—such his experience in the art!—the puns at their
poorest are at least practicable. But turn to the earlier
Perseus and Andromeda, and to the sea-monster's entrance
with

> Hullo! Fe-fi-fo-fum! What, no alarm?
> Have then those words of terror lost their charm?
> Time was when fe-fi-fo-fum all compelled,
> To pay the *fief I've of 'em* so long held;

or to Andromeda's appeal to Perseus:

> Fly! save yourself! His I alone must be,
> So you must needs give up your *share o' me*.
> My fate is sealed, so's yours if he attacks;
> So get *away for* else you'll get the *whacks*.

"Sealed" may make *wafer* and *wax* just comprehensible:

but how "*fief I've of 'em*" and *chère amie* were conveyed, even by the most glib-tongued actor, to the sharpest eared audience (without the help of a note on the programme) I find it hard to imagine.

Brough can also provide us with a fair example of the cumulative pun. In *King Arthur*, written for the Haymarket in 1863, we have Merlin entering alone with

> Some mortal eye is watching me I find;
> That *mortal I* advise his eye to mind,
> If *more to lie* in wait for me he dare—
> I say no *more till I* find out—Who's there?

But there was more to him as a burlesque writer than his trick of punning. He could project a genuinely comic character. Mahoud, the surly grumbler in *The Caliph of Bagdad*, is excellent, with his

> Why am *I* not a Caliph? Why, indeed?
> No gongs or cymbals ring out when I feed,
> Yet I can eat as much as he can!

—and, when Haroun al Raschid's night-prowling name of Al Bondocan is disclosed:

Mahoud (aside). Oh fate unjust! What has this Caliph done
That he's allowed two names while I've but one?
Mesour. He comes.
All (shouting). Long live the Caliph!
Mahoud (aside).   Now who's he,
That they should wish him longer life than me?

His *Perdita or the Royal Milkmaid*, done for the Lyceum in 1856 (Miss Marie Wilton as Perdita), which must have gained special point from Mr Charles Kean's recent production of *A Winter's Tale* at the Princess's (Miss Ellen

Terry as Mamilius), is alive with genuinely comic ideas.
Kean had evidently been pedantically providing Bohemia
with a legitimate sea-coast by changing its name to
Bithynia; and there is good play with that. "Time"
comes in useful too. The moment Camillo and Polixenes
have fled the Court, Leontes and "Time" enter simultaneously.

> *Leontes.* Camillo gone!
> *Time.*   Stop, you don't know it yet.
> *Leontes.* I beg your pardon!
> *Time.*   Time must first elapse.
> But there's no arguing with you jealous chaps!
> (*To audience.*) So I must leave to your imagination
> The time required for this embarkation.
> Suppose them nearing now with favouring breeze
> Bohemia or Bithynia—which you please.
> Now then, your Majesty, you may go on.
> *Leontes.* Then, as I said before: Camillo gone!
> Oh, traitor, villain, false disloyal slave....

He can exploit the comic value of an anti-climax quite
admirably. Leontes raves on to Antigonus and the
courtiers.

> Go, bid the waves be calm when tempests roar.
> Bid ratepayers be calm when at the door
> The poor-rate calls. Bid those by rail who travel
> Be calm when Bradshaw's mysteries they'd unravel.
> Bid studious men be calm when 'neath their windies
> An organ boy kicks up his fearful shindies.
> Bid anyone you please be calm, but don't
> Bid me—
> *Antigonus.* Well then, your Majesty, we won't.

This is better than pedestrian punning. The plot of *A Winter's Tale* is in itself near enough to absurdity for burlesquing to have to do it no undue violence. Antigonus is not killed and eaten, of course; and when in the last scene he re-enters, *"followed by the bear respectably dressed"*, we may even feel that Brough for the moment has perhaps a better sense of the fitness of things than had Shakespeare.

A caricaturist, it would seem, will only *amuse* us while he preserves—and subtly encourages in us—some respect and affection for his originals; beyond this pale lie the savageries of Hogarth and Gillray. You cannot, for this reason, burlesque Shakespeare's tragedies very ruthlessly, since we so innately respect them; though when you have a Frederick Robson to write for (of whom Henry Morley's admiring complaint was only that he did not play the parts themselves, Shylock, Macbeth, Lear) it may seem worth while to try. Macbeth's entrance upon the blasted heath with Banquo *"under an umbrella"* will be funny enough for a start; but when it comes to the murder of Duncan, one is only conscious of insult. The Greek Legends are more removed: we few of us feel an instinctive aesthetic loyalty to Zeus and the Heroes. But even here there is all the difference in effect between Planché's treatment of them and, say, Burnand's. It would be a difference hard to prove in a court of law; one cannot weigh taste and tact in such scales. The impertinences are ponderably the same, and we cannot swear that even Planché never slips uncomfortably near the edge of vulgarity. But there is a redeeming fancifulness about him, a touch of romance, the necessary latent

respect. Talfourd sets gods and heroes alike playing the
fool outrageously; even so, he knows how to keep a
spice of dignity in reserve. Brough will at least preserve
some sense of character in all he does. But with Burnand it
will be buffoonery unashamed![1] Operas and melodramas
seem, on the whole, to serve best for burlesquing; they
are near enough to the edge of the ridiculous already to
be pushed over without difficulty. And the Arabian
Nights prove a useful storehouse for somewhat the
same reason: with them we are in a fantastic world
already.

It was the pun, doubtless, which did most to sap the

[1] One may quote Henry Morley as witness for the prosecution here,
and his *Journal of a London Playgoer*. "Take, for example, that notorious
burlesque of Ixion, in which the brother of a Viscount not long ago made
his début as an actor and was thus advertised: 'Great success of the Hon.
Lewis Wingfield as Minerva. Other characters by the loveliest women
in England'.... The whole success of the piece was made by dressing up
good-looking girls as immortals lavish in display of leg and setting them
to sing and dance, or rather kick burlesque capers, for the recreation of
fast blockheads. If Miss Pelham only knew how she looks in the eyes of
the better half of any audience when she comes forward with sandy
beard and moustaches disfiguring her face, and with long pink legs
wriggling her body into the ungainly gestures of burlesque toeing and
heeling, the woman in her would rise in rebellion against the miserable
vulgarity of the display. As for the Hon. Lewis Wingfield, who dressed
his thin figure in petticoats and spoke falsetto as Minerva—every man to
his taste! His great success was an idiotic dance in petticoats that might
stand for something in competitive examination for admission into the
Earlswood Asylum, but as a gentleman's first bid for the honours of the
English stage was a distressing sight to see." Morley was by no means
a kill-joy critic. He has constant praise for Planché, and for Brough,
Talfourd and Byron too, when they will let their natural merriment tell.
"Only the blockheads", he says, "would be enemies to broad burlesque;
grotesque absurdity is fair source of recreation...." But he has no
tolerance for vulgarity; and he is, it may be mentioned, very definitely
down upon the pun. His judgment passed upon it is too long to quote;
it can be found (should anyone have occasion to cast a punster forth
from Club or Common Room with due formality) on p. 247 of the
1891 edition.

vitality of the burlesque of the 'sixties—though, indeed, by the end of them, and before, the thing had had its day and was fit for death. Byron came at last to punning as a stammerer stammers, till the very sense of his nonsense would be obscured—and nothing, of course, needs to be made clearer. They punned and punned, he and the rest, till there were no puns left to make. Then they could only repeat them; and, really, the pun served up cold for the seventh time is pretty poor fare. At its best and freshest it is mechanical humour; and what is mechanical, in humour as in all else, unrenewably wears out.

But it was not the pun, good or bad, which had won burlesque its success. Talfourd could write really good comic verse when he chose; and he so enjoyed doing it that we often find passages asterisked "to be omitted in representation"—the hall-mark, this, of the "literary" dramatist. Brough and Reece had their strong sense of comic character, and Byron can at least do excellent parody. Take the description of the "palace lifting to eternal summer" in *The Lady of Lyons*. In the burlesque it is, most appositely, the Crystal Palace, then lately set up on Sydenham Hill.

> *Claude.* If thou wouldst have me paint—
> *Pauline.*   I would. Be quick!
> *Claude (aside).* Then I must lay it on extremely thick.
> (*Aloud.*) The home to which, could love fulfil its prayers,
> This hand would lead thee (*aside*) up no end of stairs!
> (*Aloud.*) A flight of beauty such as ne'er did man see
> (*Aside.*) But in this instance quite a flight of fancy!
> (*Aloud.*) A palace in the winter and the summer
> Open to every decently dressed comer,

Who with the humble shilling can come down
(On Saturdays the charge is half a crown);[1]
With marble halls—each end a glassy tower
(The trains start every quarter of an hour).
At noon, when cooler much the air becomes,
We'd sit among the Megatheri*ums*.
And others with hard names—I scarce can tell 'em
One from the other—nobody can spell 'em.
We'd have no friend with us the livelong day;
Third parties, dear, are always in the way.
And when night came, down at the railway station,
Midst hundreds in a state of agitation,
We'd guess which carriage should convey us home,
As to the platform's side the train would come—
Say, dost thou like the picture?

But now, perhaps, no one remembers the original; so
the joke falls flat. He can do a very stirring curse. Take
Edgar's parting from Lucy in *Lucia di Lammermoor*:

Edgar. . . . What d'ye mean? I'm in a fog! Desist.
Lucy. Continue in your fog; you won't be *mist*.
Edgar. A heartless, venerable joke! (*Music tremoloso.*)
    Oh, may
You find that matrimony doesn't pay!
May you soon find your fond adoring hub
Pass his whole time at his convivial club,
Until you *hate* him; then when you can't bear him
May nothing from your presence ever tear him!
May every play you go to turn out dull!
May every evening party prove a mull!

[1] *Was* this so? It ought, surely, to have been the cheap day. The
social historian of the period will do well to glance through these
burlesques; they abound in clues.

May he deny each debt by you incurred!
May your dressmaker never keep her word!
          (*Lucy whimpers; agony on all sides.*)
May you get table beer instead of Bass;
Have something always wrong about your gas!
May you, when you to breakfast come down late,
Find they've black-leaded your steel-polished grate!
May Mudie never send you a new book!!
And may you never get a sober cook!!!

There is the right shadow of the tragic behind this, and it throws a revealing light upon middle-class domesticity in the Eighteen-Sixties.

One thing, by the way, must be remembered about these burlesques; they were not lengthy affairs. Planché had after a while elaborated his extravaganzas into two acts, for the sake, supposedly, of more scenic display, and this may well have been a mistake. But the typical burlesque was the affair of an hour, not more, split into five or six scenes for variety's sake (front cloths alternating with full sets, and nothing very elaborate even about these) played through without any interval—this was most important—for reflection. At the Strand there would be at least two, but more probably three plays in the programme, which began at seven; that meant a comedy and a farce besides. The burlesque would come at the end or in the middle. If you had booked your seat you could dine comfortably and take it as a digestive; and such was the manly habit of the day. It was a romp, a riot of absurdity, and it pretended to be nothing else.

But much skill went to such romping; and here is another thing to remember. The actors who made their

name at the Strand—and made its name also—were not
the old-fashioned clowning low comedians. They were
to be the accomplished comedy actors of the next decade
or so; and one reason at least for the Strand's decline
was that they found this new vocation. Marie Wilton,
Lottie Venne, David James, Thomas Thorne, Edward
Terry; and, from elsewhere, Carlotta and Rose Leclercq,
Mrs John Wood, Lionel Brough, and even Charles
Wyndham[1]—it was the blending of their sort of skill
with the quieter, dryer style of Bancroft, Hare and the
Kendals which produced the standard comedy acting of
the two or three decades to follow—and a pretty high
standard too! There were critics who said of Mrs Bancroft
that she never quite lost the bounce of her burlesque days.
For "bounce" read "vitality"—and we may add that it
was as well she didn't, that it would have been as well,
moreover, if this particular quality had not been allowed
to peter so politely to vanishing point in a yet later phase
of English acting.

GILBERT

Gilbert threw his hat into the ring in 1866 with *Dulcamara; or the little Duck and the Great Quack*, a burlesque
of Donizetti's *L'Elisir d'Amore*. He owed the commission
for it to T. W. Robertson and he wrote it in ten days
(he could have found no great difficulty in doing that!).
It was a success, and he went industriously to work upon
others: a *Robert the Devil*; a *Merry Zingara, or the Tipsy
Gipsy and the Pipsy Wipsy* (*The Bohemian Girl*); a *La
Vivandière, or True to the Corps* (*The Daughter of the
Regiment*); a *Pretty Druidess* (*Norma*); not to mention a

[1] The list could be lengthily added to.

pantomime, *Harlequin Cock Robin and Jenny Wren*. No one would pretend that the Gilbert of the operas is patent in them, he was to be the result of much evolution. The interesting thing is rather that they are cut quite to conventional pattern, that the jingling dialogue may sometimes be as poor, the puns as execrable—and often worse—than was usual; and (to have done with this side of it) that there are even passages in sufficiently bad taste. The authentic Gilbert can be discerned there, nevertheless.

There are two ways of developing ability in an art. The one, and doubtless the nobler, is to go out into the desert and await inspiration, and when it has worked its will on you—well, what you have written you have written. But this, for some reason, seldom proves to be the right approach to the vulgar art of the theatre. The other plan is to serve your apprenticeship as you would to carpentering or house-painting, carrying out your orders with quickness and despatch and making the momentary best of them, such as they are. Then, when you are master of your trade, produce masterpieces—if you can. This was Shakespeare's plan, and (comparisons apart) it was Gilbert's too.

He brings, needless to say, immediate vigour to the business. He can, for instance, rival, if not better, his instructors with the British priest's tirade in *The Pretty Druidess* against the practical jokes of the Roman soldier who has been billetted on him (whose sense of humour was apparently not unlike the youthful Gilbert's own):

> *Oroviso.* The fellow's one interminable hoax,
> Begins his senseless irritating jokes
> As soon as he gets up—while still it's dark.

Adalgise. A healthy custom—*rising with the lark!*
Oroviso. Who stuffs the priest's armchair with pins
and needles?
Who fills the priest's umbrella with black-beadles?
Who pulls the priest's moustachios by the roots?
Who sends the priest fictitious cheques on Coutts?
Who places cactus in his trouser legs,
Who takes and hard boils all his new laid eggs?
Who treads upon his toes until he limps?
Who fills his sacerdotal boots with shrimps?...

and so on and so on. He can do an excellent knock-down
pun as when (in *The Merry Zingara*) Thaddeus and Max
confess:

We're refugees from Poland, all the way.
Our country shall avenge our wrongs some day.
Warsaw triumphant once we thought we foresaw;
That isn't now the case, but *wice-Warsaw!*

—and do as well and better with the pun-cumulative;
when Thaddeus a little later saves Arline from the deadly
attack of—a small sucking pig, which he brings in upon
one arm, the child clinging to the other.

Thaddeus. Your daughter safely to you I restore,
My trusty Enfield settled that *small bore.*
No thanks—a t-*rifle!*
Florestein.   He don't care a fig.
Call that a small boar—why, it's very *pig!*
Count. That she's uninjured let me be assured;
Her body's safe, although her skirt is *gored.*
Thaddeus. My bullet reached his heart before he
crunched her.
The beast had almost munched her.

Count.   What a *munchter*!

Florestein (sees wound in Arline's shoulder). He's been a-
biting her—her life blood drawing.

Count. A-biting? Oh dear me, this is *a-gnawing*!
Her fate was almost sealed—a frightful death.

Florestein. A fact that this in*denture* witnesseth!

Count (to Thaddeus). She would have perished in the
monster's jaws,
If you'd not introduced your saving *claws.*
You'll join our sports—among our friends we rank you.
You'll stop a day?

Devilshoof (officiously). We will. A month.

Count (coldly).   Oh, thank you!

(Fondling Arline.) I love this very best of pipsy-wipsies.

(Shaking hands with Devilshoof.) I've a particular respect for
gipsies.

(Shaking hands with hunters.) Hunters, I worship, as I said
before.

(Shaking hands with Florestein.) I love all nephews. *(Kissing
Buda.)* Nurses I adore.
Mankind at large I love, my heart's so big;
(Sees pig.) I'm also very fond of sucking pig.

He must indeed be young and superior who cannot
laugh at that. Notice, incidentally, the skill and economy
with which the effects are made; the puns come in with
the right emphatic rhythm, and there is not a wasted line.

And here, very certainly, at the opening of *Robert the
Devil* is the authentic, if still immature Gilbert:

> *Lord Margate and five companions discovered at the Grand Mulets
> on Mont Blanc.*

Lord Margate. Marquis of Cranborne's Alley's leave I cry,
Lord Pentonville's, and yours, Sir Peckham Rye.

You all remember, when we left the shore
Of Rule Britannia, we in concert swore
We'd do our best on reaching these localities
To show our undisputed nationalities;
To show contempt in everything that we did.
Tell me, my comrades, how have we succeeded?
   Marquis of C. A. I've sworn at all who hindered my re-
      searches.
   Lord P. I've worn my hat in all the foreign churches.
   Sir P. R. On all their buildings I've passed verbal strictures,
And poked my walking stick through all their pictures.
I only carry it about for that use.
   Marquis of C. A. I've decorated all their public statues.
   Lord P. When Frenchmen have conversed with me or
      you
I've always turned the talk to Waterloo.
   Lord M. I've half a dozen Frenchmen tried to teach
That I'm twelve times as brave and strong as each;
And showed that this corollary must follow,
One Englishman can thrash twelve Frenchmen hollow.
In fact, my friends, wherever we have placed ourselves,
I may say we have thoroughly disgraced ourselves.

From the beginning, too, Gilbert scored notably by his faculty, amply developed as Bab in the pages of *Fun*, for turning out amusing lyrics. There was the heavy handicap that they had to be written to well-known tunes. This custom in burlesque had inevitably left that side of it poor; even Planché's aptitude for neat rhyming had been at a loss. The only gain lay in an entire parody of some popular song; but this, at best, was a mechanical business. Gilbert's metrical agility had its final training over these obstacles. But he detested them; and, in after years, one

of the greatest sacrifices he could make to Sullivan was
to set words to a tune.

A trio in *Robert the Devil* to the tune of *Le Dieu et
la Bayadère* is forward-looking:

> Oh, animosity and villainous verbosity,
> Perpetual precocity and fabulous ferocity,
> And venomous velocity and every other -ocity
> In planning an atrocity or compassing a crime!

He was to ring many useful changes upon that. And here,
in the probationary *Dulcamara*, is something almost as
typical; a quartette to be sung to the air of *The Sugar
Shop*—whatever that was! The "happy villagers" are
welcoming Sergeant Belcore and his soldiers:

> *Adina.* If you intend to stay with us, before you've been
>   a day with us,
> You'll learn the proper way with us, of saying what you
>   say to us.
> Each speech should have a pun in it, with very foolish
>   fun in it—
> And if you can't bring one in it—you'd better stop away.

But there is further significance in this. Set it beside the
quite unusually elaborated "apology" to the audience,
which ends *The Pretty Druidess*, written three years later;
the last of these conventional burlesques that he was to
write:

> *Norma.* So ends our play. I come to speak the tag,
> With downcast eyes, and faltering steps that lag.
> I'm cowed and conscience-stricken; for to-night
> We have, no doubt, contributed our mite
> To justify that topic of the age,

The degradation of the English stage.
More courage to my task I p'raps might bring,
Were this a drama with real everything;
Real cabs, real lime-light too, in which to bask,
Real turnpike keepers, and real Grant and Gask![1]
But no, the piece is commonplace, grotesque,
A solemn folly, a proscribed burlesque!
So for burlesque I plead. Forgive our rhymes;
Forgive the jokes you've heard five thousand times;
Forgive each breakdown, cellar flap and clog,
Our low-bred songs, our slangy dialogue;
And—above all—oh, eye with double barrel,
Forgive the scantiness of our apparel.

It could not be better, and it could not be more loyally done; but Gilbert must have known from the beginning—how should he not?—what this burlesque game was worth, and now he is pretty certain that the game is up. And the history of his career, in its consequence to the English theatre, is the history of his creating something of permanent value (though intensely individual and not to be further developed after him) out of the wreck and the rubbish of it; Savoy Opera, that is to say. His progress is instructive; from the throwing over of the pun, through the abandoning of jingling rhyme for prose (in *Thespis*, his first work done with Sullivan), the insistence upon original music

[1] C.f. *The Princess* (the skit upon Tennyson's poem that was the foundation of *Princess Ida*), Scene 3.

Let Swan secede from Edgar—Grant from Gask,
Sewell from Cross—Lewis from Allenby—
In other words, let Chaos come again.

I have not so far identified the actual drama, which so abounded with "real everything." I suspect something by Boucicault at the Adelphi.

written to his lyrics, the rejection of the men playing
women and the women playing men, the forbidding of
"gags", and finally to the stern discipline of his stage-
management at the Savoy itself. Very trivial matters,
no doubt, *sub specie aeternitatis*; and they consummate
mere triviality! But if we are to heed them and the fruit
of them at all we must take them as seriously as Gilbert
had to in his strivings.

His later work is outside my present province. He
earned the reputation of being a "difficult" man. He
was probably no more difficult than any man will be
who knows what he wants and is determined to get it.
He had laboured tenaciously and patiently at his own
task, and he could be unremittingly patient with his
actors labouring at theirs—as long as he saw that it was
honest and modest labour. But he knew well enough
that what he wanted, simple as it might seem in its final
effect, was not to be gained without an infinite taking of
pains. Over twenty years he had taken pains with his own
talent, till it could rank, in its kind, as genius. Set *Dulcamara*
beside *The Mikado* and measure the difference between
the two. The old slapdash days had been jolly enough;
he could always affectionately laugh at the memory of
them. But now, if anything was to be done with English
dramatic art, discipline was needed.

It was, I believe, this disciplinary change in the conduct
of the theatre upon which its phenomenal advance towards the end of the century was based. Macready had
bitterly complained of the sordid condition of things,
Charles Kean and his wife had done their best to reform
them, Phelps was an honest worker; but the 'fifties and

'sixties still saw the English theatre, as a whole, in a state of slovenly chaos, redeemed, when it could be redeemed, only by the sheer vitality of an individual figure or two. Then came its disciplining to a standard of all-round accomplishment undreamt of before, and to a standard of civilised behaviour, by Irving, the Bancrofts and the Kendals, by Hare and Wyndham, by Sydney Grundy and Henry Arthur Jones and, most particularly, by Pinero and Gilbert. And Gilbert's task was, for obvious reasons, the hardest of all. But single-handed he succeeded; where Planché—aiming, it is true, a little differently— had but aspired and (for all the charm of what he did amid much merited applause) finally failed. Out of the débris of extravaganza and burlesque Gilbert made something consistent in form, and sanely comic in spirit, worthy to rank as art.

There is a scene in *The Yeoman of the Guard* where Jack Point takes service under the Lieutenant of the Tower, who listens with set face to his sample jests:

Lieut. Can you give me an example? Say that I had sat me down hurriedly on something sharp?

Point. Sir, I should say that you had sat down on the spur of the moment.

Lieut. I don't think much of that. Is that the best you can do?

Point. It has always been much admired, sir, but we will try again.

Lieut. Well, then, I am at dinner and the joint of meat is but half cooked.

Point. Why, then, sir, I should say—that what is *under*done cannot be helped.

Lieut. I see. I think that manner of thing would be some-what irritating.

Point. At first, sir, perhaps; but use is everything, and you would come in time to like it. . . .

But there is no sign that the Lieutenant will. He de-parts, looking very much as a man may look after read-ing a round dozen of those mid-Victorian burlesques. After him exit Jack Point, crestfallen. And exit with him and finally (did Gilbert think as he wrote it?), following Planché's benigner shade, Byron, Brough, Burnand, Reece, Talfourd and the rest. Well they had served their turn! Of how many of us will much more be said?[1]

1 The material for this slapdash study has been by no means easy to come by, and I record my thanks for much kindly help in my search for it—first to Lady Gilbert herself; to Mr Cyril Hogg and Mr Arthur Elsbury of French's, to Mr Towneley Searle, of whose bibliography of Gilbert I have made full use; to Mr Rupert D'Oyly Carte, Mr Geoffrey Chilton, Miss Rowland Grey, Miss Ethel Dickens, Mr J. G. Wilson, and, needless to say, to the staff at the British Museum and at the London Library.

PUNCH IN THE 'SIXTIES

By *C. L. Graves*

Punch, founded in 1841 by a group of journalists and authors, in the course of the next twenty years developed from a free-lance journal of distinctly Radical colour into an interpreter of enlightened middle-class opinion, and was already a household word and almost a national institution.

This development was in no respect more marked than in *Punch's* altered attitude towards the Monarchy. It had begun even before the death in 1857 of his most truculently democratic contributor, Douglas Jerrold, whose attacks on Court patronage, courtiers, and above all on the Germanism, the alleged intervention in high politics, the notions of sport and passion for tailoring of the Prince Consort, were merciless in their frankness. Though loyalty to the person of the Queen was maintained, she was not exempt from disrespectful caricature —as in the cartoon of the old and prolific woman who lived in a shoe. The acute animus of this anti-Albertianism abated, as the result of the Prince's signal services in connection with the Exhibition of 1851, after which he was granted a comparative immunity from ridicule, but the revulsion of feeling did not manifest itself fully until his death in 1861. It is worth noting that Thackeray,[1]

[1] Thackeray ceased to be an active member of the staff in 1854, though he attended the weekly meetings till a few days before his death in 1863.

the most famous of all the members of the *Punch* staff
who took an active part in this baiting of the Prince—
witness the terrible sonnet on his exploits as a slayer of
stags—resigned his post on the "table" largely in consequence of Douglas Jerrold's acrimonious attacks on
Napoleon III, whose life was subsequently written in
a spirit of sustained eulogy by Jerrold's eldest son.

Gilbert à Beckett (Thackeray's à Beckett the Beak)
died in 1856, and Henry Mayhew, another of the
founders, and the first of philanthropic journalists who
took the poor of London as their theme, had quitted the
table before 1860. The Editor, Mark Lemon, ex-brewer
and tavern keeper, was a most prolific journalist and
playwright, Falstaffian in physique, as his portraits show,
and convivial in temperament. He was known as
"Uncle Mark", but he was neither a wicked nor a
usurious uncle. He worked at first for a salary of thirty
shillings a week and saved the paper in its early days from
disaster by the money he earned from his plays. The
debt that *Punch* owes him is generously summed up in
Lord Sumner's article in the *D.N.B.* when he says that
"during the twenty-nine years of his control *Punch* not
only attained the position of a social power, and numbered
amongst its contributors almost all the humorists of the
day, but it was singularly free from all virulence, undue
personality, or grossness—the best proof that there can
be of the purity and good nature of Lemon's singularly
amiable and honest mind".

Mark Lemon in early years had proved his capacity of
asserting himself in signal fashion when, against the
opinion of his entire staff—who considered it unsuitable

for a comic journal—he decided to publish Hood's *Song of the Shirt*, the greatest poem that ever appeared in *Punch*. More than twenty years later, when the unhappy memories of the American War were still fresh, and before the resentment caused by the attitude of England had altogether died down, he showed his good judgment and good feeling by inviting Artemus Ward to contribute to his columns. It was accepted with alacrity, for Artemus Ward had long cherished the ambition of writing for *Punch*, and led to the series *Artemus Ward in London* which appeared in 1866.

The inner staff in 1860 consisted of Mark Lemon, editor, Tom Taylor, Horace Mayhew, Shirley Brooks, Percival Leigh, John Leech, John Tenniel, and Henry Silver.

Percival Leigh, who when he died in 1889 was the last survivor of the early writers in *Punch*, was the intimate of Thackeray and Leech and, like so many of the *Punch* men, a good amateur actor. He is best remembered for the text of *Mr Pips hys Diary* (1849), illustrated by Doyle, and was one of the earliest humorous writers to apply ancient phraseology to modern life and manners, and remained a valued contributor till his death.

Tom Taylor, Fellow of Trinity College, Cambridge, and for a while Professor of English Literature at University College, London, was one of the most popular dramatists of his time, and was the friend and holiday companion of Charles Kingsley and Tom Hughes.

Henry Silver, though he was a regular and voluminous contributor during the dozen years or so during which he belonged to the "table", is chiefly worthy of grateful remembrance for his service in introducing Charles Keene to the notice of Mark Lemon. He is also remarkable for being the only *Punch* man who amassed a fortune—though not by his pen—for he died worth a million.

Horace Mayhew, the brother of Henry, did not carry great guns, but excelled as a sprightly paragraphist.

Shirley Brooks, editor of *Punch* from 1871 to 1874, when he was succeeded by Tom Taylor, was, in the words of Mr Spielmann, the historian of *Punch*, "perhaps the most brilliant and useful all-round man who ever wrote for *Punch*". He was equally successful in verse and prose, excelling in poems on ceremonial occasions or on departed worthies—the verses on Lincoln were from his pen—he was the chief cartoon-suggester in his time, and, last but not least, conceived and carried out for twenty years the idea of a weekly summary of the debates at Westminster under the title of "Essence of Parliament". These articles differ *toto caelo* from those of the late Sir Henry Lucy in which personalities and points of procedure were so effectively exploited; but they are incomparably superior in their handling of really important measures. Shirley Brooks was a great journalist and something more; he had grace and a real insight into the things that matter. His report of the Debate on the Reform Bill (May 20, 1867), in which John Stuart Mill nearly converted *Punch* to Woman Suffrage, is both ampler and fairer than many of the dramatised reports of important discussions in Parliament which appear in the daily press of to-day.

Frank Burnand, whose first contribution in 1863 soon led to his promotion to the "table", made his mark at once by his burlesques of novelists, and above all by his *Happy Thoughts* (1866) originally published in serial form, the best of all his works, relying on humorous observation and almost entirely free from the puns which were his besetting sin.

Yet, strong though *Mr Punch's* team was on the literary side, the men of the pencil in the 'sixties conferred an even greater lustre on his fame. Charles Keene, by general consent the greatest black-and-white artist who ever adorned the pages of *Punch*, had made his first appearance in 1851, but was not promoted to the "table" till 1860. He never took a prominent part in the discussions over a cartoon, seldom originated a joke, and was almost entirely dependent upon his friends—notably Mr Joseph Crawhall—for suggestions; was never at his ease in depicting "swells" or great ladies; but has left in his pictures for *Punch* a wonderful "Comédie Humaine" of the middle-class England in mid-Victorian times, drawn with a faithfulness which appeals to the many and a technical mastery that can only be appreciated by the few.

John Leech, who died in 1864 while still in full command of his powers, left a gap which has never been filled. His career had many phases, for he was responsible in the early numbers of *Punch* for some of the most powerful cartoons that ever appeared in its pages— notably the *Poor Man's Friend* (Feb. 22, 1845) showing Death standing over the gaunt emaciated figure of a victim of the "Hungry 'Forties" lying on a truckle bed. He could be daringly unconventional, as in the picture of a woman of the street, *The Social Evil*; but his most conspicuous services were rendered in his social and hunting cuts, in his delineation of ingenuous youth, of precocious schoolboys, and above all of the buxom, artless, unintellectual young person—at archery meetings or on the seashore, or in the ballroom. Leech's girls did not shine in repartee or wit; they were sentimental, feminine, and unsophisticated, but always good-humoured and good to look at. His hunting pictures were based on first-hand experience. Some of his followers have excelled him in drawing a horse or in the suggestion of the hunting landscape; none have approached him in his appreciation of the humours of the chase.

John Tenniel, who joined the staff in 1850 and was at the top of his form in the 'sixties, was marked out for the post of *Punch's* premier cartoonist, as Mr Spielmann has epigrammatically observed, not only by Nature but by the Pope. Had it not been for the "Papal Aggression" campaign—caused by the Pope's appointing archbishops and bishops to English sees—Richard Doyle would not have resigned and no opening would have been made for Tenniel. The strength and limitations of Tenniel are admirably summed up by Mr Spielmann in his *History of "Punch"*. Tenniel's school training was negligible, his anatomy was often to seek, he never bothered about accuracy of details, in regard to which he was the diametrical opposite of Sambourne, whose work, by the way, he cordially admired. But he had a natural instinct for the grand style, which enabled him to treat great subjects greatly, though, as we know, he was equally successful as an illustrator of the fancies of little people.

Of all the "new boys" who were enlisted under the banner of *Mr Punch* in the 'sixties none was more happily endowed for the enlargement and refinement of his outlook than George du Maurier. Born in 1834 he contributed his first picture to *Punch* in 1860 and was promoted to the "table" in 1864. Thus, for four years he acted as a most valuable complement to Leech in dealing with the manners and modes of society before entering on his unchallenged reign, which lasted till his death in 1896, as the supreme delineator of Victorian Society in its old exclusive phase before it had become amorphous, unwieldy, cosmopolitan and plutocratic. To borrow what I have written elsewhere, "he was the finest and best equipped of the commentators and critics of the old régime, who recognised its distinction and its drawbacks and satirised with impartial ridicule decadent aristocrats and vulgar intruders".

Du Maurier was an early promoter of the *entente cordiale* by refusing to perpetuate the old tradition of representing the Frenchman as a fussy, gesticulating figure, ridiculous in the hunting-field or in the domain of sport. As the writer of the memorial lines in *Punch* after his death rightly observed:

> He brought from two great lands the best of both
>   In one fine nature blent.
> Lover of English strength and Gallic grace,
>   Of British beauty, or of soul or face.

Unlike Leech he credited women with wit—his girls were not "shallow brained". He was always happy in his legends, some of them contributed by Canon Ainger, but mostly his own, and always in keeping with the personages depicted. They talked as they looked—thoroughbred; not like the genteel suburbanites of most of his successors. Nor must one forget his admirable skill and fidelity in portraying the elegances and eccentricities of fashion, gorgeous and insolent flunkeys, and huge but benovolent dogs, or his excursions into the realm of nightmare. Like Keene, he took little interest in politics, and Sir Bernard Partridge has told me that at the weekly dinners, when the business of the evening began, he would put up his legs on another chair, cover his head with a handkerchief, and say: "Now while you clever old cockalorums are settling your cartoons, I'm going to have forty winks".

Linley Sambourne, who began to draw for *Punch* in 1867, soon improved out of all recognition on the pleasing but almost amateurish small cuts which he contributed in the late 'sixties. His development was truly astonishing, and in fifteen years—his best work was done in the 'eighties—his consummate draughtsmanship, combined with a truly masterly command of design, went far to justify the view, strongly upheld by many good judges, French as well as English, that he and not Charles Keene was the greatest of our black-and-white artists. His style was his own and inimitable; he did not influence the younger artists as Leech, du Maurier, and Keene had done. But it is worth recording that Phil May once said in reply to a question as to his training, "all I know I learned from Sammy". "Sammy" was not only a great artist but a most lovable and genial companion, with a wonderful gift for Malapropisms—which he was suspected of deliberately cultivating—and endeared to his colleagues by his engaging foibles as well as his goodness of heart.

The movement of *Punch* from the Left to the Left Centre and then to the Right Centre was not only due to the disappearance of Jerrold and the increasing popularity of the Monarchy; it was in no small measure due to the influences which conspired to make the 'sixties peaceful and prosperous. For this decade chronologically and spiritually represents mid-Victorianism *in excelsis*. It was the age of non-intervention: the only war in which we were actively engaged was the Abyssinian campaign. The ambitions and enterprises of the French emperor caused England no little anxiety, and gave a stimulus to the volunteer movement. *Punch* reluctantly acquiesced in England's neutrality in the matter of the Schleswig-Holstein campaign and its formidable sequel. His sympathies with the Risorgimento and with Garibaldi, who on his visit to England was described as "a dear old weatherbeaten angel", were freely expressed but involved no risk of our being drawn into the conflict.

In the War of the North and South his record is less immune from criticism. He "backed the wrong horse" throughout, though it may be urged in extenuation that the cause of the South was favoured by all classes; that it appealed to Mr Gladstone—of whom *Punch* was a fervent admirer in the 'sixties—and that the Duke of Argyll and John Bright were the only British statesmen, and *The Spectator* the only British newspaper of any standing who supported the North. But there is no excuse for *Punch's* failure to recognise the existence of any idealism in Lincoln, whom he persistently maligned and misrepresented until his death. His *amende* was handsome and complete:

> Yes, he had lived to shame me from my sneer,
>   To lame my pencil and confute my pen—
> To make me own this hind of princes peer,
>   The rail-splitter a true-born King of men—

but the tribute lost its virtue by being delayed until the death of the greatest of Americans.

Much more inexcusable was *Punch's* failure to render justice to the idealism of our cotton operatives who espoused a cause which was not only unpopular, but the promotion of which entailed the maintenance of that blockade which caused widespread distress and misery. The real heroes in English public life in 1861–5 were the Lancashire cotton-spinners.

In spite of local distress, the general prosperity of England was enough to minister to national complacency. *Punch* was a Free-Trader and he was confirmed in his adhesion to that doctrine by the wonderful series of Gladstone's budgets in the 'sixties, when there never was a deficit, when expenditure hardly ever exceeded £70,000,000, and when the income-tax was reduced to 4d. *Punch* recognised the great qualities of Lord Palmerston—while alive to his opportunism—and of Lord Derby, and handsomely acknowledged the courage and persistence of Disraeli, but on the whole Mr Gladstone was the statesman who throughout the 'sixties secured his most benevolent consideration, while Disraeli, alike by his policy and his physique, lent himself most readily to criticism and caricature. *Punch* was not an anti-Semite, and had vigorously supported the long campaign for Jewish emancipation from civil disabilities, but the Oriental strain in "Dizzy", his flamboyant rhetoric, and the love of gorgeous upholstery in his novels which inspired the parodies of Thackeray, were distasteful to the John Bullishness of *Punch*, and this antagonism emerges again and again in the cartoons and political articles of this period.

Punch's insularity was not so intense as in the 'forties and 'fifties, but he cannot be said to have been a lover of foreigners. He distrusted their rulers and statesmen, and combined a reluctant acquiescence in our neutrality in 1864 and 1866 with strong and bitter criticism of Austria and Prussia—especially the latter, whose desire to possess a Fleet in particular inspired him to rather silly sarcasm alternating with serious misgiving. It is hard to dissociate his espousal of the cause of Poland from the fact that Russia supported the North in the American civil war, or his enthusiasm for Garibaldi from his antipathy to the Vatican. In the recurrent invasion scares which agitated this period *Punch* pooh-poohed the extravagance of the alarmists, but cordially supported the Volunteer movement, and deprecated its disparagement by the Regulars, though fully alive to the humours of amateur soldiering. On the question of the Suez Canal in 1861 *Punch* committed himself to the rash assertion that this "impossible trench" would never be cut, and applauded the Government view that if it could be made, "we ought not for political reasons to allow it, but as it could not be made, the wise course was to let the speculators ruin themselves and diddle the Pacha".

ROME. 1866.

"Welcome the Coming, Speed the Parting Guest."

It is easy to be wise after the event, and as a set-off to
Punch's unfulfilled or wholly erroneous forecasts we may
note that he predicted aerial air service to Paris in 1870,
anticipated even earlier the advent of Big Berthas and
air raids on a colossal scale, and when the typewriter was
exhibited in London in 1867 gave a fantastic but sub-
stantially accurate summary of the possibilities of an
invention which has revolutionised the prospects of the
superfluous woman.

In the sphere of Home politics, *Punch's* record is
marred by very few lapses from a consistent support of
all measures that made for progress, humanity, and the
fusion of classes. Much as he admired Palmerston, he
welcomed the end of the regime of "masterly inactivity"
which retarded the enlargement of the Franchise, though
admitting that the Bill of 1867 was robbed of much of its
grace by the party strategy summed up in Lord Derby's
famous phrase about "dishing the Whigs". It is true
that *Punch* had adopted a more critical attitude towards
the working man, and the tyranny of the Trade Unions,
but this did not prevent his espousing the cause of the
workers when the conditions were bad—e.g. domestic
servants—the hours long and the wages inadequate. As
the champion of working children, he was heart and soul
with Lord Shaftesbury in his successful crusades against
the Agricultural gangs and the tyrannies of master
sweepers, and in his institution of Ragged Schools. He
never wearies in his onslaughts on the maladministration
of the Poor Law by lax and ignorant guardians. *Punch*
may claim to have been one of the pioneers of the "Play
Centres" movement by advocating "Ragged play-

grounds" on the excellent principle that "if we mean to teach the ragged young idea, we must give heed to the ragged body likewise". *Punch* thought that reclamation should begin at home. He had no sympathy with Borrioboola-Gha, and a famous cartoon of Tenniel's represents a little London street Arab appealing to Britannia as she looks through a telescope at missionaries overseas, with the words "Please 'm, ain't we black enough to be cared for?" Sweated labour in the West End millinery shops comes under his lash in 1863. Where hygiene, housing, and sanitation were concerned *Punch* refused to believe that landlords were altogether to blame, but does not acquit the Government officials, and at times felt that a little more paternal government *à la* Bismarck would be a good thing.

Punch had no fear of the growth of industrialism if humanely and wisely controlled and directed—as by Henry Schneider, the founder of the Barrow Steel Works. He did not, however, favour the direct representation of Labour in Parliament, and his assumption that "the best and broadest Liberalism" sufficed for the needs of the working classes has long since gone by the board. In earlier years he had strongly combated the maintenance of capital punishment, and it is remarkable to note that his abandonment of this attitude was largely due to the speech made by John Stuart Mill—a true humanitarian if ever there was one—on the measure introduced in 1868 to make executions private. In this same speech Mill had defended flogging as "a most objectionable punishment in ordinary cases, but a particularly appropriate one for crimes of brutality, especially against women". Mill, it may be added, had been in the forefront of the movement for securing the prosecution of General Eyre for his drastic suppression of the riots in Jamaica. *Punch* supported General Eyre throughout, and on the question of capital punishment may have been influenced by the principle *fas est et ab hoste doceri*, even though the opponent was undermining his own position. On more general grounds *Punch*, as an independent observer, might well admire and be impressed by the candour and detachment from party ties which marked Mill's political career.

In the 'fifties *Punch* had carried on a vehement campaign against Papal aggression. In the 'sixties he was still capable of banging the "No Popery" drum as loudly as ever—witness his fury at the exultation of the Irish Roman Catholics who "hurrooed" for the Pope and groaned for Garibaldi, when Rome was occupied by the French at the close of 1862. Rome—Papal Rome—was still to him the Scarlet Lady, a red rag to John Bull, but the more immediate objects of his animosity were the Ritualists and supporters of the Confessional in the Anglican Church. High Anglican Ritualism was to him the chambermaid of the Vatican: as for the Confessional, it was "a dangerous and disgusting practice". This animosity led to the publication of many pictures and cartoons—notably that of "the Brompton Area-Sneak" —which verged on the brutal. His attacks on Father Ignatius throughout 1864 and 1865 were sometimes amusing, for the "mock monk" laid himself open to ridicule, but more often deviated into sheer scurrility. *Punch* treated all, or nearly all Ritualists as if they were on the level of Father Ignatius, an extreme obscurantist who fulminated against the Higher Criticism and all liberal theologians. *Punch* himself, it should be noted, was by no means an orthodox Churchman, for while he professed to represent the majority of English Protestants and was avowedly Erastian in maintaining the supremacy of the Law Courts in all cases, he was no rigid upholder of Evangelicalism; Kingsley and Maurice and Stanley were his heroes, and he was an ardent supporter of Jowett and Colenso against the heresy-hunters; and when Stanley's appointment to the Deanery of Westminster excited the lamentations of the *Record*, the organ of ultra-orthodox Evangelicalism, he sarcastically hailed its disapproval as a convincing proof of the wisdom and justice of the appointment. Still, this was an improvement on his references to the "viperine expectorations" of the Editor of the *Tablet* in earlier years.

On the vexed question of Irish Disestablishment, *Punch* supported Mr Gladstone and acquiesced in the measure though not without misgivings lest it should be interpreted as a concession to Fenian intimidation. Thus in the cartoon *Justice to Ireland*, the figure of Justice is shown blindfolded, with sword and scales enthroned in the background. In front and at her feet Gladstone, laying the Irish Church on a flaming altar, says: "This is a sacrifice to Justice, not to Papists or assassins." But in the main *Punch* in these years stood for comprehension and toleration: he had far more sympathy with underpaid curates than opulent bishops and had little respect for the episcopal bench, if we except Temple and Tait. As in

JUSTICE TO IRELAND

THE BRITISH MINISTER: "This is a sacrifice to Justice, not to Papists or assassins. And if they——"

earlier years he vigorously combated the notion that Sunday should be a day of gloom. The extremes of Sabbatarianism invariably excited his indignation and derision, as when early in 1861 a controversy arose in Scotland as to whether the sale of milk was permissible on Sunday. The Day of Rest in his view need not be divorced from cheerfulness, but he had no sympathy with efforts to "brighten" religion by sensationalism in the pulpit.

But *Punch* did not confine his criticisms to dissent and Romanism. He found the leaders of the Church of England lacking in the larger vision which he recognised in Livingstone and Maurice. The Pan-Anglican Synod of 1867 moved him to compare the assembled bishops to a chorus of old washerwomen, who refused to be "worrited" with the great questions, theoretical or practical, which concerned the very existence of the Church of England, and were governed in their deliberations by "impotent caution and misplaced decency"—a phrase which he borrowed from the *Pall Mall Gazette*.

Punch certainly could not be charged in the 'sixties with an excess of caution in the sphere of religious controversy. But in closing this summary of his incursions into the theological arena, I think he deserves unqualified praise for his handling of the attempts which were made to discredit Disraeli on the score of his religion—or irreligion—at the time of his first Premiership. *Punch's* attitude was all the more creditable because Disraeli was not one of his heroes. *Punch* admired his great abilities, and congratulated him on achieving his ambition in spite of failures and rebuffs. But it was a reluctant

admiration, quite unlike that accorded to his great rival
and opponent Mr Gladstone. Disraeli had himself anticipated the attacks of the anti-Semitic critics in his first
speech as Premier on March 5, 1868, when he said that
in his position there were personal and peculiar reasons
which would aggravate the burden and augment the
difficulties.

Punch's protest against this "campaign of curiosity" took
the form of an article headed "The Modern Inquisition":

Perhaps the Premier, who has now got to make a Bishop
of Hereford will write one more letter and satisfy the British
Booby on the subject of "Mr Disraeli's Religion", which
appears to afflict divers. Scarcely a day passes but some new
conjectural impertinence, or some particularly unnecessary
information is tossed out. Mr Disraeli knows that *Punch*
has not refrained from a great lot of good-natured allusions
to the nationality of which the former is so justly proud; and
it is possible that we may have many another cartoon of
which he will be the smiling or scowling hero. But we
protest...against sneaking into a gentleman's study, and
taking notes as to whether Prayer Book, Missal, Watts's
Hymns, Koran or Shaster, be most thumbed, and publishing
inferences....Is this England or America? We do not
habitually admire French legislation, but the late Edict
against ransacking Private Life is not without its merits.
Somebody will be asking about our religion next, and will
need all his own to bear the consequences.

Space prevents my dealing with *Punch's* multifarious
intrusions into other spheres of serious activity, and
I must content myself with the briefest summary.
Towards Feminism in all its phases he had replaced

ridicule—often tasteless ridicule—by respect. He was within an ace of being converted to Woman Suffrage by Mill, but in the end came down on the other side of the fence. He was with some reserves on the side of throwing open the professions to women, and approved of the foundation of women's colleges. He was critical of our public schools and the excessive adulation of athletics, and strongly supported the reform of our older universities. In his patronage of art and letters he made no mistake in dealing with mediocrities: and he recognised Whistler and Meredith and Fred Walker long before their genius was generally recognised. He was hopelessly wrong about Wagner, but so was nearly everyone in the 'sixties, when the Parisian Jockey Club hooted down *Tannhäuser* and cried "À bas Wagner, c'est le petit-fils du Duc de Wellington".

Punch's activities as a critic of fashion in dress in the 'sixties were chiefly displayed in his long, unremitting and as he himself candidly admitted, ineffectual campaign against the monstrosity of the crinoline. It lasted as long as the siege of Troy—ten years—for it began in 1857 and it was not pronounced "gone" till 1867, the year in which another monstrosity loomed on the horizon in the person of the Claimant, whose arrival in England and recognition as the rightful heir was announced in the columns of *Punch*. Even at the outset of the campaign *Punch* seems to have recognised its futility when he wrote:

> The more you scoff, the more you jeer,
> The more the women persevere
> In wearing this apparel queer.

But his pessimism did not cause him to relax his efforts. All his resources of pen and pencil were mobilised for the attack, which was begun by Leech and carried on by du Maurier and Sambourne. When the monster fell it was not by force of arms assisted by guile as in the parallel campaign against Troy, but by its own absurdity, through the weariness of its supporters, and above all in consequence of its adoption by domestic servants.

Crinolines passed, but *Punch* soon found a new grievance in the very long skirts—*robes à queue* as they were called, which dragged their slow length on the pavement to the discomfort of everybody—and in the minute bonnets attributed to the fashion of the chignon, a mode of coiffure, revived from the eighteenth century, which reached the summit of extravagance in the mid-'sixties, and afforded endless opportunities to Sambourne and to du Maurier. The most striking of these caricatures is that entitled *Stupendous Triumph of the Hairdresser's Art*, in which a lady is seen riding a pony with its mane and tail fluffed out to harmonise with her chignon. Sambourne's best effort shows a lady bent nearly double under an enormous chignon, making her figure closely resemble that of a coal-heaver shouldering a sack of coals in the background.

In the artificial enhancement of beauty the 'sixties showed an enterprise culminating in the astonishing career of the once famous Madame Rachel, an obscure adventuress who rose from keeping a fried fish shop to fame and fortune as an enameller and vendor of cosmetics in New Bond Street, with an expensive house in Maddox Street and a box at the opera. *Punch* openly warned his female readers against her in 1862 when the wife of an officer was ordered to pay £1000 for the process of enamelling: "Ladies", he wrote, "take warning. Be natural rather than artificial. Never appear in society with a mask on, no matter how beautiful the mask may be. From the above you should learn in time how much it may cost you for being double faced".

The warning passed unheeded, and Madame Rachel, who professed to make women beautiful for ever, continued to reap a golden harvest for five years. In 1867 she was sentenced to five years' penal servitude for swindling a customer out of £5300 and was burned in effigy on Guy Fawkes' Day. But *Punch* was premature in speaking of her "last appearance". Released on a ticket of leave in 1872, she renewed her operations in the West End and continued them till 1878 when she was sentenced to a second term of five years' penal servitude, dying in Woking prison in 1880. I doubt whether she would have suffered so heavily to-day; but her fall cannot excite much sympathy, for she was a forger and a blackmailer, and the reminiscences of Sergeant Ballantine, who knew her in her early days, and of Montagu Williams, neither of them given to squeamishness, agree in describing her as a wicked and dangerous woman. Her fame, it may be added, was not confined to one hemisphere. One of the springs on the shores of Lake Rotorua in New Zealand was named "the Madame Rachel Bath" in virtue of its medicinal and rejuvenating qualities. Against dyed hair and wasp-waists *Punch* tilted vigorously; the mode of carriage known as "The Grecian bend" was satirised by Sambourne. *Punch* was sceptical as to the possibility of our ever being able to extricate ourselves from the tyranny of the tailor and the milliner, but when a writer in *The Times* fell foul of the dowdiness of Englishmen and Englishwomen abroad, he was up in arms at once. He admitted that British tourists did include specimens both of the Guy and the Gorilla, but vigorously protested against any wholesale indictment of his compatriots *en voyage*, and maintained that English travellers of both sexes were as a rule the best-dressed travellers in the world and that the English abroad were the best-mannered travellers, and at home the best-mannered dealers with travellers to be found in the circle of civilized nations.

In the realm of pastime, archery was still in favour, though croquet was far more frequently referred to. Both, so far as *Punch* is concerned, are regarded as mainly an excuse for flirtations between the bewhiskered Charles and the becrinolined Clara, while at croquet, still in its unscientific infancy, cheating was regarded as quite fair game. Tall hats had gone out and caps come in at cricket, where, before the days of billiard-table pitches, players suffered a good deal from bumping balls. The establishment of clubs at Lisbon and Oporto prompts *Punch* to suggest international games—Turks and Chinamen, Dutch and Japanese—an example of a mock prophecy fulfilled in a way which the prophet never expected. The references to football are mainly confined to the practice of "shinning" or "hacking" as then permitted by the Rugby code, *Punch* ranging himself on the side of a "Surgeon" who had condemned it in *The Times*.

THE BALL

Harry Bullfincher, who is ever so much better across Country than when he mixes in the Merry Dance (especially after Supper) has come to grief over a stool during a Polka, and is shouting for someone to *"Catch his horse!"*

Mr Spencer Poffington makes a Morning Call. He will wear an Eye-glass—and skips like Lord Dundreary—and comes to grief over a Croquet iron, taking a header into the arms of Lady Honoria Bouncer!

Punch, though he had not entirely outgrown the ferocity of his early days in political controversy, was in the main so humane and humanitarian in his general outlook that we are hardly prepared for his remarkable eulogy of the Prize Ring in 1860. For this was the year of perhaps the most famous of all the fights recorded in the annals of boxing—when the American Heenan (the "Benicia Boy") and Tom Sayers the English champion were matched for £200 a side at Farnborough on April 17th. The contest did not excite unanimous approval, as may be gathered from the comments of the Rev. W. N. Molesworth, the friend of Bright and Cobden, in his *History of England 1830–1874*:

Half London endeavoured to be witnesses of it and though comparatively few of those who attempted to reach the scene of action succeeded in reaching it, the number of spectators was enormous. But that which will most astonish our posterity to learn is that peers, members of Parliament, clergymen, men of highly cultured minds, men remarkable for artistic taste and artistic power, were amongst the foremost spectators of this disgusting and unlawful exhibition.

Lord Palmerston in the House of Commons declared that he saw nothing more demoralising in a boxing match than in the ascent of a balloon. But *Punch* went much further, chronicling the fight in a poem, in the manner of Macaulay's *Lays of Ancient Rome*, which occupied a whole page, describing the train journey to Farnborough in the grey dawn, the exalted personages present, and the details of the fight—all told with a fervour that borders on ecstasy. *Punch's* prophecy as to the degeneracy of the race of milksops destined to succeed the "fighting covies" and "sporting swells" of the 'sixties has been curiously falsified, but the verses, spirited and sincere, seem to show how strangely *Punch's* humanitarianism was leavened and influenced by primitive instincts in the domain of sport. It is only fair to add that a few years later he flagellated, with a happy mixture of ridicule and contempt, an abortive attempt to introduce bull fighting at the Agricultural Hall, Islington, and pilloried the "tame-pigeon-shooting nobility and gentry" who introduced that degrading sport at Wormwood Scrubs.

In conclusion I trust I may be acquitted of undue partiality in this review of *Punch* in the 'sixties. It is impossible for anyone who has had the honour—as I think it—of serving him, however obscurely, for nearly thirty years not to regard *Punch* with a certain filial affection. Looking back to the 'sixties I like to think of *Mr Punch* as on the whole a benevolent old gentleman, mostly on the side of the angels, more urbane and mellow than he was in his youth, less fond of the indiscriminate use of his truncheon in battering any head that excited his antipathy, and though reflecting the national complacency of that prosperous and pacific age, not free from moments of self-criticism and misgiving.

HISTORIANS IN THE 'SIXTIES

A NEW ERA

By *Frederick S. Boas*

In the volumes surveying the Eighteen-Seventies and the Eighteen-Eighties our attention has been claimed by poets and dramatists, writers of fiction and wits, critics, scholars and divines. But, except for a short vivid section of Dr Macan's essay on Oxford in the 'seventies, historians have been little noticed. Hence it may not be out of place that they should be the subject of the first lecture in a series that will deal with the Eighteen-Sixties. And that decade, as I hope to show, marks, from various points of view, a new era in the writing and study of history in England. It is from that angle that I wish to approach the 'sixties. I will not attempt to assess the general value of the work of any individual historian, for in nearly every case only part of it comes within our range. Still less will I venture to pronounce upon the soundness or otherwise of their particular views or conclusions. That is the province of the specialists in each branch of the subject, and even they do not always agree. My aim is to indicate some of the ways in which the period saw important changes in the conception of the scope of historical study, and no less important changes in the methods by which it was pursued.

I must ask for just a little grace in the matter of dates, though one of first-rate significance is almost uncannily pat to my purpose. On December 28, 1859, died Lord Macaulay, the greatest figure among those who, in the first half of the nineteenth century, had sought to interpret the past not primarily to scholars and academicians, but to the general reading public. For the ancient world Thomas Arnold, Grote and Thirlwall, for the mediaeval Milman, Lingard and Hallam are among the outstanding names. From the printed materials accessible to them they aimed at the reconstruction of the life of the periods with which they dealt. Most of them were influenced by their political or religious views, but they did not attempt to formulate a philosophy of history as a whole, or bind themselves to an unduly austere service. "I shall cheerfully bear the reproach of having descended below the dignity of history", wrote Macaulay, "if I can succeed in placing before the English of the nineteenth century a true picture of the life of their ancestors", or as he put it in a characteristically highly-coloured way in a letter: "I shall not be satisfied unless I produce something which shall for a few days supersede the last fashionable novel on the tables of young ladies". How marvellously he succeeded is known to all.

The four completed volumes of Macaulay's *History of England* appeared between 1849 and 1855. While he was engaged on what was to be the unfinished fifth volume, a work made its appearance, the first volume of the *History of Civilisation in England* by Henry Thomas Buckle, which was intended to effect a revolution in historical study in this country. Buckle, born in 1821, was a man of means, but of delicate health, who had little formal education. But he was an omnivorous reader, had a remarkable gift for learning languages, and had travelled for a year on the Continent. The ferment throughout Europe in the middle years of the nineteenth century was causing men to dive deeper than before into social origins, and Buckle had come particularly under the influence of Comte, whose *Cours de Philosophie Positive* had been completed in 1842. It was in 1857 that Buckle published the first volume of his *History*. On that account, and for another reason to be given later, that year may be taken as our starting-point. The second volume (1861) falls strictly within our mathematical limits.

In the opening chapters of his work Buckle proclaimed that he was inaugurating a new era in historical method. "Of all the great branches of human knowledge, history", he states, "is that upon which most has been written....And it seems to be the general opinion that the success of historians has, on the whole, been equal to their industry." And so far as the collection of materials is concerned, this belief may be admitted to be true. Buckle gives a summary of those materials which are ripe for use, ranging from the compilations of political and military annals to the statistics of births and deaths and prices of commodities. But where the error lies, and where a new way must be taken, is in the use that has been made of these materials:

The unfortunate peculiarity of the history of man is that although its separate parts have been examined with considerable ability, hardly any one has attempted to combine them into a whole, and ascertain the way in which they are connected with each other. In all the other great fields of

D   12 inquiry the necessity of generalisation is universally admitted, and noble efforts are being made to rise from particular facts to discover the laws by which those facts are governed.

Buckle may have had here in mind such works as William Whewell's *The History of the Inductive Sciences* (1837) or J. S. Mill's *System of Logic* (1843) and *Principles of Political Economy* (1848). Between the publication of the first and second volumes of his *History* an even more exact illustration was to be provided by the appearance in 1859 of Charles Darwin's *On the Origin of Species by Means of Natural Selection*.

In contrast with the writers in other fields of research, historians, according to Buckle, have the strange idea that their business is merely to relate events which they may occasionally enliven by such moral and political reflections as seem likely to be useful. And this narrow conception of their office has prevented them from equipping themselves adequately to grasp their subject in the whole of its natural relations:

Hence the singular spectacle of one historian being ignorant of political economy; another knowing nothing of law; another nothing of ecclesiastical affairs and changes of opinion; another neglecting the philosophy of statistics, and another physical science; although these topics are the most essential of all, inasmuch as they comprise the principal circumstances by which the temper and character of mankind have been affected, and in which they are displayed.

The result is that "for all the higher purposes of human thought history is still miserably deficient and presents that confused and anarchical appearance natural to a subject of which the laws are unknown and even the foundation unsettled". It was Buckle's aim to "bring up this great department of inquiry to a level with other departments", and in so doing he may be said, in Bacon's phrase, to have taken all knowledge to be his province. He starts off by boldly plunging into a discussion of the fundamental problem whether Chance or Necessity, Free-will or Predestination is the arbiter of events. His conclusion is that it is not necessary to accept either doctrine. All that we need believe in order to construct a science of history is

that the actions of men being determined solely by their antecedents must have a character of uniformity, that is to say, must, under precisely the same circumstances, always issue in precisely the same results. And as all antecedents are either in the mind or out of it, we clearly see that all the variations in the results, in other words, all the changes of which history is full, all the vicissitudes of the human race, their progress or their decay, their happiness or their misery, must be the fruit of a double action; an action of external phenomena upon the mind and another action of the mind upon the phenomena. Thus we have man modifying nature and nature modifying man; while out of this reciprocal modification all events must necessarily spring.

The historian therefore was bound to effect a coalition between the work of two separate, and at that time often antagonistic, parties, the students of nature on the one hand, and the moralists on the other.

Buckle therefore first turns to the investigation of "the influence exercised by physical laws over the organisation of society and over the character of individuals". And the four most powerful physical agents he groups as Climate, Food, Soil, and the General Aspects of Nature. The production of wealth in the earliest stages depends entirely on soil and climate, "the soil regulating the returns made to any given amount of labour; the climate regulating the energy and the constancy of the labour itself". With an abundance, not to say a super-abundance, of illustrations, Buckle drives home the point that in Asia and Africa the condition was a fertile soil, causing an abundant return; in Europe it was a happier climate causing more successful labour. European civilisation, therefore, though later, has been the more permanent because "the only progress which is really effective depends not on the bounty of nature, but on the energy of man".

That energy is dependent not only on climate but on food, and Buckle is thus led to a somewhat rambling discussion, physiological, economic and geographical, upon food supply and its influence. "If two countries, equal in other respects, differ solely in this," he declares, "that in one the natural food is cheap and abundant, and in the other scarce and dear, the population of the former country will inevitably increase more rapidly than the population of the latter. And by a parity of reasoning, the average rate of wages will be lower in the former than in the latter, simply because the labour-market will be more amply stocked." Such confident generalisations make us rub our eyes. They could only apply to a purely static world. There is no idea of the revolution that was soon to be wrought by transport which was to turn America into the granary of Western Europe; or of the

transformation in industrial conditions that was to be
effected by the growth of trade unions.

Buckle then passes from climate, food, and soil, which
concern the accumulation of wealth, to what he calls
"the Aspects of Nature" that concern the accumulation
and distribution of thought. These Aspects may be
sublime, terrible, and dangerous, including the earth-
quakes and volcanoes of tropical regions, which stimulate
the imagination at the expense of the reasoning faculties.
Or they may be homely, gentle and beneficent, em-
boldening the understanding and inspiring man with
confidence in his own resources. In illustration Buckle
draws a detailed contrast between the Greek and the
Indian civilisations.

But Buckle limits the working of the understanding to
inductive methods. He devotes a special chapter to an
attack on metaphysicians, whose method, he declares, is
the direct opposite of the historical, the metaphysicians
studying one mind, the historian studying many minds.
And in what is perhaps the most challenging section of
his work he contrasts the "stationary aspect of moral
truths with the progressive aspect of intellectual truths":

There is unquestionably nothing to be found in the world
which has undergone so little change as those great dogmas
of which moral systems are composed. To do good to
others; to sacrifice for their benefit your own wishes; to love
your neighbour as yourself; to forgive your enemies; to
restrain your passions; to honour your parents; to respect
those who are set above you; these and a few others are the
sole essentials of morals; but they have been known for
thousands of years, and not one jot or tittle has been added to

them by all the sermons, homilies, and text-books which moralists and theologians have been able to produce.

And in a note he adds "to assert that Christianity communicated to man moral truths previously unknown, argues on the part of the asserter either gross ignorance or else wilful fraud". Whatever view may be held as to the claims of Christianity, it is of course a complete misconception to think of it as merely communicating moral truths, old or new. If so, its first propagandists would not have turned the world upside down and ranged against themselves the imperial power of Rome. But without entering upon such high themes, we may appropriately at the present time consider Buckle's more detailed arguments in support of his general thesis. He maintains that the decline in the frequency of wars is due in no way to any change in men's moral feelings but is entirely the result of intellectual progress. Every increase in knowledge increases the authority of the intellectual classes between whom and the military classes he assumes that there is a necessary antagonism. Writing in the days of the Crimean War, how little he foresaw the alliance between the German General Staff and the Professoriate in propagating *Kultur*. A subsidiary cause of the decay of the martial spirit was the invention of gunpowder, resulting in the formation of standing armies distinct from the main body of citizens who were left to carry on their peaceful pursuits. The millions of nationals of every country arrayed in opposite camps in the Great War are a sufficient answer to this claim. Nor has Time endorsed Buckle's championship of the orthodox Political

Economy and the improvement of Locomotion as necessarily contributors to the decline of the war spirit.

But, right or wrong, it is such doctrines that seem to me to give his work permanent value rather than the sketches that follow of historical developments from the sixteenth century in England, France, Spain and Scotland.

Enough has perhaps been said to account both for the resounding success of *The History of Civilisation in England* on its publication and the comparative eclipse that has overtaken it. In its introductory chapters it set forth in lucid and confident style a linked series of impressive generalisations which frequently challenged orthodox or traditional views. These generalisations claimed to be inductions based on accumulated masses of facts. But the facts, drawn almost entirely from printed sources, were unequal to so massive a super-structure.

And the work appeared at what, after the first flush of success, was to prove a curiously unfavourable time. Buckle writes throughout as if he were dealing with a static world, with a vast mechanical order, where what is true to-day will be true to-morrow and for all time. But, as already mentioned, Darwin's *Origin of Species* appeared between his first and second volumes. The theory of development or evolution was to change the whole conception of history into that of an organic process. Hence Buckle's work, so revolutionary in aim, has to-day an old-fashioned air.

None the less, it would be unwise to underrate its interest and influence. It succeeded in the early 'sixties in drawing away the young Irishman, W. H. Lecky, from biographical sketches of Leaders of Public Opinion in his own country to the study on a wide canvas of *The Rise and Influence of the Spirit of Rationalism in Europe*, followed in 1869 by *The History of European Morals from Augustus to Charlemagne*. Lecky himself spoke of these two works as belonging to a school, of which Buckle was the English representative, which looks at history not as a series of biographies or accidents or pictures, but as a great organic whole. Lecky, as everyone knows, reverted in the next decade to his earlier love, for in his *History of England in the Eighteenth Century* there are no more attractive chapters than those dealing with Ireland. But we are told that *The History of European Morals* remained his favourite work.

Buckle has found a more thorough-going champion in Mr J. M. Robertson, who has replied vigorously to his critics, and has re-edited in 1904 *The History of Civilisation*. Had this work never been written, would *The Outline of History* by Mr H. G. Wells have taken exactly the form that we know? And are not the Cambridge physicists and astronomers, to whom we are all listening so eagerly to-day, giving an undreamt-of extension to Buckle's claim that history could only be written when a coalition had been effected between the students of nature and the moralists?

Sir Arthur Eddington and Sir James Jeans are not, in the ordinary sense, historians. But in their cosmological speculations the destiny of man on this planet has its place. And they are raising again in far more subtle form those metaphysical questions which Buckle thought were permanently solved. With him causality was a bed-rock principle. But in opposition to this the modern physicist brings forward the principle of Indeterminacy, and we are told that "Science withdraws its moral opposition to free-will". Sir Herbert Samuel, whom we usually associate with other spheres, discusses the bearing of these problems in *The Contemporary Review* for January, 1931, and they are fundamental to the history of civilisation.

I have said that, in addition to its being the date of the publication of Buckle's first volume, there is another reason for taking 1857 as our starting-point. It was this year that saw the beginning of two series of official publications, the *Calendars of State Papers* and the *Rolls Series*, that have remodelled our methods of historical investigation. In making documentary sources accessible to students England had hitherto lagged behind France, where the *École des Chartes*, as a permanent institution, dated from 1829, and Germany, where *Monumenta Germaniae Historica* had begun to appear in 1826.

A tentative beginning had been made in 1830 with the publication of a volume of State Papers relating to the reign of Henry VIII. But it was not until 1857 that a systematic scheme became effective by the publication of the first *Calendar of State Papers, Domestic Series, of the Reigns of Edward VI, Mary, Elizabeth, 1547–80*. A similar volume soon followed dealing with the earlier years of James I, 1603–10, and another in 1858 with the first two years of Charles I. The early 'sixties saw the beginning of the "Foreign Series" and "Colonial

Series" Calendars, and Calendars of Archives preserved at Simancas and Venice bearing upon the foreign relations of England in the Tudor period. Thus began those invaluable sets of Calendars of official archives which are still in progress and with which it is a primary duty of every student of history, and in many cases of literature, to become familiar.

The purpose of these publications was admirably expressed in his preface by the editor of the first volume, Robert Lemon, and his words may be repeated here:

Each separate paper or document is briefly abstracted, the leading facts stated, and the persons and places to which it relates are mentioned, sufficiently to indicate to what particular subject it belongs. The student, whether of history, biography, genealogy, or general literature, at however remote a distance he may be placed, can thus ascertain precisely the amount of information existing among the State Papers on whatever may be the subject of his inquiry. Everyone acquainted with, or in the habit of consulting, original documents will know that it is impossible to compress within descriptions, necessarily so brief, all the information that may be required. Such slight entries rather point out where information may be found than supply the information itself; but for the full satisfying the purposes of study recourse must be had to the originals.

It is only when the warning in the last words is disregarded that the Calendars may become something of a snare.

On January 26th, 1857, the Master of the Rolls submitted to the Treasury "a proposal for the publication of materials for the History of this Country from the

Invasion of the Romans to the Reign of Henry VIII". He suggested "that these materials should be selected for publication under competent editors..., without mutilation or abridgment....the most correct text should be formed from an accurate collection of the best MSS....the editor should give an account of the MSS. employed by him, of their age and their peculiarities; he should add to the work a brief account of the life and times of the author, and any remarks necessary to explain the chronology; but no other note or comment was to be allowed, except what might be necessary to establish the correctness of the text".

The Lords of the Treasury accepted the proposal, with some slight modification, and in 1858 the first volume of *Rerum Britannicarum Medii Ævi Scriptores* or *Chronicles amd Memorials of Great Britain and Ireland during the Middle Ages* was published. It was, appropriately, *The Chronicle of England* by John Capgrave, edited by the Rev. F. C. Hingeston from two MSS. preserved at Cambridge. Capgrave, a fifteenth-century friar of Lynn in Norfolk, thought it necessary to go back to the year one of the Creation, under which is entered: "The first man Adam was mad on a Friday, withoute modir, withoute fader, in the feld of Damask; and fro that place led into Paradise, to dwell there: after dryvyn oute for synne. Whanne he had lyved nyne hundred yere and XXX. he deied, byried in Hebron: his hed was lift with the Flood, and leyd in Golgatha".

There is a blank for "Anno 2–11", but under 12 there is an entry beginning, "This yere Eve bare too childirn at o birth, the man hite Cayn, the woman Calmana".

This may not seem a very auspicious beginning to a set of publications selected "to fill up the chasms existing in the printed materials of English history". But Capgrave gradually narrows the scope of his work, and the second half of it deals almost entirely with the annals of his own country from the accession of Henry III in 1216 to 1417, when it suddenly breaks off. For the events of the period falling within, or not long before, his own lifetime, he is a valuable authority.

Capgrave's *Chronicle* was speedily followed by other volumes, and, by the end of the 'sixties, the *Rolls Series* included just over fifty publications, many of them in numerous parts. Among these were *The Anglo-Saxon Chronicle*, with a translation by Thorpe, Higden's *Polychronicon*, the minor works of Roger Bacon, the *Itineraries* of Giraldus Cambrensis, the *Muniments of the Guildhall*, edited by H. T. Riley, *Political Poems and Songs* edited by T. Wright, *Memorials of Henry VII* edited by James Gairdner. Even this short selection illustrates the range and varied interest of the Series, and the discrimination shown in the choice of editors. But the greatest name among them has yet to be mentioned—William Stubbs.

It was in 1864 that Stubbs, who then held a living in Essex, began a connexion with the Series which lasted for a quarter of a century. His first *Rolls Series* publication consisted of *The Chronicles and Memorials of Richard I*. This was followed in 1867 by an edition of the Chronicle of Benedict of Peterborough, and in 1868–71 by one, in four volumes, of Roger of Hoveden. His later contributions to the Series fall outside our present survey, but his "massive prefaces", as Dr G. P. Gooch has called them, were, one and all, collected in 1902 by Arthur Hassall in a well-known volume. Stubbs was pre-eminent among his colleagues not only for learning but for mastery of a trenchant style. Dr Gooch's statement that "he wrote under the immediate impression of his sources" may be given a more extended application. Whatever the historical value of these mediaeval and early Tudor chronicles or documents might be, they were written for the most part, so far as they were not in Latin, in the simple nervous English of their day, in forcible, concrete vernacular. Editors in daily contact with them could not but be insensibly influenced, and frame for themselves models of historical style different from the glossy and rhetorical periods which had been an inheritance from the less admirable traditions of later eighteenth-century prose.

Two years after his first publication for the *Rolls Series* Stubbs was appointed in 1866 to the Chair of Modern History at Oxford. The two Regius Professorships of History at Oxford and Cambridge had existed since 1724. But it was not till after 1850 that modern history became recognised in the academic curriculum, with a "School" or a "Tripos" in which it formed a subject leading to a degree.[1] Thus we may say broadly that it was in the 'sixties that organised academic

[1] The first class-list at Oxford in Law and Modern History was issued in the Easter Term 1853. Henry Hallam was one of the Examiners. The first class-list in Modern History alone appeared in the Michaelmas Term 1872. Among the Examiners were Mandell Creighton, the future Bishop, and Sidney J. Owen, afterwards my father-in-law.

teaching of the subject began in England, and that the professional historian took the first steps to supplant the amateur. In this way too the 'sixties mark a new era. Hence it was of the greatest moment to historical study that a scholar of the eminence of Stubbs should be appointed to the Oxford Chair. With his predecessor, Goldwin Smith, master of a lucid and forcible style, history had been, in the main, a political handmaid. At Cambridge the Chair was filled by Charles Kingsley, who has many claims to remembrance, but not as a specialist in historical study. To Stubbs the subject was one to which he had dedicated his full powers and to whose teachings, as he declared in his Inaugural Lecture on February 7th, 1867, "I feel myself indebted for whatever power of judgment, critical experience, or speculative equity...I am conscious of possessing". He fought shy of the claim of being himself a teacher, preferring to be looked on as a "helper and trainer in a school in which every man has to learn his own lessons". And it is true that he kicked against the pricks of academic regulations, against the statutory obligation to deliver a prescribed number of lectures every session. As an undergraduate I was present at his farewell lecture, on May 8th, 1884, after he had been made Bishop of Chester, when, in retrospect over his seventeen years' tenure of the Chair, he asserted that he would rather have broken into his concentrated work of historical research by giving a lecture on Euclid or Algebra, than by coming down to an elementary discourse in his own subject. And I well remember how he further startled his hearers by his almost final words: "I have never been able to reconcile myself with smoking, late hours, dinner parties, Sunday breakfasts, or University sermons".

But though Stubbs may thus not have been the ideal Professor, according to the pattern approved by a University Commission, what an inspiration and source of strength it was to a new "School", which had not yet fully established its place among the older traditional Oxford studies, to have at its head a master of his craft, who combined vigorous scholarship with a finely edged literary style. Nor was historical study, in his eyes, to be divorced from present-day issues. It had a twofold purpose: "it is at once the process of acquisition of a stock of facts, an ignorance of which unfits a man from playing the very humblest part as a citizen, or even watching the politics of his own age with an intelligent apprehension; and it is an educational discipline directed to the cultivation of powers for whose development, as it seems to me, no other training is equally efficacious". These words from his Inaugural Lecture Stubbs reiterated in his farewell discourse, in slightly expanded form, as representing his unchanged conviction. They help to explain why he made constitutional history his chief field. But his great achievements there lie just beyond our present scope. His classic volume, *Select Charters and other Illustrations of English Constitutional History to the Reign of Edward I*, appeared in 1870, and was followed by the first volume of *The Constitutional History of England* in 1873. It was in the work of the 'sixties for the *Rolls Series* and in his earliest Oxford lectures that the foundations for these masterpieces of research and exposition were well and truly laid.

When E. A. Freeman was chosen to succeed Stubbs it was probably largely with the aim of securing continuity, for Freeman at the time had recently completed in 1882 his *Reign of William Rufus*, the sequel to his chief work dealing with mediaeval English history, *The Norman Conquest of England*, of which the first volume had appeared in 1867. But though their interests in the relations of Normans and Saxons overlapped, and though they were close personal allies, Freeman's general attitude to history, and his methods, were very different from those of Stubbs. With his appointment, in a sense the amateur again replaced the professional in the Oxford Chair. He was a Somerset county gentleman whose first love had been architecture and who had published a history of the subject in 1849. In the following year he had written *An Essay on the Origin and Development of Window Tracery in England*, with illustrations by himself. When he turned to history it was at first to some of its wider mediaeval and classical aspects in *The History and the Conquests of the Saracens* (1856) and *Ancient Greece and Mediaeval Italy* (1857). It was while he was engaged in such studies that he formulated the doctrine that he preached, in season and out, of the Unity of History. Hence the very title of a Chair of Modern History was an offence to him and in his Inaugural Lecture, which I attended, I remember his suggesting, to the amusement of his hearers, the call of Abraham as an appropriate date for the beginning of the modern period. Freeman's doctrine of continuity, though, so far as I know, not directly influenced by the Darwinian theory of evolution, was in tune with the organic conception of man's development due to that theory, which had superseded the more mechanistic views of Buckle. But as Dr Gooch has pointed out, fruitful as was Freeman's doctrine, the continuity that he preached was of action, rather than of thought and feeling, and it was limited in range to the western world.

Freeman's professorial activities in the 'eighties lie, of course, outside of our period, and except for his Inaugural Lecture my own memories of them are slight. My more vivid recollections are of visits to his house in St Giles's where I was introduced to the game of badminton, at which a Balliol contemporary, now our leading Franciscan scholar, nearly "did for" a daughter of the house by an unwary use of his racket; and where before their professional appearance on the stage I saw Miss Violet Vanbrugh (as she is now known) act in doublet and hose one of the forest scenes from *As You Like It* and heard her younger sister, Irene, recite *The Jackdaw of Rheims*. Perhaps such incidents may serve as footnotes to the theme of the Unity of History.

But it is chiefly through his *History of the Norman Conquest of England* that Freeman comes into our present survey—the first volume was published in 1867.

Here Freeman concentrated his powers on the elaboration of one great historical theme, though in the earlier chapters dealing with the Norsemen in France, and the Danish Kings in England, he worked on a wider canvas. He was stimulated to his gigantic labours by a fiery zeal for representative institutions and by an exaggerated belief in their Teutonic origin. Godwin and Harold, the leaders of the English, thus became the heroes of his story, and in the meetings of the Witan in the later years of William's reign he seeks to find the preservation, amid the upheaval of the Norman conquest, of the old-established constitutional liberties. With the question of the historical truth of these views we are not here directly concerned. What we have to ask is how far was Freeman's work typical of a new era in historical methods. In two respects it was not. He subordinated all other features of national life to those that were purely political. And comprehensive as was his knowledge of the printed materials for his period, he neglected, for he was no palaeographer, the manuscript sources. On the other hand, he had an eye for those concrete memorials which the palaeographer is apt to overlook. "He was", in Dr Gooch's words, "the first English historian to realise the importance of an exact knowledge of the geographical site and historical remains in the recon-struction of events." Here his early architectural in-terests and his love of travel helped to make him a real pioneer, who did for mediaeval history something of the same service as Schliemann and his successors have done for that of classical antiquity. And Freeman's ardent passion for the England and the English of the pre-Conquest period powerfully stimulated not only the interest in the history of the Anglo-Saxons but in the prose and poetry they have bequeathed. He helped to make it impossible to begin the story of our literature with Chaucer instead of with *Beowulf*. And his own style, though lacking in grace and variety, caught at its highest the forthright strength and energetic rhythm of old English speech. Take one illustration from the description of the stricken field of Hastings when all was over:

Night had closed in and those among the English host who had not fallen around their King had left the field under cover of the darkness. William now came back to the hill, where all resistance had long been over. He looked around, we are told, on the dead and dying thousands, not without a feeling of pity that so many men had fallen even as a sacrifice to his own fancied right. But the victory was truly his own; in the old phrase of our Chroniclers, the Frenchmen had possession of the place of slaughter. A place of slaughter indeed it was, where from morn till twilight, the axe and javelin of England, the lance and bow of Normandy, had done their deadly work at the bidding of the two mightiest captains upon earth. Dead and dying men were heaped around and nowhere were they heaped so thickly as around the fallen standard of England. There, where the flower of England's nobility and soldiery lay stretched in death, there, where the banner of the Fighting Man now lay beaten to the ground, the Conqueror knelt and gave his thanks to God, and bade his own banner be planted as the sign of the Victory which he had won.... He was hailed by the loud applause of his troops, likening him to Roland and Oliver and all the heroes of old. Again he gave thanks to God, again he thanked his faithful followers, and sat down to eat and drink among the dead.

The last words, in their austere and primitive grandeur, might have come from a northern saga.

The appointment on Freeman's death in 1892 of his bitterest critic, J. A. Froude, to succeed him in the Oxford Chair was one of Lord Salisbury's characteristically cynical gestures. But Froude was like Freeman in this respect that he had been too long away from academical surroundings to fit into them easily or to exert much influence on the work of the "School". Nor could the man who in his youth had been associated for a short time with the Oxford Movement, and who after his recantation in *The Nemesis of Faith* (1849) had been deprived of his fellowship, be expected to feel himself at home in the transformed Oxford of "forty years on". It was in the reaction from his early Anglo-Catholicism, and under the influence of Carlyle, that Froude had embarked on the great undertaking, *The History of England from the Fall of Wolsey to the Defeat of the Spanish Armada*, of which the earlier and more challenging volumes began to appear in 1856 and the later ones fall exactly within the limits of our period.

Everyone is now familiar with what were Froude's main objects—to vindicate the Protestant Reformation in England from what he looked on as prejudiced and partisan attacks; to substitute for the "blue-beard" conception of Henry VIII the picture of a patriot King whose matrimonial affairs were dominated by the over-mastering need of providing a male heir to the throne. Henry becomes again in Froude's pages what he was to Gray in *The Installation Ode*:

> The majestic lord
> That broke the bonds of Rome.

His daughter, Elizabeth, fares less well at Froude's hands, for in his researches he became convinced that she did much to check the vigorous Protestant policy of her ministers. It is Burleigh whom he exalts as "the solitary author of Elizabeth's and England's greatness". Mary,

Queen of Scots, is painted in the darkest colours in contrast with the Regent Murray and John Knox. It is not
for me here to discuss the truth of Froude's presentation.
None of us can approach questions so closely inter-
linked with present-day controversies without pre-
possessions on one side or the other. But it can be said
without doubt that no one is qualified to give an estimate
of the careers of Henry VIII and Burleigh who has not
made himself familiar with Froude's revaluation of
them. Perhaps after all it was an act of poetic justice
when Burleigh's Victorian descendant honoured the
panegyrist of his Elizabethan ancestor.

In any case Froude showed that he belonged to the new
era by his extensive use of documents. He transcribed
long extracts from archives at home and abroad, especially the Spanish papers at Simancas. He was not a
careful copyist, and he sometimes substituted his own
abstracts for the original texts. He thus laid himself
open to charges of inaccuracy, which were exaggerated
by hostile critics into those of falsification. These have
not been sustained, though Froude doubtless selected
among his materials those that would give support to his
particular views.

Charges of manipulation of sources were the more
readily believed of a historian who was not only a
propagandist, but that suspicious character, an artist in
prose. Froude's *History*, though not without defects of
balance and proportion, is the finished prose epic of the
Protestant Reformation in England, with its climax in the
defeat of the Armada, as Macaulay's *History* is the unfinished prose epic of the later Whig Revolution.

The style of the twelve-volume work, as flexible as
it is lucid, is admirably suited to a long sustained narrative.
Professor Saintsbury has detected in it "something of the
cool, clear, silvery note" of his early master, J. H.
Newman, "variegated and flourished up". At times too
"flourished up"! Some of the famous purple passages,
for all their subtle and haunting melody, are so deliberately worked up that they seem to me to be not of
the vital essence of the *History*, but exquisite outward
adornments. Let us linger again for a moment over the
most familiar of them all, the elegy upon the passing of
the mediaeval world:

For indeed a change was coming upon the world, the
meaning and direction of which even still is hidden from us,
a change from era to era. The paths trodden by the footsteps
of ages were broken up; old things were passing away, and
the faith and the life of ten centuries were dissolving like a
dream. Chivalry was dying; the abbey and the castle were
soon together to crumble into ruins; and all the forms, desires,
beliefs, convictions of the old world were passing away,
never to return. A new continent had risen up beyond the
western sea. The floor of heaven, inlaid with stars, had sunk
back into an infinite abyss of immeasurable space; and the
firm earth itself, unfixed from its foundations, was seen to be
but a small atom in the awful vastness of the universe. In the
fabric of habit which they had so laboriously built for themselves, mankind were to remain no longer.

And now it is all gone—like an unsubstantial pageant
and faded; and between us and the old English there lies a
gulf of mystery which the prose of the historian will never
adequately bridge. They cannot come to us, and our imagination can but feebly penetrate to them. Only among the

aisles of our cathedrals, only as we gaze upon their silent figures sleeping on their tombs, some faint conceptions float before us of what these men were when they were alive; and perhaps in the sound of church bells, that peculiar creation of the mediaeval age which falls upon the ear like the echo of a vanished world.

Under the enchantment of these seductive strains our critical faculties are lulled, and we are moved to cry:

> Here will we sit and let the sounds of music
> Creep in our ears.

Froude's style in such passages may not be the pure Attic, but it is that of one who never forgot that the historian is the servant of a Muse.

While Froude was engaged on the Tudors another historian, of a very different type, had begun what was to be his life-work on the Stuarts. Only four volumes of S. R. Gardiner's *History of England* which appeared at intervals between 1863 and 1901, and covered the years from 1603 to 1656, fall within our period. They deal with the reign of James I, till the episode of "the Spanish Marriage". It was not till Gardiner's work had reached a later stage that its significance was fully recognised. But even in the 'sixties it had become manifest that the dominant Whig conception of the relations of King and Parliament in the first half of the seventeenth century would have to be revised in the light of the labours of this indefatigable scholar. Without forensic arts, by the exhaustive analysis of contemporary authorities, and by the patient disentanglement of trains of policy, especially in foreign affairs, he made it impossible even for those whose sympathies are with the popular side to cling to the purely traditional views of the issues and personages in the great constitutional struggle.

While Froude was seeking to rehabilitate Henry VIII, the master of his later life, Carlyle was doing the same for Frederick the Great. The six volumes of Frederick's *Life* which appeared between 1858 and 1865 are neither such a work of art as *The French Revolution* nor such a contribution to historical research as *Cromwell's Letters and Speeches*. They dispelled the current superficial views of Frederick's character and they proved that Carlyle retained his trenchant power of portraiture and description and the passionate zeal for accuracy in detail that led him to undertake two journeys to the scenes of Frederick's battles. But he was overweighted with his materials and the book, as a whole, has not the sustained energy and glow of his earlier works. It looks back rather than forward. It will always be, whatever its shortcomings, one of the historical treasures of the 'sixties, but it does not help to mark the new era.

For the justification of that title we must look elsewhere—to the wider conception of the range of the historian due to Buckle and his followers; to the more intensive methods of investigation followed, in different ways, by Stubbs, Freeman, Froude and Gardiner; to the opening up of documentary sources by the earlier publications of the *Rolls Series* and the *Calendars of State Papers*; to the growth of modern history as a subject of academic study, especially in Oxford; and, at the very close of our period, in 1869 to the appointment of J. R. Seeley to the Cambridge Chair, where history was once again to enlist in the service of statesmanship and become the interpreter of a new imperial ideal.

ENEAS SWEETLAND DALLAS

By *John Drinkwater*

A few particulars of the life of Eneas Sweetland Dallas, as given in the *Dictionary of National Biography*. He was born in Jamaica in 1824, but was brought to England as a child and was educated at Edinburgh University. Adopting journalism as a career, he became one of J. T. Delane's staff on *The Times*, to which paper for many years he was a leading contributor. He married an actress in 1853 and was divorced in 1874. Dying in 1879 at the age of fifty-five, he was buried in Kensal Green cemetery. "He had", says his biographer, "a singularly handsome presence and charming manners, and his conversation was bright and courteous."

Dallas appears to have published three books. By far the most popular of these was Kettner's *Book of the Table*—a manual of cookery which appeared in 1877. In 1852 he published his *Poetics*, and in 1866 *The Gay Science*, a large work in two volumes, which is the occasion of this paper. The title was taken from a term used by the troubadours to designate the art of poetry, and Dallas's theme is an elaborate inquiry into the foundations and principles of poetic criticism. The book, published by Chapman and Hall, seems to have made no impression whatever on the reading public. "The subject", says the *Dictionary* biographer, "was too abstruse for the general reader, and the book did not meet with the attention which it deserved." Philosophic criticism that abstains from all biographical interest has never made easy or popular reading, and it is not surprising that Dallas's quite formidable treatise should have received little immediate recognition. What is surprising is that it somehow failed in succeeding years to attract any notice at all, and of several English scholars to whom I put the question not one had even heard of Dallas's name. This, I say, is surprising. It is common enough for a work of difficult distinction to be little noted at the time of its appearance, but it is very unusual for such a work in the course of time not to attract a word of testimony here and another there until at last it has acquired a secure reputation that is handed on from age to age by a few discerning readers. *The Gay Science* is a highly distinguished contribution to English poetic criticism; on many claims, I think, it cannot be refused admission to the first rank. And yet to-day it is lost in an obscurity from which, indeed, it never seems to have emerged. It was by mere chance that in casting about for a subject apposite to the eighteen-sixties I happened upon a single casual reference to *The Gay Science* in Professor Walker's *History of Victorian Literature*. The name took my fancy, and as the book belonged to the right period I sought a copy of it. The London Library did not fail me, and after reading a few pages I was astonished to find myself under the spell of a quite remarkable critical intelligence.

Since *The Gay Science* is so little known, or one should say so entirely unknown, it would be purposeless at this stage to debate its arguments and conclusions. If, as I hope, some publisher should have the courage to give us a reprint of the book, the scene will then be set for such a discussion, but in the meantime Dallas can best be served by an attempt to give a brief summary of the book itself. In making this attempt I shall employ quotation as freely as possible.

The plan of the argument is this. Poetry itself, according to the troubadours, is a science. How much more then should scientific system govern that less creative, less unpredicable process of the mind, poetic criticism. But it is precisely in this system that criticism as a whole has been deficient. Lacking any clearly defined and commonly accepted intention as a basis, it has evolved not into an organised science, but into a display of loose if often brilliant impressionism, illuminating in its detail, but unaware of a presiding tradition, and uncertain always in direction. Dallas insists that the criticism of poetry cannot achieve its potential values until we have agreed as to some basic agent in poetry for which the tests of criticism must be applied. What, in a word, is the purpose of poetry? Let us decide that; and then of any poem our first question will be, Does it fulfil this purpose? The purpose of poetry and, indeed, of all art, we are told, is pleasure. And Dallas then proceeds by an investigation of great length to ascertain what pleasure is.

First we may note a few of the general features of his inquiry. He writes excellent prose, copious in vocabulary, easy in analogy, with grace and force equally at his command. His learning is wide, assured, and never paraded. He can furnish his argument at ease with illustrations drawn from the critics and philosophers of

many languages, and he is intimate with the doctrines of
all of them from Plato down to Matthew Arnold.
Tasso, Horace, Lessing, Schiller, Goethe, Bacon,
Wordsworth, Coleridge, Shelley, Aristotle, Kant, Locke,
Mill, Ruskin, Dryden, Cervantes; he knows what all of
them have said that is pertinent to his matter. And with
great respect for authority, he is never afraid of it. Plato
and Aristotle may be the springs at which all subsequent
criticism has refreshed itself, but neither was immune from
the snares of nonsense. And it is doubtful whether
Matthew Arnold, who was forty-four when *The Gay
Science* was published, and so only two years older than
Dallas, was treated as a critic with as much intelligent if
sometimes rather tart discrimination by any other contemporary writer.

It is difficult enough to determine what is originality
in the poet, the creator. It is even more difficult to
determine what is originality in the critic, the thinker. If
only we know enough, we shall detect in the course of
the most seemingly original thinker old trails that
remind us once more that there is no new thing under the
sun. By the most exacting standards, Dallas may not be
an original thinker, but he is certainly a very stimulating
one. So far as thought will take him, he is tireless in
tracking an idea to its origins. When you have read *The
Gay Science* you may be in doubt as to whether he has
succeeded in proving a case. In following his elaborate
analysis you may even sometimes be uncertain as to what
precisely the case is that he is intent on proving. And if it
comes to that, I suppose there is no accredited philosophic
system in the world of which it is generally allowed that

that is that, and that there is no more to be said about it.
The real interest in Dallas, as in any other philosopher,
lies not in what he does or does not prove, but in his
manner of attempting to prove it. And here Dallas goes
on for some seven hundred pages with an energy that can
be robust or subtle at will, and, it may be added, with a
gaiety that does credit to the title of his book.

In introducing Dallas now to your attention in his
own words, I make no apology for doing so in a passage
of considerable length that displays at once the felicity of
his style and his power for consecutive reasoning:

Now this method of confounding fact and fiction, in
order that fiction may appear to rise to the assurance of fact,
was not peculiarly Italian, but existed in full force among the
Greeks. It was an essential feature of their drama. The most
marked characteristic of the Greek drama is the presence of
the chorus. The chorus are always present,—watching events,
talking to the actors, talking to the audience, talking to
themselves,—all through the play, indeed, pouring forth a
continual stream of musical chatter. And what are the
chorus? The only intelligible explanation which has been
given is that they represent the spectator. The spectator is
introduced into the play and made to take part in it. What
the Greeks thus did artistically on their stage, we moderns
have also sometimes done inartistically and unintentionally,
but still to the same effect. We have had the audience seated
on the stage, and sometimes, in the most ludicrous manner,
taking part in the performance. When Garrick was playing
Lear in Dublin to the Cordelia of Mrs Woffington, an Irish
gentleman who was present actually advanced, put his arm
round the lady's waist, and thus held her while she replied to
the reproaches of the old king. The stage in the last century

was sometimes so beset with the audience, that Juliet has been seen, says Tate Wilkinson, lying all solitary in the tomb of the Capulets with a couple of hundred of the audience about her. We should now contemplate such a practice with horror, as utterly destructive of stage illusion; and yet we must remember that it had its illusive aspect also, by confounding the dream that appeared on the stage with the familiar realities of life.

From all this, however, it follows that if the Greeks made a confusion between fact and fiction, art and nature, they were not peculiar in so doing. What is peculiar to them is this, that they gave a critical character to their doubt as to the limits of truth in art. It was fairly reasoned. If it showed itself sometimes as a childish superstition, sometimes as the mere blindness of a prosaic temper, and sometimes as an enjoyment of silly illusions, it also at times bore a higher character and rose to the level of criticism. The Greeks were the first to raise this subject of the truth of art into an important question which they transmitted to after times.

This is not the place to enter into a discussion whether they were right or wrong, and whether fiction be or be not falsehood. That discussion will be more fitly handled when we come to examine the ethics of art. Here we need only record and confront the fact that the objection to the pleasure of art which most frequently puzzled the Greek thinkers, was that it appeared to be mixed up with lies. Plato, as I have already said, exhausted his dialectical skill in showing the untruthfulness of art. He condemned it as an imitation at third hand. He meant, for example, that a flower in the field is but the shadow of an idea in the mind of God; that the idea in God's mind is the real thing; that the blossom in the meadow is but a poor image of it; and that when a painter gives us a copy of that copy, the picture stands third from the divine original, and is, therefore, a wretched false-hood. Plato's statement as to the truth of art is thus grounded on his theory of ideas, and when that theory goes, one would imagine that the statement should go also. It is a curious proof of the vitality of strong assertion, that his opinion (but it would be more correct to say the opinion to which he gave currency) abides with all the force which his name can give to it, while the theory of ideas from which it sprung and derived plausibility, has long since gone to the limbo. It is incredible that mankind should find enduring pleasure in a lie. There cannot be a more monstrous libel against the human race than to say that in the artistic search for pleasure, we have reality and all that is most gracious in it to choose from; that we look from earth to heaven and try all ways which the infinite beneficence of nature has provided; that nevertheless we set our joy on a system of lies; and that so far the masterpieces of art are but tokens of a fallen nature, the signs of sickness and the harbinger of doom.

As Plato took one side of the question, Aristotle took the other, and in the writings of the latter we have the final conclusion and the abiding belief of the Greek mind upon this subject of the truth of art. The view which he took was concentrated in the saying that poetry is more philosophical than history, because it looks more to general and less to particular facts. We should now express the same thing in the statement that whereas history is fact, poetry is truth. Aristotle does not set himself formally to answer Plato, but throughout his writings we find him solving Plato's riddles, undoing Plato's arguments, and rebutting Plato's objections. Many of his most famous sayings are got by recoil from Plato. Thus his masterly definition of tragedy, which has never been improved upon, and which generation after generation of critics have been content to repeat like a text of Scripture, is a rebound from Plato. And the same is to be said very nearly of Aristotle's doctrine concerning the truth of art. It is so clear and so complete that it has become a common-place of criticism. It asserted for the Greeks, in the distinctest terms, the truthfulness of art; it showed wherein that truthfulness consists; and, as far as criticism was concerned, it at once and for ever disposed of the notion that art is a lie. Greeks like Gorgias could see vaguely that if art be a cheat, it may, nevertheless, be justifiable, as we should justify a feint or other stratagem in war. It was reserved for Aristotle to put the defence of art on the right ground—to deny that it is a cheat at all—and to claim for it a truthfulness deeper than that of history.

This, then, is one of the earliest lessons which the student of art has to learn. The first lesson of all is that art is for pleasure; the second is that the pleasure of art stands in no sort of opposition to truth. We in England have especial reason to bear this in mind, for we are most familiar with the doctrine that art is for pleasure, as it has been put by Coleridge; and it is not unlikely that some of the repugnance which the doctrine meets in minds of a certain order may be due to his ragged analysis and awkward statement. He rather prided himself on his anatomy of thought and expression, but he hardly ever made a clean dissection. Mark what he says in this case. He says that the true opposite of poetry is not prose, but science, and that whereas it is the proper and immediate object of science to discover truth, it is the proper and immediate object of poetry to communicate pleasure. This is not right. Coleridge has defined science by reference to the external object with which it is engaged; but he has defined poetry by reference to the mental state which it produces. There is no comparison between the two. If he is to run the contrast fairly, he ought to deal with both alike, and to state either what is the outward object pursued by each, or what is the inward state produced by each. He would then find that, so far as the subject-matter is concerned, there is no essential difference between poetry and science, it being false to say that the one possesses more of truth than the other; and he would define the difference between the two by the mental states which they severally produce—the immediate object of science being science or knowledge, while that of poetry is pleasure. To say that the object of art is pleasure in contrast to knowledge, is quite different from saying that it is pleasure in contrast to truth. Science gives us truth without reference to pleasure, but immediately and chiefly for the sake of knowledge; poetry gives us truth without reference to knowledge, but immediately and mainly for the sake of pleasure. By thus getting rid of the contrast between truth and pleasure, which Coleridge has unguardedly allowed, a difficulty is smoothed away from the doctrine that the end of art is pleasure, and that of criticism the analysis of pleasure. His statement has an air of extraordinary precision about it that might wile the unwary into a ditch. All his precision goes to misrepresent the pure Greek doctrine.

Here we see the range of his scholarship, his gift for co-ordination, the shrewdness of his thought, and, in the observations on Coleridge, the candour of a mind that can perceive greatness without being infatuated by it. The passage will, I am sure for most of my readers, be their first introduction to Dallas, and in order to emphasise the impression I will take leave to quote another passage of like length in which he expounds his theory of pleasure as the immediate end of art.

If the unity of the arts does not lie in the possession either of a common method which they pursue, or of a common theme which they set forth, wherein does it consist? Manifestly the character of an art is determined by its object; and though the critics have made no use of the fact, yet it is a fact which they admit with very few exceptions, that poetry and the fine arts are endowed with a common purpose. Even if poetry and the arts could boast of a common method and a common theme, still every question of method and the choice of theme must be subordinate to the end in view. The end determines the means, and must therefore be the principal point of inquiry. If, then, we inquire what is the end of poetry and the poetical arts, we shall find among critics of all countries and all ages a singular unanimity of opinion—a unanimity which is all the more remarkable, when we discover that, admitting the fact with scarcely a dissentient voice, they have never turned it to account— they have practically ignored it. It is admitted that the immediate end of art is to give pleasure. Whatever we do has happiness for its last end; but with art it is the first as well as the last. We need not now halt to investigate the nature of this happiness which poetry aims at, whether it is refined or the reverse, whether it is of a particular kind or of all kinds; it is enough to insist on the broad fact that for more than two thousand years pleasure of some sort has been almost universally admitted to be the goal of art. The dreamer and the thinker, the singer and the sayer, at war on many another point, are here at one. It is the pleasure of a lie, says Plato; it is that of a truth, says Aristotle; but neither has any doubt that whatever other aims art may have in view, pleasure is the main—the immediate object.

Here, however, care must be taken that the reader is not misled by a word. Word and thing, pleasure is in very bad odour; moralists always take care to hold it cheap; critics are ashamed of it; and we are all apt to misunderstand it, resting too easily on the surface view of it as mere amusement. There is in pleasure so little of conscious thought, and in pain so much, that it is natural for all who pride themselves on the possession of thought to make light of pleasure. It is possible, however, in magnifying the worth of conscious thought, to underrate the worth of unconscious life. Now art is a force that operates unconsciously on life. It is not a doctrine; it is not science. There is knowledge in it, but it reaches to something beyond knowledge. That something beyond science, beyond knowledge, to which art reaches, it is difficult to express in one word. The nearest word is that which the world for thirty centuries past has been using, and which sky-high thinkers now-a-days are afraid to touch—namely, pleasure. There is no doubt about its inadequacy, but where is there another word that expresses half as much? If art be the opposite of science, the end of art must be antithetical to the end of science. But the end of science is knowledge. What then is its antithesis—the end of art? Shall we say ignorance? We cannot say that it is ignorance, because that is a pure negation. But there is no objection to our saying— life ignorant of itself, unconscious life, pleasure. I do not give this explanation as sufficient—it is very insufficient— but as indicating a point of view from which it will be seen that the establishment of pleasure as the end of art may involve larger issues, and convey a larger meaning than is commonly supposed. What that larger meaning is may in due course be shown. In the ninth chapter of this work I attempt to state it, and stating it to give a remodelled definition of art. In the meantime, one fails to see how, by any of the new-fangled expressions of German philosophy, we can improve upon the plain-spoken wisdom of the ancient maxims—that science is for knowledge, and that art is for pleasure.

14-2

But if this be granted, and it is all but universally granted, it entails the inevitable inference that criticism is the science of the laws and conditions under which pleasure is produced. If poetry, if art, exists in and for pleasure, then upon this rock, and upon this alone, is it possible to build a science of criticism. Criticism, however, is built anywhere but upon the rock. While the arts have almost invariably been regarded as arts of pleasure, criticism has never yet been treated as the science of pleasure. Like the Israelites in the desert, who after confessing the true faith went forthwith and fell down to a molten image, the critics no sooner admitted that the end of art is pleasure, than they began to treat it as nought. Instead of taking a straight line, like the venerable ass which was praised by the Eleatic philosopher, they went off zigzag, to right, to left, in every imaginable direction but that which lay before them. Art is for pleasure said the Greeks; but it is the pleasure of imitation, and therefore all that criticism has to do is to study the ways of imitation. So they bounced off to the left. Art is for pleasure said the Germans; but it is the pleasure of the beautiful, and therefore all that criticism has to do is to comprehend the beautiful. So they bounced off to the right. In the name of common sense, let me ask, why are we not to take the straight line? Why is it that, having set up pleasure as the first principle of art, we are immediately to knock it down and go in search of other and lesser principles? Why does not the critic take the one plain path before him, proceeding instantly to inquire into the nature of pleasure, its laws, its conditions, its requirements, its causes, its effects, its whole history?

This turning aside of criticism from the straight road that lay before it into by-paths has been owing partly to the moral contempt of pleasure, but chiefly to the intellectual difficulty of any inquest into the nature of enjoyment, a difficulty so great, that since the time of Plato and Aristotle it has never been seriously faced until in our own day Sir William Hamilton undertook to grapple with it. Whenever I have insisted with my friends on this point, as to the necessity of recognising criticism as the science of pleasure, the invariable rejoinder has been that there is no use in attempting such a science, because the nature of pleasure eludes our scrutiny, and there is no accounting for tastes. But the rejoinder is irrelevant. All science is difficult at first, and wellnigh hopeless; and if tastes differ, that is no reason why we should refuse to regard them as beyond the pale of the law, but a very strong reason why we should seek to ascertain the limits of difference, and how far pleasure which is general may be discounted by individual caprice. It is not for us to parley about the difficulties of search, or the usefulness of its results. Chemistry was at one time a difficult study, and seemed to be a useless one. Hard or easy, useful or useless— that is not the question. The question is simply this: If there is such a thing as criticism at all, what is its object? what is its definition? and how do you escape from the truism that if art be the minister, criticism must be the science of pleasure?

As the plan of his book develops, Dallas undertakes to show that the profoundest pleasure of which man is capable is that which is engendered in the imagination, and in three chapters entitled "On Imagination", "The Hidden Soul", and "The Play of Thought", he investigates the nature of the imagination with an insight that is no less profound than the execution is brilliant. To these chapters I will return, but in the meantime let me give a few examples of the engaging detail with which Dallas embellishes his argument.

Confessing at the outset of his work that all critical

exploits are questionable, he quotes the opinion of
G. H. Lewes: "The good effected by criticism is small,
the evil incalculable". And adds on his own account,
"Critics have always had a strong cannibal instinct. They
have not only snapped at the poets: they have devoured
one another". Allowing that Porson was a giant, he
nevertheless girds at his pedantry, and proceeds:

Nor was Porson alone; he had disciples even worse.
Many a youth of wild temperament wishes for something
to break his mind on, like the study of Armenian, which
Byron found useful in that way. Let him read Elmsley on the
Medea. If Porson was a kind of Baal, a lord of flies, Elmsley
was a literary dustman. The criticism of detail which both of
them studied has an invariable tendency to stray further and
further from science, and to become Rabbinical. It ends in
teaching Rabbis to count the letters of a sacred book backwards and forwards until they can find the middle one.

Of Aristotle, whom he admits to hierarchical rank, he
says:

His leading principle, which makes all poetry, all art, an
imitation, is demonstrably false, has rendered his Poetic one-
sided...and has transmitted to all after criticism a sort of
hereditary squint.

Pleading for the recognition of standards in art, he says:

The difference in England between a contest of racers and
a contest of poets, painters, or essayists, is to be found in this,
that the pace of two horses admits of measurement. There is
a standard to which all give assent; the race is won by a nose,
or a head, or a neck, or a length. There need be no mistake in
the comparison; and if the rewards are tempting, we may be

pretty sure that the best horses will run, and that the result may be taken as a fair test of merit. If there were any doubtfulness about the test the owners of the best horses would never allow their favourites to run. But in any contest between painters or sculptors, poets or essayists, there is just that dubiety as to the standard of measurement which would prevent the best men from competing.

Pleading the necessity of scientific criticism, he says:

We believe in insects as fit objects of science; but the mind of man is beyond our science, and we give it up in despair. Mr Kingsley, who has written one book to show that a science of history is impossible, has written another to show the great and religious advantage at watering-places of studying science in the works of God—that is, in sea-jellies and cockle-shells.... When a man goes to the sea-side, and, taking the advice of the same author, begins to study natural history, can tell the number of legs on a crab, the number of joints on a lobster's tail, names one kind of shell a helix, another kind of shell a pecten—that is called studying the works of God.... Or if he analyses a quantity of earth, can tell what are its ingredients, whether it is better for turnips or for wheat, and whether it should be manured with lime or with guano—that is studying the works of God.... Amid all this cant of finding God in the material and not in the moral world, and of thence lauding the sciences of matter to the neglect of the science of mind, who but must remember a sermon in which the speaker, it is true, invited his audience to consider the lilies of the field and to behold the fowls of the air, but only that he might drive home the question—Are ye not much better than they?

Eighty years after his death Wordsworth's fame is at its zenith. Authoritative critical opinion has advanced him to the third place among the poets of our race, subordinate only to Shakespeare and Milton. In this, we may allow, the great Lake man gets no more than his deserts. And yet the most devoted recognition of his poetry cannot but be tinged at moments with a feeling that he was subject to moods of philosophic infirmity against which both Shakespeare and Milton, and, it may be added, many smaller masters, were immune. Dallas in 1866 was in no doubt as to Wordsworth's durable greatness, but he diagnosed the infirmity with unerring touch:

This antithesis between the works of God and the works of man, which we find in the science of our time, seems to have begun in a misanthropical vein of thought belonging to a considerable portion of the poetry of the nineteenth century. Byron, of all our recent poets, would be most easily accused of this misanthropy; but it is not of Byron that we have to complain: it is of Wordsworth and his incessant harping on the opposition between nature and humanity. It was from Wordsworth's region of thought that the petty controversy arose, many years ago, as to the materials of poetry. Bowles contended that poetry is more immediately indebted for its interest to the works of nature than to those of art; that a ship of the line derives its poetry not from anything contributed by man—the sails, masts, and so forth; but from the wind that fills the sails, from the sunshine that touches them with light, from the waves on which the vessel rides—in a word, from nature. The essence of this criticism is misanthropy; it is such misanthropy which Byron fought against manfully, and with which he was incapable of sympathising. We can trace this misanthropy downwards to Mr Ruskin, at least so long as he was under the influence of Wordsworth.

In his earlier criticism he was always quoting that poet; his whole mind seemed to be given to landscape painting, and he conceived of art as the expression of man's delight in the works of God. He has long outgrown the Wordsworthian misanthropy, and has learnt to widen his definition of the theme of art; but still in his eloquent pages, as in the strains of Wordsworth, and as in the tendency to landscape of much of our poetry and painting, the men of science will find some sanction for the hollow antithesis which sets the works of God against those of man.

The view here taken of the malady may be an unnecessarily gloomy one, but it cannot be dismissed as untenable.

In his historical survey, Dallas says:

Speaking roundly, there are but two great systems of criticism. The one may be styled indifferently the classical system, or the system of the Renaissance. It belongs to ancient thought, and to the modern revival of classicism; and it chiefly concerns itself with the grammatical forms of art. The other is more distinctly modern; it first made way in Germany, and, philosophical in tone, chiefly concerns itself with the substantial ideas of art.

This is the kind of generalisation in which he is so skilful, and, generally, so sound. And while many may be found to dispute his daring, none can fail to admire it when it marches thus:

It may be remembered that Wordsworth, in a celebrated preface, enters into elaborate antiquarian researches, to show that the neglect which he suffered from his contemporaries was only what a great poet might expect, and that the most palpable stamp of a great poem is its falling flat upon the world to be picked up and recognised only by the fit and few.

Now, in art, the two seldom go together; the fit are not few, and the few are not fit. The true judges of art are the much despised many—the crowd—and no critic is worth his salt who does not feel with the many. There are, no doubt, questions of criticism which only few can answer; but the enjoyment of art is for all; and just as in eloquence, the great orator is he who commands the people, so in poetry, so in art, the great poet, the great artist will command high and low alike. Great poetry was ever meant, and to the end of time must be adapted, not to the curious student, but for the multitude who read while they run—for the crowd in the street, for the boards of huge theatres, and for the choirs of vast cathedrals, for an army marching tumultuous to the battle, and for an assembled nation silent over the tomb of its mightiest. It is intended for a great audience, not for individual readers. So Homer sang to well greaved listeners from court to court; so Aeschylus, Sophocles, and Euripides wrote for the Athenian populace; so Pindar chanted for the mob that fluttered around the Olympian racecourse.

As an example of his mischievous phrase, may be quoted:

Scudéry's statement of the precious (i.e. *les précieuses*) doctrine of pleasure will be found in the preface to that grand epic bug—his poem of Alaric.

And again:

Nothing, however, looks half so big as Coleridge's definition. "The imagination I consider either as primary or secondary. The primary imagination I hold to be the living power and prime agent of all human perception, and as a repetition in the finite mind of the eternal act of creation in the infinite I AM. The secondary I consider as an echo of the former." Oh, gentle shepherds! what does this mean? Is it something very great or very little? It reminds me of a splendid definition of art which I once heard. When the infinite I AM beheld his work of creation, he said Thou ART, and ART was.

Of incidental felicities, one last instance may be given, namely a reference to "one of our least known poets, but a true one, Matthew Green". The critic of English poetry who in 1866 knew *The Spleen* for the fine poem that it is was very wide awake. And even then one could wish to make further levies upon this author's fertile wit. So resourceful in illustration, as when quoting Malebranche's lovely aphorism, "Attention is the prayer of the intellect"; so cunning in its perception, as when it observes of Shakespeare's art that "it is built on a vast expenditure of facts, on a wonderful exposition of knowledge. Through the splendid collision of facts, we learn to catch at something which is not in the facts".

I have left myself but inadequate space in which to deal with Dallas's theory of the imagination. Briefly, it amounts to this. The philosophers, says Dallas, have expounded many fragmentary opinions as to the nature of imagination, but no more than this. Some have identified imagination with memory, some with passion, some with reason, and, again, some have represented it "as a faculty by itself—different from the other powers of the mind". In each degree there is a difference: "It is reason out for a holiday; it is perception in a hurry; it is memory gone wild; it is the dalliance of desire; it is any or all of these together". Against all these views, Dallas

advances his own view that the imagination is the
activity of any or all of the mind's faculties conditioned
by a specific if not precisely definable mood. "I propose
this theory, that the imagination or fantasy is not a
special faculty but that it is a special function. It is a
name given to the automatic action of the mind or any of
its faculties—to what may not unfitly be called the
Hidden Soul." The Hidden Soul in turn he relates to the
lubber fiend of legend, "who toils for us when we are
asleep or when we are not looking....He will not lift a
finger that we can see; but let us shut our eyes, or turn
our heads, or put out the light, and there is nothing
which the good fairy will not do for us". It is in this
sub-conscious, or semi-conscious region of the mind, of
all the faculties of the mind, that the imagination
operates; or, more strictly, this sub-conscious or semi-
conscious activity is the imagination. In this condition
the mind works with a power, a cunning, a magic, which
are beyond the scope of what is generally termed con-
sciousness. It is here possible to give no more than this
crude summary of a case that Dallas argues at great
length, and, as it seems to me, with admirable persuasion.
It leads him to conclusions of which not the least notable
is embodied in one last passage which I will submit from
his book, in the hope that some attention may be drawn
to a writer whose merits have been strangely overlooked.

There is no word in the language which has so many
meanings and which has been so used and abused as *nature*.
Sometimes it is opposed to art, sometimes to grace, sometimes to man, sometimes to affectation; and in the foregoing
paragraph I have opposed it to conscience. Now, the

necessity for explanation here arises out of the fact, that the man of most authority as a moral philosopher in this country, Bishop Butler, runs all his arguments up to the point of proving that virtuous action is according to nature. The remark of Sir James Mackintosh, however, must be remembered, which was to the effect that no man so clear-headed has, perhaps, ever been so dark-worded as Butler. His obscurities of diction are more than enough to make one doubt the truth of the well-known maxim, that to write clearly, you have only to think clearly. It is not because the language of a sermon is unfit for philosophic accuracy that he thus fails. From the pen of Hobbes, of Berkeley, of Hume, has flowed language far more homely, but seldom or never wanting in precision. Now, Butler's argument is, that a life according to conscience is a life according to nature, because conscience is part of human nature. It is a question of words which in itself is not worth looking at; but which, nevertheless, cannot be disregarded by anyone who knows how the metaphysicians, whenever they get near the subject of conscience, begin to wrangle about words, and to display all the craft of the casuist. To speak of action led by conscience as natural, in the same sense in which we speak of action led by impulse as natural, is to confound speech. In common parlance, we speak of a good-natured or an ill-natured man; we say it is the nature of cherubim to know, the nature of seraphim to love. Thus, a man may be so gentle, that not for his life could he do anything unkind; or so high-minded, that it would be impossible for him to descend to any meanness, and he is never once visited by that fear of vulgar minds lest peradventure they may do something shabby. This is to act naturally; it is to act instinctively. But to act by the law and rule of conscience is altogether different; it is natural in a much lower sense. Innocence is nature, holiness is second nature; but virtue is not nature as innocence and holiness are; it is in contrast to these affected; it is, if I may so speak, artificial. And I hope I have rendered it sufficiently clear that art, as a moral force, tends to create or to establish a nature. It is the part of art not only to hide its own art, but to be opposed to art. It is born of nature, it follows nature, and it creates nature.

No sooner have we reached this idea of art—that in so far as it is pure and noble, it cherishes the inborn nature which we call innocence, and the engrafted or implanted nature which we call holiness, but has little to do with virtue, or the life according to conscience—than we are met in full front by the philosophers. They cannot indeed tell us that the cultivation of natural impulse, and the trusting to it, is immoral; but they insist on the inferiority of impulse to conscience, of sensibility to the sense of duty. Dugald Stewart, in this country, and Victor Cousin, in France, for example, maintain that conscious endeavour after the right is something higher than instinct, that struggle and victory are something better than peaceful possession. But surely these are as shoemakers sounding the praise of leather. Intense consciousness is the all-in-all of philosophy; therefore, philosophers think that it must be the all-in-all of life. By the same rule, it would be better to eat and drink, not guided by appetite, but by a kind of animal conscience, formed out of chemical calculations, and called the sense of food. There are poor wights to whom almost everything eatable has become a forbidden fruit. Hunger and thirst can no longer be trusted, and a new faculty arises, built of the ruins of appetite, the purchases of experience, the findings of reason, and the advice of the doctor, in one word, and in the old use of that word—a conscience; not unlike to which in its higher sphere is that conscience known as the sense of duty. Banished from the paradise of our innocence, with dispositions to good either froward or weak, troubled with sorrow and trial, cursed with shortcomings and backslidings, full of longings that have waxed and waned moon by moon, and of vows that have sprung with the spring, but have too often fallen long ere the fall of each returning year; man, tossed about and torn asunder by the discordancies of his life, is guided by a faculty of conscience built out of and upon the ruins of natural inclination.

I have taken more than my allotted space, and I am still conscious that I have given but a very inadequate summary of the seven hundred pages that are so closely knit in Dallas's unknown work. The most that I can hope is that I have been able to indicate in a fugitive way that it is a work of great, and greatly underestimated, merit.

GEORGE WHYTE-MELVILLE

By *The Hon. Sir John Fortescue*

For two hundred years England was governed by her country gentlemen, and it was under their guidance that the British Empire was built up. Their sons, mostly their younger sons, supplied officers to Navy and Army, and they themselves looked to the paying of the bill. They were a curious lot, of many grades and conditions. At the top were the great magnates, mostly, though not all of them, peers, but these were often mere upstarts of Henry VIII's time, and there were numbers of little squires who could and did boast of longer pedigrees and longer possession of coat-armour. The pride of all these squires was immense, and their faith in the virtue of coat-armour unquenchable. The eighteenth century was their golden age. Some never moved from their estates from year's end to year's end. The knights of the shire of course went up to London for the Parliamentary session, and the wealthier made the Grand Tour abroad, learned French and Italian and bought pictures, statuary and books. When a great magnate started for London, his horses, coaches and waggons filled the road and flooded the inns. But roads were so bad that the richest as well as the poorest made most of their journeys in the saddle.

One characteristic, which was shared by all alike, was passion for sport—and by sport I mean sport in the old sense of hunting, shooting, fishing, hawking, horse-

racing and, I suppose that I should add, cock-fighting.
Of these, hunting was the chief and the most universal.
Countless little squires possessed, if not a pack of hounds,
at least a cry of dogs, and the yeomen, farmers and
humbler folk kept up what were called trencher-fed
packs. The wild deer was the noblest quarry, and the
hare the humblest. The Norman invaders had taught the
English all about the chase of these, and the hunting-
cries, such as "Tally-ho", "Eleu", and so forth, were all
derived from the French. Moreover, though the English
had evolved their own woodcraft, distinct from the
French, the only books about sport were still translations
from the French. But the English had also evolved an
entirely new sport of their own, fox-hunting, unknown
in any other country, and the fox-hunting squire was a
favourite butt of novelists and playwrights, a character
never to be spoken of without ridicule. But in due time
there rose up a champion, William Somerville, born in
1742, who celebrated divers kinds of the chase in blank
verse and, though he chose that rather inappropriate
form for his thoughts, understood very well what he was
writing about. He was quickly succeeded by the father
of all fox-hunting literature, Peter Beckford, a Dorset-
shire squire; and with him fox-hunting acquired a new
dignity. Beckford was very remote from the type of
Squire Western. He was a good classical scholar, he was
a master of French and Italian, having travelled and
hunted in both countries—in short he was a gentleman
of culture and refinement, though there never was a
better sportsman nor a keener fox-hunter. His first
letter on hunting is dated 1779, and it is evident from its

pages that the modern foxhound was then far advanced towards perfection, and that the noble science was well understood.

For long the country-folk of all grades had their sport to themselves, and all the better sport because most of England was much less heavily enclosed than at present. It is reckoned that in the finest part of Leicestershire and Northamptonshire the number of horsemen that met the hounds did not exceed thirty. But in the cruel years which followed upon the long war that was finally concluded in 1815 at Waterloo, great changes trod quickly one upon the heels of another. Railways and macadamised roadways came in almost simultaneously to improve communications, and people were able to travel for long distances to hunt. Sir Richard Sutton, when an undergraduate, would gallop with relays of hacks from Cambridge to Leicestershire for a single day's hunting. Lord Althorp would gallop in like manner all night from the House of Commons to Northamptonshire for a day with the Pytchley. Less wealthy individuals would travel all night by coach to meet the hounds. Moreover, well-to-do tradesmen took to hunting with enthusiasm, and would steal a day from business to enjoy a run even from London in the days when Balham and Highgate were still rustic villages. The fields grew larger and larger, the votaries of hunting were multiplied; the drawing and reproduction of sporting prints became remunerative, and there were readers enough to maintain magazines devoted chiefly to sport.

But meanwhile heavy blows had been struck at the country gentlemen and at rural England at large. The

Reform Act of 1832 took the first step in depriving the country gentlemen of the government of England, and the repeal of the Corn Laws in 1846 deliberately sacrificed British agriculture to what is called industrialism and laid the country under the heel of the towns. Factories had already destroyed the village arts and crafts, and legislation as deliberately ruined British agriculture. The country squire was hurled from his high position, and he received no sympathy. He had long enjoyed power and, since all power corrupts, he had not always exerted it wisely. Moreover, a rather muddle-headed Anglo-Judaeo-Portuguese stockbroker, named David Ricardo, had laid it down that the interest of the landowner is always opposed to the interest of every other class in the community. It is true that he argued from false premises which could not fail to lead him to a false conclusion; but the foolish world loves such teachers as Ricardo and Rousseau though they are the principal causes of civil and external war.

Thus the English country gentleman, who had made England great and created that rare type which is (or used to be) known as the English gentleman, was sentenced for his pains to ruin. But the crash came gradually. Old habits and traditions kept him and his country-side, tottering indeed but standing, for a full generation after 1832 and 1846; and thus it is that in the 'sixties, despite of the spread of railways and the malignities of radical manufacturers, we can catch our last glimpse of old rural England.

The principal chroniclers of that interval (from the country gentleman's point of view) are two. The first,

Robert Smith Surtees, younger son of an old Durham family, was born in 1803 and began life as a solicitor, but before middle age succeeded to the family estate upon the death of his brother and became a squire. He opened up a new vein in following the imaginary career of a tradesman of the city of London with whom fox-hunting was a mania, and who is known even to the present generation under the name of Mr Jorrocks. Surtees was a really good sportsman, as is evinced by the one piece of excellent work that he ever did—the account of the trencher-fed pack in the opening chapters of *Handley Cross*. He knew his Beckford by heart and understood his teaching. But Surtees was first of all a satirist, and he chooses for his satire all the most unpleasant types that are to be found in the hunting world. Remembering as he did the old England that was before railways, Macadam and industrialism, he draws very bitter pictures of the successful tradesmen who had made fortunes and thrust themselves in among the country gentlemen. But he does not spare profligate peers, nor eccentric peers, and the cruellest portrait of all is that of the degenerate country squire, Mr Jawleyford. He is not less hard upon servants; and the character of Dick Bragg, of his relations with his master, Mr Puffington, who had inherited a fortune built on starch, is one of the cleverest things that he ever did. Nevertheless, Surtees's persistent preference for shady and unpleasant characters becomes monotonous. Some of them are skilfully drawn, but one feels the lack of a foil to set them off. Surtees must have known many country gentlemen and many servants of the best possible type,

but he very rarely attempts to depict them.   He is a
slovenly writer, also, who is too often content to fill up
his pages with dull vulgar trash; and a great deal of his
humour turns, as in the early work of Dickens, upon
drunkenness, which has lost its savour for the present
generation. In fact a great deal of his popularity is due
not to himself but to John Leech, whose illustrations are
really the best part of his books. And Leech pointed with
his pencil the fine distinctions which Surtees was too
lazy or too clumsy to point for himself. For instance, the
guests at Lord Bramber's are, as one can tell by a glance
at Leech's drawings, gentlemen, and Lord Bramber's
groom of the chambers is a gentleman's servant.
Contrast these with the drawings of Captain Guano
shortening his stirrup, of Charlie Slapp talking to
Frostyface, and of Spigot, the drunken old reprobate of
a butler at Jawleyford Court. When Surtees fairly gets
away with a fox he is at his best, and it is always good to
follow him. We may thank him too for much shrewd
observation of country life in his time, but, without
John Leech, an incomparably greater man, he would
have been long ago forgotten.

"By the way, have you read *Digby Grand*? Grand
book it is too." With these words in the mouth of his
favourite character, Mr Jorrocks, Surtees generously
appreciates the young writer who was to be his successor.
George Whyte-Melville, eldest son of a Scottish laird,
was born in 1821. He was educated under Hawtrey at
Eton, where he imbibed a love of Horace and, in a lesser
degree, of Homer which he cherished to the end of his
life. He joined the 93rd Highlanders after leaving Eton,

served with them in Canada, exchanged into the
Coldstream Guards and shortly afterwards, leaving the
Army, brought out his first book *Digby Grand* in 1853.
Upon the outbreak of the Crimean War he volunteered
for military service and went to the front with a corps
of irregular cavalry, but was never seriously engaged,
though he saw enough of the operations to give him
material for another book, the *Interpreter*. Then, at the
conclusion of peace, he finally renounced a military for a
literary career and poured out novel after novel, to the
number of nearly thirty in all, until while out hunting in
1878 his horse came down with him galloping over an
open field, and he was killed on the spot. His father
survived him, so that he never was a laird himself, but
no man in England knew better or loved better the
life of an English country gentleman and his favourite
diversion of fox-hunting.

Beyond all question Whyte-Melville possessed a very
considerable literary gift. He knew how to tell a story
and how to draw a character; his style was simple, easy and
correct. He knew his own tongue, not the worse for a
good knowledge of French and German, and respected it
as an honest writer should; he had abundant humour and
frequently remarkable felicity of phrase. Underlying all
were a strong tinge of romance and a vein of melancholy
and sentiment that could not be suppressed. His marriage
was not a happy one, which may have deepened his
natural sadness, but he is never bitter nor misanthropic.
He cherished always a chivalrous reverence for women
and a sympathy with his fellow-men which was
quickened by his lively sense of the ridiculous. Above all

he was always clean, and could write the life of a confirmed rake, such as Digby Grand, without dwelling
upon doubtful incidents. Modern readers will no doubt
wax impatient over the long pages of moralisation which
interrupted his narrative, and some will fret over the
frequent quotations from Horace which are scattered all
over his pages. But such things were expected of a
novelist in those days. Every intelligent boy learned the
Odes of Horace by heart in those days as, for that matter,
I and my contemporaries did thirty years later; so that the
lines came very readily to his tongue. His heroes generally
come to a good end and sooner or later marry the
woman they love, and his villains, some of them very
genial villains, are not too hardly punished; but their
careers are traced with very shrewd knowledge of human
nature. Once, in *Market Harborough*, he follows Surtees
in sketching the adventures of a country squire whose
morality, in the matter of horseflesh, was extremely
doubtful. "He delighted in a five to two sort of hat, with
a flat brim and a backward set, which denote indis-
putable knowledge of horseflesh and a sagacity that
almost amounts to dishonesty." But Whyte-Melville,
unlike Surtees, introduces real gentlemen as a foil to this
individual; and when his hero sells to one of these
gentlemen a brute of a horse for four times its value,
Whyte-Melville contrives a delightful form of retribu-
tion. This book, which turns wholly upon fox-hunting,
is probably the only one of his works that still lives, being
much esteemed by hunting-men for its shrewd wit and
bubbling humour.

More than once Whyte-Melville essayed historical

novels, without great success. He stumbled into the pitfalls which always await the amateur historian, as when he made Cromwell drill the Ironsides according to the drill-book of 1842 instead of 1642, not apparently realising that there was any difference between the two. He is far happier when he writes of the society in which he lived and moved all his life, well-to-do folk who had houses and hunters in the country and another house and hacks in London. In fact he is the only novelist of his time, or since, who writes with conviction about ladies and gentlemen, for he was one of the few writers who knew them by heart as being one of themselves. The world of the novel and the stage is thickly populated with titled folk of every degree, but they are mere puppets and lack the intimate touches which make them real. Whyte-Melville, indeed, was less a novelist than a country gentleman who wrote novels. Without being wealthy he was comfortable and could afford to live and hunt without the help of his pen. I have been assured by one who knew him that he was never really well mounted; but if he were satisfied with his horses that was his own affair. Modest and unassuming he gave himself no airs as an author, though every new book of his found an instant place upon every drawing-room table in the West End. He mixed in no literary society, for he was first of all a country gentleman with a passionate love of horses and hunting, and he preferred to live among his own kind. It was supposed by his friends that he wrote only for his amusement, and one of them once confided to me, with an air of some bewilderment, that he had it from George Melville himself that writing a novel was very hard work. Whyte-Melville certainly published a great many volumes in twenty-five years, and latterly he visited hunting countries that were new to him—Ireland and Exmoor for instance—to gather material for fresh books. He must have made first and last many thousands of pounds by his literary labours, but he gave every penny of it to charities and benevolent institutions connected with hunting. Altogether he is something of a curiosity in the literary world.

But his sketches of the circle in which he lived are most interesting. Let us glance at them first in London. It was a London in which everyone—even pedestrians— paid toll to cross Waterloo Bridge; where Piccadilly and St James's Street were paved like Hay Hill and the clatter of the traffic was appalling; where the turnpike-gate at Hyde Park Corner was still standing or had only just been removed, and where the railings round Hyde Park were no bigger than those round Berkeley Square until they were pulled down by a mob (I remember seeing the wreck of them next day) and replaced by the present, so deeply entrenched and firmly established as to defy any mob in the world. To such a London a few hundred families migrated from the country in May, and till the middle of July the West End hummed like a beehive. Beautiful carriages and beautiful horses thronged the streets, and in some of the narrower thoroughfares the block of traffic was almost modern. The rule of the road was not too carefully observed, but good coachmanship saved accidents. Rotten Row was given up exclusively to riders of both sexes, for the most part excellently mounted, and the footways were

thronged with men, all members of the same exclusive
society, who came to see and admire. Then in the evening
appeared the family coaches, gorgeous in heraldic
ornament, with a cocked-hatted coachman on the
hammer-cloth and two cocked-hatted footmen behind,
all in resplendent liveries; and away rolled the pleasure-
seekers to dinners, theatres, operas, balls or drums. There
were always fine horses in those coaches, for without
any load of human beings they weighed thirty hundredweight. London was worth seeing in the season in
those days.

One of Whyte-Melville's heroines, Kate Coventry,
exults in the fact that she lived in Lowndes Street, in
which rustic neighbourhood she could go out into the
adjacent market gardens unattended; and she protests
like any modern girl against the conventions that for-
bade her to move about London at large without a
chaperon or a protector of some kind. She forgot, as
modern girls forget, that until the Metropolitan Police
were formed in 1829 London was an exceedingly
dangerous place, and, though the streets might have
been safe in her mother's time, there were still the old
traditions of peril carefully preserved by her grand-
mother and great-aunts. The female sex is extremely self-
assertive in these days, but it never occurs to them that
they could not be so without the police. And the police
in the 'sixties had just thrown off their original tall hats
and blue coatees in favour of the modern helmet (for a
short time a combed helmet) and tunic.

Gentlemen at that time were infinitely better turned
out in London than at present, and they rode all over

London, on their business or their pleasure. Two old gentlemen continued this habit into the 'nineties, when they were both octogenarians, but they were obliged to yield to the traffic at last. In the 'sixties mounted grooms could be seen all over Mayfair and Belgravia holding their masters' horses (often very handsome horses) before the doors which their masters had entered, and there used to be a crowd of them round the Houses of Parliament when in session. Members of both houses even then were most of them good sportsmen according to the old tradition. Of the older statesmen Lord Althorp has already been mentioned; but Sir Robert Peel had been mad about partridge-shooting; Lord John Russell was above the average both as a horseman and a shot, and Lord Derby was an enthusiast over racing.

For the rest, the chief personal preoccupation of women was bonnets and of men whiskers. Both have vanished for the moment, but in old masculine dressing-cases there may still sometimes be found the mysterious instrument called a bostrokizon (a tiny metal comb in a neat metal cylinder) which was used for whisker-curling. Curled whiskers, however, were going out in the 'sixties, though I remember one pair that survived until the 'nineties.

So these migrants from the country held on from May until July, never, however, losing touch with the country. Their flowers, fruit and vegetables were all sent up from their own gardens, and they shrank from the produce of Covent Garden Market with suspicion and disgust. Some, who had boys at school, lingered on to the end of

July, but before August all with one accord rushed back joyfully to their homes in the country, quite content to stay there, with little if any diversion or variety, until the following May.

The West End became a dismal wilderness of closed houses and silent streets, and the sentries before St James's Palace and Marlborough House had St James's Street and Pall Mall almost to themselves. The annual artificial life of "society" in the town was over, and the natural life in the country had begun. There was still a rural England in the 'sixties. Railways had thrust their hideous tentacles deeply into much of it. Industrial mechanics had killed out the old village arts and crafts. Agriculture, though sick unto death, was not yet dead. There was still a village life and a provincial town life. The little market towns had all of them their two or three little local banks which issued their own notes; and in those notes, much soiled and greased by wear, farmers of the old school still paid their rents. The bank managers and the town attorney were nearly always good sports- men, keen riders with the hounds when they could give themselves a holiday, and sometimes very good shots. The parson and the doctor were of much the same stamp; and all alike talked the local dialect. If their plate included no more than a few silver spoons, they possessed instead beautiful cut glass, which was the pride of their hearts; and some of them could trace descent from old- established families.

As to the villages, each possessed, besides a black- smith, a tailor and a cobbler, at least a rat-catcher, a mole- catcher and a thatcher, for the beautiful craft of thatching had not yet been displaced by abominations of purple slate and corrugated iron. The agricultural labourer knew his business, which is far more varied than ignorant townsmen suppose. In these days unfortunately he too often does not. Half the young fellows in the country now do not know how to hang a gate or how to make a faggot-binder; and indeed it needs a real craftsman to make a binder out of brittle material such as laurel. But the old agricultural labourer was a master of his profession in all of its branches and, though occasionally even in the 'sixties he could not read or write, he was none the less a highly educated man. As Cobbett very truly said, a man who can drive a straight furrow is an educated man. This mastery of his calling gave the agricultural labourer a natural dignity and courtesy, for he respected himself and looked for respect from others. Of course there were many varieties of him, good and bad, but perhaps he was seen at his best on the estate of some good squire, whose family, like his own, had lived on the same spot for generations. He was condemned by radical townsmen as servile because he punctiliously saluted the squire and all of his family, and brought up his boys to take off their caps and his girls to drop a curtsey even to the youngest of them. But there was no servility in this. There was only courtesy, and a courtesy which was as courteously returned. Nowadays too many people think that they can only assert their independence by familiarity or sheer incivility; and this is only a form of snobbishness. These country-folk were not snobs but nature's gentlemen.

An English gentleman—the phrase is little understood

now though once so potent. "I told him", said the old Duke of Wellington when a slight was put upon him by King Louis XVIII, "that not only was I Commander-in-Chief of the Allied Armies of occupation etc., etc., but that, *more than that*, I was an English gentleman." So too in our military code misconduct is not merely a military affair, it is "conduct unbecoming an officer and a gentleman". "It takes three generations to make a gentleman", says a proverb attributed to Sir Robert Peel. "Three generations from clog to clog", echoes the proverb of Manchester. What is an English gentleman? He is (or was) something which can hardly be defined and certainly cannot be imitated. Peers of the realm are scattered broadcast over our drama and our literature of fiction; but rarely does one find (outside the pages of Whyte-Melville) the portrait of an English gentleman. Let Whyte-Melville give his own definition:

"My own idea", he says, "is that neither birth, nor riches, nor education, nor manners suffice to constitute a gentleman, and that specimens are to be found at the plough, the loom, the forge, in the ranks, before the mast, as well as in the officers' messrooms, the learned professions and the Upper House itself. A gentleman is courteous, kindly, brave and high-principled, considerate towards the weak and self-possessed among the strong. High-minded and unselfish, he does to others as he would they should do unto him, and shrinks from the meanness of taking advantage of his neighbour, man or woman, friend or foe, as he would from the contamination of cowardice, duplicity, tyranny or any other blackguardism."

By no means all squires came up to this standard and

by no means all labourers, but there were many fine
specimens of gentlemen in all ranks—squires, parsons,
yeomen, farmers and labourers. Moreover, there was
nothing in the training of the old village schools to
hinder the continual production of gentlemen in the
labouring class. The old-fashioned schoolmaster understood that reading and writing are only a small part of a
man's education, and that equality is but a mathematical
abstraction, having no existence in nature. He trained
his children for service, which is the duty of us all; and in
those days the most welcome career to village boys and
girls, as a rule, was domestic service in the "great house".
There, if they were steady, diligent and intelligent, they
could rise to be house-stewards, butlers and house-
keepers, well fed, well housed and well cared for. Sometimes they stayed in the same place for life. Sometimes
they were advanced by promotion to the household of
some relation or some friend, and might so pass into
a wider circle. Their masters and mistresses took an
interest in them and were proud and happy when they
did well. The best of them ended less as servants than as
trusted and treasured friends, whose death or retirement
caused not merely sorrow but consternation in the family
with which they lived. Since they had no expenses they
could save money—I knew one who had honestly
amassed £9000—and frequently some couple of them
would marry and keep lodgings. Mount Street, Mayfair,
before it was rebuilt in its present form, was full of such
lodgings where ladies and gentlemen from the country
could find hosts and hostesses who understood their ways
and needs. The modern idea that domestic service is

degrading is mere snobbishness. Servants of the old stamp, being natural ladies and gentlemen, would have scorned to entertain it.

And so we come to the special charm of the English country-side—sixty or seventy years ago—its comparative freedom from vulgarity. The country-folk were content to give to others that respect which they gave to themselves, and being natural and simple they eschewed all shadow of pretention. The women thought none the worse of themselves because they wore pattens at home and sun-bonnets abroad, nor the men because the smartest addition which they made to their daily wear of fustian was a coloured plush waistcoat. On Sundays they went to church or chapel, the women in bonnet, shawl and sober-coloured skirts, the men in black broadcloth and tall hats inherited from their forbears; and there were always musicians enough to form a little band which led the hymns from the gallery. The parson donned the surplice for the service and his black gown for the sermon before the eyes of the congregation, and, for all that he might be a scholar and a gentleman, very often spoke in good county dialect. There were of course good and bad—even very bad—parsons, but nearly every one, good or bad, kept a horse, and there were few who did not from time to time use that horse as a hunter. Many were right good sportsmen and not the less acceptable to every one of their parishioners upon that account. There were some who gave themselves up excessively to hunting but these were not the least popular with all ranks in the country. Women are said to love a priest, but men love a man.

And here I pass to a striking characteristic of those days, the part played by the horse in the life of man. Cycles, then called velocipedes, were still in their infancy, and bicycles (then made of wood) were seen, if seen at all, at circuses and the like displays. Railways had not so many branches as at present and the horse still held his own. Everyone above the rank of labourer had—or seemed to have—a horse of some kind. The village cobbler frequently had a pony, and even the rat-catcher contrived to ride some miserable old beast. The saddle was still the favourite means of locomotion. The squire rode to his highway boards, petty sessions and quarter sessions; the doctor rode the round of his patients, though sometimes he preferred a gig; the bank manager rode out to farms before granting overdrafts; the lawyer rode out to his clients with the draft will in his pocket, and the parson rode round his parish. Some old gentlemen rode out to dine and sleep with their dress-clothes in saddle-bags, and turned out spotless for dinner like the old fellow in *Mr Romford's Hounds*. No one who has seen a pair of old saddle-bags (good saddle-bags were a matter of *cut* quite as truly as a frock-coat) will feel any surprise at this. Briefly there were more horsemen than drivers on the road, and among them were the extinct race of postilions.

When branch railways were still few, posting was the usual way of traversing the long distances from railway station to country house. Any little inn in any little town would turn out a pair of horses and a postilion— clad generally in a light blue jacket with many metal buttons and a black velvet cap. I remember as a boy seeing a newly married couple drive off in a barouche with four grey horses and two postilions in light drab jackets and tall white silk hats—all supplied by a neighbouring inn. Postilions, supplemented by out-riders, were equally common in private houses. These always wore the same smart short jackets, whether with a pair of horses or with four. Sir Peregrine Grand, the pompous old father of Whyte-Melville's Digby Grand, thought it beneath his dignity ever to drive out with fewer than four horses; and in great houses postilions and four were a matter of every day. Now it is rare to see postilions except in the royal carriages. Probably it would be hard to find a young fellow (unless trained in the Army) who knows how to ride-and-drive. Few people would recognise a postilion's whip or understand its peculiar properties if they saw it.

The all-pervading use of the horse led to a courtesy of the road which has for the present disappeared. The essence of that courtesy was that every man thought not only of his neighbour but of his neighbour's horse. Any rider who saw a piece of broken glass in the road would dismount and throw it into the ditch. Some would do as much for a single loose stone, knowing that it might throw a horse down in the dark, and would soundly rate any carter who put a stone under his wheel and left it in the middle of the road. All alike respected a rider with a led horse, and were careful to pass him on the side where the led horse was not. The young were taught to behave themselves on the road whether riding or driving, and to beware of three principal dangers—a pig, a cow and an old woman. The most awkward thing occasionally encountered on the road was a travelling menagerie with walking elephants and camels, for even if you got your horses safely past the elephants they were sure to shy at the scent of the camels. But such obstacles were rare and were not enough to disturb the courtesy of the road. That courtesy was first upset by the bicyclists, who, being townsmen, were very lax in observing the rule of the road, and, until they became familiar to horses, always made them shy. Bicyclists learned manners after a time, and it is to be hoped that motorists may do likewise.

Such was, very briefly, the country to which members of "society" returned after the intoxicating life of the London season. How they rode and hunted and danced at county balls may be read abundantly in the pages of Whyte-Melville. What he does not describe so fully was possibly less familiar to him. But, on reaching home, the girl who was besieged by partners in every London ballroom sought out instantly all of her humble friends in the village, heard their news and told them her own, bringing little delicacies for the sick, toys for the children, and a cheering presence to the aged and the suffering. And the rest of her family, parents, brothers and sisters, were not behind her in this courteous service. For it was not what is called charity or benevolence which led them (and happily in some places still leads them) to this duty, but the obligation of courtesy towards old and valued friends, an obligation far more binding than that of leaving cards at a London house where she had danced during the night before. No two classes understand each other so well as the so-called highest and lowest in rural

England, for none have more feelings and sympathies in common.

That understanding urban agitators have for the best part of a century been striving in the name of progress to undo. The matter is beyond their comprehension, and they therefore distrust it. There is only one thing which beyond all question has made most lamentable progress in my time, and that is vulgarity. Townspeople, utterly void of courtesy and dignity, are more than ever pervading the rural districts, destroying all that is left of those qualities among the country people, and reducing them from the old status of natural gentlefolk to their own degrading level. Many doubtless will rejoice in the fact. I am old fashioned enough to regret it. "It takes three generations to make a gentleman"; and it is a sad thought to me that the good old type of countryman may be extinct for a full century, if it be not extinguished altogether. But I am happy at least in having seen and known it, and in the prospect of being before long delivered from the pain of seeing the world made safe for that most unsafe and lowering of influences, vulgarity.

SCIENCE IN THE 'SIXTIES

By *Sir Oliver Lodge*

Just before the 'sixties began, *The Origin of Species* was published: that was in the year 1859; and the 'sixties accordingly reverberated with the controversies aroused by that work. The end of the 'sixties was marked by the inauguration of the important weekly paper called *Nature*, which took the whole of physical science, including the various departments of Biology, for its province, and is a recognised organ through the continents of Europe and America. The first number appeared in 1869, with an Introductory Article by Thomas Henry Huxley, in which he quoted the aphorisms of Goethe with keen approbation. This was a rhapsody on the subject of Nature; and Huxley said it had been a delight to him from his youth up, and that

no more fitting preface could be put before a Journal, which aims to mirror the progress of that fashioning by Nature of a picture of herself, in the mind of man, which we call the progress of Science. A translation, to be worth anything, should reproduce the words, the sense, and the form of the original. But when that original is Goethe's, it is hard indeed to obtain this ideal....Supposing, however, that critical judges are satisfied with the translation as such, there lies beyond them the chance of another reckoning with the British public, who dislike what they call "Pantheism" almost as much as I do, and who will certainly find this essay of the poet's terribly Pantheistic.

Goethe himself admits something of the kind, for he says that the paper was written between 1780 and 1790, when he was himself chiefly occupied with Comparative Anatomy, the metamorphosis of plants, and the theory of the skull. He says:

> There is an obvious inclination to a sort of Pantheism, to the conception of an unfathomable unconditional humorously self-contradictory Being underlying the phenomena of Nature; and it may pass as a jest, with a bitter truth in it. If we consider the high achievements by which all the phenomena of Nature have been gradually linked together in the human mind; and then, once more, thoughtfully peruse the above essay, from which we started, we shall, not without a smile, compare that comparative, as I called it, with the superlative which we have now reached, and rejoice in the progress of fifty years.

To this Huxley adds:

> Forty years have passed since these words were written, and we look again, "not without a smile", on Goethe's superlative. But the road which led from his comparative to his superlative has been diligently followed, until the notions which represented Goethe's superlative are now the commonplaces of science—and we have a super-superlative of our own.

And he predicts that

> When another half-century has passed, curious readers of the back numbers of Nature will probably look on our best, "not without a smile"; and, it may be, that long after the theories of the philosophers whose achievements are recorded in these pages are obsolete, the vision of the poet will remain as a truthful and efficient symbol of the wonder and the mystery of Nature.

Well, there are certain things in the science of the 'sixties on which we can look back with a smile; for instance, in the very first number of *Nature* there is an article by Norman Lockyer on a solar eclipse, in which he seriously contemplates the suggestion that the solar corona may be an illusion due to a lunar atmosphere; and he hails the application of the spectroscope to Astronomy as a revolutionary novelty, which no doubt it was.

But there are things in the science of the 'sixties at which this generation can by no means afford to smile. We recognise there the beginnings of great developments both in Pure and in Applied Science. Indeed, the two departments have worked hand in hand. Sometimes an engineering application demands a theoretical advance in knowledge: sometimes a theoretical discovery bears as its fruit a revolutionary practical application. I propose to take a concrete instance of an example of both these remarkable developments.

In 1857 the first Atlantic cable was laid; but it only lasted a few weeks, being destroyed by the electrical ignorance of that generation. Then there entered on the scene William Thomson, Professor of Natural Philosophy at Glasgow, who, with a European reputation in Mathematical Physics and all manner of achievements to his credit, turned his attention to the problems of cable telegraphy. He showed that signalling under the ocean was a very different problem from signalling across land. A thin wire separated by a narrow insulator from the ocean, over a length of two thousand miles, had problems which had never been faced or contemplated by the old telegraphists. He showed that the problem was something like trying to signal along a bar of metal by applying heat and cold alternately at one end, and watching the fluctuations of a thermometer at the other. The problem of the conduction of heat had been worked out by Fourier with wonderful skill, in what Thomson and other good judges considered a mathematical poem, and Thomson applied this poetico-mathematical treatment of the diffusion of heat to the problem of telegraphy through a submarine cable. A type of cable necessary and sufficient was designed and constructed in accordance with his theory. Instruments of surpassing delicacy were designed to receive the signals: tests were devised which could be applied at every stage of the proceedings, and signals were arranged so that they could be sent all the time it was being laid. The whole length of cable was manufactured near the mouth of the Thames, was then coiled up in large tanks in "The Great Eastern", which had been gutted for the purpose, and was the only ship big enough to take it; and so in 1865 it was laid, not without accident and much anxiety. The cable on that occasion never reached the American coast, but the expedition returned full of hope and with the certainty of ultimate success, so that in 1866 it started again with another cable on board, and, meeting with no misadventures, succeeded in uniting the two continents for the first time in a permanent manner.

Then came a remarkable part of the epic, namely an attempt to grapple with and pick up the 1865 cable, which lay broken two miles down on the bottom of the Atlantic. It was found, it was hauled up, it was spliced to another length, and thus that cable was completed too.

The captain of "The Great Eastern" became Sir James Anderson, the chief financial supporter became Sir John Pender, Professor William Thomson of Glasgow became Sir William Thomson, subsequently known to this generation as Lord Kelvin; and America and England have never since been separated.

This was an engineering and navigational and scientific triumph of the eighteen-sixties. For in those days electrical science was in its infancy. Measurement, on which everything depended, was extraordinarily difficult: there were no units in which to measure things. Physical agents do not lend themselves readily to measurement: the only things that can naturally be measured are discrete things that occur in units that can be counted. There is no counting to be done on a physical quantity that has the property of continuity: it must be split up into artificial units first. There was no recognised unit for an electric current or electrical pressure in those days. The idea of electrical capacity was new in engineering, and self-induction had not been born. Indeed, that last was a later development, not taken account of in Sir William Thomson's theory, but applied in modern times with great results by the more complete theory of electric cable signalling, due to the genius of Oliver Heaviside. A British Association Committee however had been appointed to consider the question of electrical standards. It continued its labours for many years, and to it we owe the nomenclature, the specification, and many of the modes of measurement of those things which are now familiar household words, the ohm, the volt, the ampere, and the microfarad. Those terms have been suggested and adopted all in my own lifetime: they represent as it were the outer husks which are apparent enough even to those who know nothing of the kernel inside them, and have no suspicion of the immense amount of skilled work which has gone to their exact determination.

The profession of electrical engineering was not born in the 'sixties: it was beginning however as the outcome of cable enterprise; The Institution of Electrical Engineers was still called The Society of Telegraph Engineers. There were no other engineers dealing with electricity, for the practical dynamo had not yet been made, though the discovery on which it was founded had been made in 1831. The first practical dynamo appeared in the 'seventies; the first electric railway and electric lighting began in the early 'eighties. By that time the electrical engineering profession had been well established, and a great body of knowledge accumulated, which enables us to look back at the early efforts of the pioneers with a respectful smile.

So far for the applications of physical science, which have so largely revolutionised the ordinary processes of life. Now let us turn to the pure science, and especially the science of mathematical physics. Here the developments have been prodigious and most extraordinary, and if we look back to the science of the 'sixties in this department, it is not with a smile that we look back, it is rather with a feeling of wonder akin to worship; for the 'sixties were undoubtedly dominated by the end of Michael Faraday, and the climax of Clerk Maxwell.

These two geniuses differed, about as widely as

possible. Faraday lived in his laboratory, was constantly making experiments, and was in touch at first hand with the phenomena of Nature that he was investigating. Maxwell, on the other hand, when he took up the subject of electricity and magnetism, had hardly made an experiment in it. He had been soaked in mathematics from his youth up, and had a most extraordinary genius in dealing with them. He took up the facts from Faraday's researches, he laid down certain equations as expressing the ideas which Faraday had dissected out; and these equations have become the wonder and the admiration of the world. They have not been superseded, they are alive to this day. They are at the basis of nearly all the discoveries that have since been made. The doctrines of Relativity and the Quantum have been grafted on to them, and now seem fairly secure, though they have not yet been finally interpreted.

I wish it were possible to give to men of letters some idea of the extraordinary Memoir which Maxwell published in 1865, the very middle of our period. It aroused interest at once, but was not understood on the Continent till much later; nor was it welcomed in every quarter even here. Not till the year 1888 did it finally come into its own. Maxwell, alas! died in 1879, at the age of 48; but some of us had already recognised the magnitude of his work and the brilliance of his generalisation.

It may be asked why a discovery of this magnitude was received so silently; in fact it was not really "received" at all. No one knew anything about it except a few students of science. This calls attention to a great change

which has come over the spirit of the scene. Einstein's
discovery was no more important, indeed it may be
questioned whether it was of equal magnitude: it was
certainly no more easily understood, and yet it aroused
public interest, and is referred to in all the newspapers.
In the 'sixties the Press and the public were asleep in the
scientific direction; they didn't expect anything sensa-
tional, they didn't expect even anything that they could
understand from science; and accordingly, except when
there was some practical application to be made, they
took no notice. Now, at the smallest hint of a discovery,
they are all agog, and are constantly writing or tele-
phoning to know more about it. They have no means of
discriminating between what is of value and what is not,
so that they are sometimes misled into advertising mares'
nests or very feeble speculations; but undoubtedly the
interest of the public in science is well maintained, and the
activity of the Press in that direction is admirable. But
in the 'sixties a great genius like Clerk Maxwell could
come and go without making any impression except on
a few scientific students. A press reporter seldom knows
how to spell his name. Electrical science has been
revolutionised; but not till now has a Literary Society
desired to hear more about the science of the 'sixties.
The reason no doubt is partly due to an increase of
general interest; but the main cause must be that there
was then no skilled expositor; in fact very few people
thought of expounding the results of scientific investigation in language intelligible to the general public.
Maxwell himself was content with having written for
posterity, and for the few students who could read his

recondite work. Even Sir William Thomson never properly assimilated it. In 1888, nearly a quarter of a century later, he was walking about the streets of Bath with a Maxwell volume under his arm, and getting FitzGerald to explain some points in it. He never really became a full disciple, though the beginnings of Maxwell's work were due to Thomson's own initiative. But Sir William was an exceptional man, who found it easier to work out things for himself than to read other people's work. Certainly FitzGerald understood Maxwell: so did Oliver Heaviside. Fleming and I understood him partially. We were at that time (about 1871) both students of Chemistry at South Kensington. It was about the time Maxwell had been appointed First Professor of Physics at Cambridge under the endowment of the Duke of Devonshire, and Fleming went to Cambridge to work under him. But we never thought then of expounding the doctrine in public; nor were we ever asked to do so. On the Continent there were rival theories, and Maxwell's never became properly known till long afterwards. The work of Hertz twenty years later made it familiar in scientific circles, but the public only awoke when Mr Marconi and Sir William Preece went about the country demonstrating an application of it, and then the public made the mistake of attributing not only the enterprising application but everything to Marconi, and assuming that that was the beginning as well as the fruition of the long-continued growth.

In Biology it was not quite the same. Darwin had no sooner written his book (in 1859) than Huxley waxed enthusiastic and promulgated his doctrine, using his great literary skill for that purpose. It needed a man of letters to make Darwin's discovery known, and controversies about it dominated the 'sixties.

At the present day it happens that people are sometimes their own expositors, and have the gift of writing not only severely and mathematically, but also to some extent popularly. Thus, Einstein would not have been known but for Eddington, who has caught the ear of the public, and has gone on to speculative results which seem to be absorbed by the philosophers. Jeans also, in spite of his great power in Physics and Mathematics, has not scrupled to popularise his views in books which have become best-sellers. The Press and the public are now keen for information in all sorts of directions; and men of letters have decided to make use of such expository powers as they can find distributed in the ranks of science, to understand a little more of the meaning and scope of it all. Which brings me back to the present day.

Perhaps now I ought to take advantage of this singular opportunity of addressing men of letters and try to expound the work of Faraday and Maxwell, which came to a climax theoretically in 1865. We realise that their achievement lent a special glory to the science of the 'sixties. Faraday had devised a non-mathematical mode of expressing the conditions in space, by surrounding the electrified and magnetised bodies he experimented on with what he called lines of force. These mapped out the region round the conductors or the magnets, so as to indicate at every point the direction of the force there; and when the lines were drawn or imagined in a systematic way, the intensity of the field was also indicated by the closeness of the lines. The importance of this mode of regarding the matter was that it diverted attention from the visible things which could be handled in the laboratory, and had hitherto received an undue amount of attention, and concentrated attention on the empty or vacuous space near them. It was in this space that all the phenomena really occurred. The visible and tangible objects were only the indications, their movements were only the appreciable outcome, of something otherwise unperceived and imperceptible. In Faraday's philosophy "matter" began to be put in its proper place, as the thing which our senses took notice of, but which itself had no activity and was entirely inert.

I have developed this doctrine since, in various ways, and have applied it not only to Physics and Chemistry but to Biology likewise; but I trace the beginnings of it to Faraday. Space, or something in space which made no appeal to the senses and was commonly called emptiness or vacuum, was the really important thing in which everything occurred. There lies all the energy, there the activity, and whatever spontaneity there may be. Maxwell took hold of these lines of force in space, threw them into a mathematical form, and then juggled with the representations of both the electric and the magnetic lines. He found that when they were superposed upon each other, so that they both affected the same region of space, that space was inevitably affected by a periodic disturbance of an unknown kind, which travelled at a rate that could be calculated from the electrical and magnetic constants, and which fell into the class of

phenomena that were called waves. We knew very little
about these waves beyond their speed of travel, we could
not even say that there was any motion in them, all we were
sure of was that the disturbance was electric on the one
hand, magnetic on the other, and that the two disturbances
were exactly in phase, and at right angles to one another.

I have said that Maxwell devised a mathematical
scheme for expressing Faraday's idea about the field of
force. Indeed, he invented a special function for this
purpose which he called "curl". Expressed in words, it
may be said that directly electricity is in motion, in
other words wherever there is an electric current, that
current has to flow in a closed circuit, and the circuit
is wrapped or curled round by magnetic lines of force.
You cannot have an electric current without such lines.
But the relation is a reciprocal one; wherever there are
magnetic lines of force they are curled or wrapped round
by an electric current of some kind. This is not obvious
in the case of a permanent magnet; but Ampère surmised
molecular electric currents which operated in that case;
and these satisfied the law. There is thus a reciprocal
relation between an electric current and a magnetic
field, one is the *curl* of the other; and when Maxwell put
the two mathematical equations together which expressed these facts, so as to get the curl of a curl, he found
that they combined into another equation which he
recognised at once as the familiar equation to a *wave*.
When I say familiar, it is a differential equation which
conveys no meaning to ordinary people, but to a
mathematician is luminous. It does not tell you in the
least what sort of wave it is, it only says that the dis-

turbance represented is something periodic in space and
time, which travels through space at a rate determined by
one of the factors; everything else is arbitrary. It may be
of any energy, any wave-length, and in general of any
speed. The speed of a wave may easily depend on the
wave-length, but the equation arrived at by Maxwell
through a study of the electromagnetic field was not of
that kind; the speed was absolutely constant for all wave-
lengths, so long as the medium was unchanged, being
thus more like the waves of sound or of light than the
waves on the surface of the sea. He surmised that these
electromagnetic waves had some relation to light, since
they existed in the ether.

He then set to work to make experiments to determine
the electric constants involved. There were two, one
was the old Faraday constant called "specific inductive
capacity" or the dielectric constant, commonly denoted
by K, and the other was a magnetic constant, recently
introduced into the science by Sir William Thomson,
under the name "magnetic permeability", denoted by μ.
Maxwell found from his wave equation that the rate at
which the energy was transmitted was the reciprocal of
the geometric mean of these two constants, or $1/\sqrt{(K\mu)}$.
He could not measure either of these two constants of
space themselves, so as to determine their real value, nor
did he know of what nature the quantities were that
were thus denoted: one was called electric, and the other
was called magnetic, but those names were no help to
any philosophic contemplation of their nature.

Still we are in ignorance about these two constants:
I have made guesses at their nature, and even at their

value, but guesses are of no use in science unless they are confirmed; and at present there is no serious confirmation: they are still unknown to this day. But Maxwell found that, though they could not be determined separately, their product might be measured. To do this you would have to measure a charge electrostatically, and also to measure it as a current when the charged body was discharged. No, it is not quite like that. Two spirals of wire were taken, so that when a current was sent through each in opposite directions they would repel each other; and yet if they were mounted on plates oppositely charged by the voltage which drove the current through the coils, they would attract. In other words, there was an electric attraction and a magnetic repulsion: and it might be possible to adjust these so that they should be equal, or at any rate have a measured ratio to each other.

Somewhat on that plan the experiment was designed, and was carried out so as to measure the product of the two space or ether constants. The reciprocal of the square root of the product of the two constants, which Maxwell had shown to be a velocity, came out astonishingly near to the velocity of light. Every experiment since made has confirmed that to the hilt. The rate of transmission of the waves thus discovered, due to the superposition of an electric and magnetic field, is simply the velocity with which light is transmitted through empty space. Immediately the supposition jumped to the mind that that might be exactly what light was, that light was not a mechanical disturbance as had previously been thought, that the ether which conveyed it was not an elastic solid, or had any other mechanical properties such as the nineteenth century had endeavoured to foist upon it, but that it transmitted light simply and solely because it had the unknown properties which we call electric and magnetic. Light was truly a periodic or wave phenomenon, but its waves were unlike any other wave; they were in their intimate nature composed of two oscillations, one electric, at right angles to the plane of polarisation, the other, perpendicular to the first, in the plane of polarisation. Moreover, there must be a close relation between the refractive index of any medium and its dielectric constant. Conductors of electricity must be opaque. All this followed. Optics became a branch of Electricity and Magnetism, so that Electricity became an imperial science.

This great discovery, now clearly and fully elaborated, was only partially made, because it had never been experimentally confirmed. Nobody knew how to produce such waves. Some doubted if it would ever be possible to make them. It seems odd to say that now, when these waves are all about us, bringing with them speech and music from all parts of the earth, crossing and recrossing without any interference, penetrating our buildings, travelling round the earth to the Antipodes, received by ships at sea and by lonely lighthouses, a means of conveying intelligence all over the world. But then we knew nothing of all that. Some of us were anxious to find a means of generating the waves, and many devices were thought of. G. F. FitzGerald of Dublin got very near to it. He reckoned that such waves would be emitted by any alternating current; but when you came to reckon the energy that would be lost from any alternating dynamo, you found it utterly insignificant. Only when the vibrations were excessively rapid, comparable to several million per second, could you expect to get an appreciable amount of energy.

So we tried the oscillations of a Leyden jar, which had the desired frequency, and we saw signs of the waves running along wires. But at the same time Heinrich Hertz at Carlsruhe, though he then knew much less of Maxwell's theory, was conducting an investigation suggested to him by Von Helmholtz, and was finding a phenomenon akin to waves in the neighbourhood of an electric discharge, by means of the little sparks which they generated when absorbed. He in fact made the discovery of Maxwell's waves in space, he generated light; for in all essentials it was light, except that the waves were several yards long instead of only the fraction of an inch. I say he generated light for the first time, knowing what he was doing. Hitherto all artificial light had been generated blindfold: a body had been made hot, and when it was hot enough it gave out light for reasons unknown. The waves emitted from a discharged conductor were exactly of the same nature, only instead of oscillating five hundred million million times a second, as the light does which affects our eyes, the oscillations were only a few million a second, and therefore had to be detected in some other way.

But I must not go into all that, since it belongs to the 'eighties and 'nineties, not to the 'sixties. But the root of the matter is in the 'sixties, as Hertz soon found. He gradually absorbed Maxwell's theory, and found that it would account for everything he had observed. And to this day in wireless telegraphy we detect either the magnetic or the electric oscillation, whichever we like; they are both equal in energy; the electric is collected by a vertical wire, the magnetic by a coil set so as to utilise the oscillation which is at right angles to the electric disturbance. Maxwell's waves have received their apotheosis; they travel with the speed of light, they are reflected and refracted in accordance with optical laws, they are polarised, they produce interference phenomena, they do everything that light does, except that they are of length too long to be visible to the eye, or to affect photographic plates.

But in speaking of wireless telegraphy we are descending once more to practical applications. The glory of Maxwell's achievement in the 'sixties is not the use that has been made of it, but the extraordinary power and intuition which dissected out the laws of electric and magnetic behaviour, and expressed Faraday's results in immortal equations, which have survived the test of time. These are the first steps towards understanding the true nature of the ether and of that etheric disturbance which brings us information from the most distant parts of the universe; an etheric disturbance which we, having a special sense organ for it, have known and been familiar with ever since humanity existed.

Looking backward is comparatively easy, we can pick out from our memories those doctrines that had a lasting effect and really contributed to the advance of knowledge, and can ignore the others. But looking forward is much more precarious. Among the crowd of new theories which are springing up under recognised authority, are we to accept them all as current coin of real value? I feel it would be rash. Heisenberg's doctrine of uncertainty, for instance, with which great play has been made, is of somewhat limited scope. Some have used it to seek some physical justification for the admission of an element of contingency amid physical phenomena, such as has been held to justify scientifically the psychical experience of free will. It is held that strict determinism vanishes from physical science, or that the law of causation may have gaps in it, when we come to deal with the smallest particles; so that their subsequent action can never be predicted, because we are inherently unable to ascertain and specify all the circumstances of their state. The attempt to ascertain those facts inevitably modifies them, I agree. They straightway become different, and the difference is in an unknown direction; apparently the result must be controlled by pure chance so far as our measurements apply. The application of light to an electron, in order to see it in a microscope and so examine its position, perturbs it in a random manner, so that even if we knew where it was we cannot tell where it will go to. Or else we cannot see it till it has gone, so we cannot tell whence it came. An exact specification of both position and speed is impossible, and hence there is a definite amount of uncertainty. The doctrine depends on the quantum, and is only applicable where the occurrences spoken of are so minute that the quantum is sufficient to perturb them. But then all events are made up of immense numbers of these minutiae, so that the discovery of the quantum is supposed to affect the deterministic philosophy in a revolutionary manner.

Now I myself sympathise with the attempt, and to some extent agree with the conclusion. I do not hold a doctrine of strict determinism—fixed fate, predestination, and the like. But then I apprehend the element of contingency as an outflow or consequence of the entry of life and mind into the scheme. Without that irruption, in the inorganic world, I see no sufficient reason to introduce anything but bare cause and effect, one event following another in unbroken sequence with absolute certainty and regularity, except when the purely physical is interfered with by life and mind. In the inorganic world prediction would be possible if we knew all the facts. Yes, it is said, that is just the difficulty, you cannot know all the facts, by the very nature of things. There is an element of fundamental uncertainty in our knowledge, which no philosophic or other reasoning can overcome. The act of *observing* carries with it inevitably an act of *perturbing*. Things are not the same after they have been observed, and you cannot tell precisely what change the act of observation has effected. Consequently you can predict no longer, the data are not accessible.

Well, inaccessibility is not synonymous with non-existence. It might be interesting if contingency ruled throughout the universe, if it affected the physical as well as the psychical: but I venture to doubt the validity of the argument. I admit all that Heisenberg and his followers have said on the physical side, I admit that with our present powers of observation we cannot tell which way the cat will jump, but I deny the philosophical and generalised deductions therefrom. Because we cannot know, it does not follow that certain events are essentially and absolutely unpredictable. Because we cannot identify a quantum and say which one will strike or which way it will deflect a path, it does not follow that the occurrence is not absolutely determined. Our seeing or perceiving the details of a phenomenon are not essential to its working. It will go on just as well if we are not observing it, i.e. if no one is observing it, and then there is nothing to perturb the inevitable sequence. The act of observation is partly a psychic phenomenon, and wherever psychic elements enter, indeterminism or free choice may be admitted; *but we have gone beyond or outside the purely physical world when we introduce an observer*. An unknown psychic element has to be postulated before we can talk of prediction; and it is well known that our predictions are all of them fallible, and are only made on the (often tacit) assumption that nothing unforeseen occurs. We must take all the data into account, and some of them may be impossible of attainment. Sometimes the affair is simple, and the neglected agencies do not matter. To predict absolutely, everything in the universe would have to be taken into account (like Tennyson's soliloquy on a flower in the crannied wall), and that is impossible.

As an example of scientific prediction the simplest and standard case is the prediction of an eclipse. That involves only accurate knowledge of the path of two bodies so massive and so isolated in space that nothing perturbs them except a few other similar bodies whose perturbing influence can be calculated. The return of a comet is another instance; but that is a body not particularly massive, and moreover is one which takes such long journeys into regions where it cannot be followed that it may encounter something unexpected, so that the prediction is uncertain. Still another example is the local condition of the earth's atmosphere, commonly called the weather, which cannot with any certainty be predicted more than a few days ahead.

It may be instructive to take a few historical instances of scientific prediction, which the event has more or less falsified. In 1892 Sir William Crookes made a forecast in *The Fortnightly Magazine* of something very like Wireless Telegraphy and Broadcasting, on the strength of having seen some laboratory experiments and exercised his imagination. But Crookes had an uncanny insight. He predicted a fourth state of matter, neither solid, liquid, nor gaseous, but something further removed from even laboratory experience, in 1879; and he did this on the strength of his own cathode ray experiments. He was rebuked at the time, but he has been entirely justified. The atoms have since been broken up into electrical charges; it was really the flight of those electrical charges that he was watching in his tubes; and though he did not know what they were, he felt instinctively that they were like no matter that had ever been seen, and they appeared to him to be in a higher than material state. We now know that they were a torrent of electrons, each of them as much lighter than the lightest atom of matter as an ounce is lighter than a hundredweight.

Crookes made other observations, some of them anathema to his contemporaries. He felt that the future would be on his side, and I am inclined strongly to agree: but the scientific world is still hostile or in doubt, and it is still left to posterity to decide. It has recently been argued that Crookes made a false prophecy about the coming scarcity of wheat, when he gave his Presidential Address to the British Association at Bristol in 1898. Well, agriculture was not his province, and I was sorry that he swerved into alien fields, but let it be noted that his direful prediction was intended as a warning that *unless certain things were done*, unless nitrogen could be extracted on a large scale from the atmosphere and applied to the soil, an untoward anticipation would follow. And now note that, whether in consequence of this warning, or in the natural course of events, the application of atmospheric nitrogen to the soil has been made, and the threatened scarcity of crops averted.

I am reminded of the prophecy of Jonah. He was told to say, "Yet forty days, and Nineveh shall be destroyed". The prophet felt that the message would secure its own falsification, and was accordingly unwilling to deliver it. He said as much, complaining that repentance would follow, that the city would be pardoned, and his reputation as a prophet irretrievably spoiled. In the end he was made to realise that he thought too much about his own reputation, and that he ought to rejoice if his message saved a number of innocent people. Even so, Crookes no doubt rejoices at the falsification of his prediction about food scarcity; and in his case we can remember that the very method he advocated for evading the trouble has been actually employed.

Another instance of not exactly prediction but of calculation falsified by subsequent discovery of fresh data is Lord Kelvin's estimate of the age of the earth, and the time it would probably last. His estimate was based on the data then known; but he was cautious enough to say that it was right "provided no entirely unknown source of heat was discovered". Soon afterwards radioactivity manifested the immense store of energy wrapped up in the very constitution of the atoms of matter, some of which was continually being liberated as heat; and accordingly the whole calculation was falsified, just as he had made allowance for.

What is the moral of all this? Do I wish to inculcate caution in accepting as true some of the predictions or philosophic speculations of our prophets to-day? Yes, I do. For instance I mistrust every conclusion based on the comprehensive generality of the second law of thermodynamics. The law was formulated by Lord Kelvin in the 'sixties; and so long as the statistical terms "heat" and "temperature" are applicable, so long as we contemplate a condition of things in which those terms are appropriate, the law is certain. But directly mind takes control and acts with design and purpose, attending to events individually, the whole of the conditions are upset and the conclusions break down. Even if they are true they are not justified by the reasoning: and I doubt if they are true. Looking ahead is very precarious, the data are uncertain, and disturbing causes that we leave out of account may have the most vital consequences.

Sir Arthur Eddington claims that disorganisation must increase; and so long as absent-minded operations like shuffling a pack of cards are carried on, that is true; but anyone giving his mind to it, and playing a game of patience, reverses the confusion and restores order. Mind is left out of account in pure physics, and accordingly prediction need not be valid.

Do I say the same of the doctrine of relativity? No, not exactly the same, but I advise caution wherever it has not been confirmed by experiment. What is called the General Theory of Relativity of 1915, where gravitation comes into notice, has been fairly verified, and is probably sound, but as regards most of the earlier and simpler doctrine dating from 1905 verification is really absent. The only confirmatory evidence, and I admit it is strong, is the consistent way in which various otherwise known phenomena can be expressed by it. The constancy of the velocity of light in free space to all observers is its sheet anchor, and this doctrine may be true. I am inclined to think that it is. But the instincts of great men were against some of the curiosities or absurdities brought forward to illustrate it; and it may be fair to the memory of the late Lord Rayleigh to narrate that he once said to me: "I wish you would seriously look into this relativity doctrine and explode it", or words to that effect. Well, I have suggested hesitation time and again, but the doctrine is very strong, it seems to stand out against all assaults, and it may be permanently true; but parts of it still lack confirmation, and are accepted as an act of faith. Faith is justified by trying if a doctrine works, and the theory of relativity does work, so perhaps it is all right.

The quantum is all right too in my judgment, but not every kind of speculation based upon it. It is as fundamental as anything can be, it covers all the interaction of matter and ether, and there is no doubt of its application to the finest and minutest transactions. In the gross and treated statistically it averages out, and therefore does not affect any branch of engineering, so far.

As to the wave theory of dynamics, it is in its infancy. I cannot tell what it is going to become. But it is a healthy infant of great promise, it shows signs of replacing material by etherial considerations, and I for one wish it well. But there is a lot to do before it can be popularly expounded. My hope is that life and mind will sooner or later come under its jurisdiction, or that the wave theory may act as their servant, their minister, and thus that these psychic entities will at last enter the scheme of physics, and justify the inclusion of a mass of evidence concerning phenomena which at present lie outside in the cold.

INDEX

à Beckett, Gilbert, 122, 150
Abercrombie, Lascelles, 1–19; *Sir Henry Taylor*, 1–19
Aberdeen, Lord, 17
Adam Bede (Eliot, George, q.v.), 52
Aeschylus, 218
After Dark (Collins, Wilkie, q.v.), 70, 83, 85, 86
Ainger, Canon, 156
Alice Through the Looking-Glass (Carroll, Lewis), 64
All the Year Round, 60
Althorp, Lord, 226, 235
Amours de Voyage (Clough, Arthur Hugh, q.v.), 22, 23, 37, 50
Ancient Greece and Mediaeval Italy (Freeman, E. A., q.v.), 192
Anderson, Sir James, 249
Anson, G. W., 69
Antonina (Collins, Wilkie, q.v.), 53, 54, 59
Arabian Nights Entertainment, The, 135
Argyle, Duke of, 157
Aristophanes, 118, 119, 120, 125; *The Birds*, 118, 119
Aristotle, 204, 207, 208, 210, 213, 214
Armadale (Collins, Wilkie, q.v.), 69, 76, 81, 82, 83, 84, 93, 97
Arnold, Dr, 20, 26, 28, 29, 30, 50
Arnold, Matthew, 21, 25, 26, 27, 28, 29, 30, 32, 33, 34, 35, 36, 38, 43, 204; *Thyrsis*, 27, 28, 30
Arnold, Thomas, 21, 76
Artevelde, Jacques Van, 3
Artevelde, Philip Van, 3, 9, 10, 11
Atlantic Cable, 247, 248, 249
Atlantic Monthly, The, 26
Austen, Jane, 85
Autobiography of Sir Henry Taylor, 3, 9, 10, 13
Ayrton, Robert, 121

Bab Ballads, The (Gilbert, W. S., q.v.), 105, 143
Bacon, Sir Francis, 107, 204
Bacon, Roger, 72, 188
Bagehot, Walter, 25
Ballantine, Sergeant, 170
Balzac, Honoré de, 68
Bancroft, Mrs (Wilton, Marie, q.v.), 68, 104, 139, 147
Bancrofts, The, 68, 139, 147; *On and Off the Stage*, 68
Barham, R. H., *Ingoldsby Legends*, 193
Basil (Collins, Wilkie, q.v.), 61, 74–6, 79–87, 98, 100
Bass's Ales, 138
Beckford, Peter, 223, 228
Beddoes, Thomas Lovell, 2, 6; *The Bride's Tragedy*, 2
"Benicia Boy, The" (Heenan), 173
Beowulf, 194
Bergson, Henri, 128; *Le Rire*, 128
Berkeley, Bishop, 221
Big Bertha, 161
Birds, The (Aristophanes, q.v.), 118, 119
Bismarck, Prince, 162
Blake, William, 5
Bleak House (Dickens, Charles, q.v.), 98
Blue Beard; or the Fatal Curiosity (Planché, J. R., q.v.), 111
Boas, Frederick S., 175–200; *Historians in the 'Sixties*, 175–200
Bohemian Girl, The, 139
Boswell, James, 62
Bothie of Tober-Na-Vuolich, The (Clough, A. H., q.v.), 23, 26, 34, 35, 36, 37, 38, 39, 50
Boucicault, Dion, 112, 119, 145; (with Brougham, J., q.v.), *London Assurance*, 112
Bradshaw's Railway Guide, 133

Index

Index 275

Index

Index

Printed by W. LEWIS, M.A., at the University Press, Cambridge